JAPAN

SEA OF JAPAN (NIHON-K

To Mabel Johnson,
a Texas lady,
a gift-giver of shelled pecans
and the best fruitcake in North America

First published 1984
Second Edition 1987
Orafa Publishing Company, Inc.
1314 So. King Street, Suite 1064
Honolulu, Hawaii 96814
U.S.A.

©1984 John W. McDermott

All rights reserved. No part of this publication may be reproduced in any form without written permission of the publishers.

ISBN: 1-55650-016-5

Typeset by Studio Graphics, Inc., Honolulu
Printed by Fairfield Graphics, Pennsylvania
Maps by Roger Suga, Honolulu

Previous books in the series:
HOW TO GET LOST AND FOUND IN NEW ZEALAND
HOW TO GET LOST AND FOUND IN FIJI
HOW TO GET LOST AND FOUND IN TAHITI
HOW TO GET LOST AND FOUND IN AUSTRALIA
HOW TO GET LOST AND FOUND IN CALIFORNIA AND OTHER LOVELY PLACES
HOW TO GET LOST AND FOUND IN OUR HAWAII
HOW TO GET LOST AND FOUND IN *UPGRADED* NEW ZEALAND
HOW TO GET LOST AND FOUND IN LONDON (Coming)

Distributed in North America by:

300 Raritan Center Parkway,
CN 94, Edison, N.J. 08818

How To Get Lost And Found In New Japan

by John W. McDermott

Edited by
Bobbye Lee Hughes McDermott

Orafa Publishing Co., Inc.
Honolulu, Hawaii, U.S.A.

List of Maps

Map of Japan	inside front cover
Tokyo	xiv
Tokyo Shopping Areas	
Shopping Villages	32
Ginza/Nihombashi	36
Akasaka Roppongi	44
Azabu Juban	44
Shibuya	46
Shinjuku	46
The Wholesale Villages	53
Central Honshu	61
Kyoto Area	71
Hiroshima	88
Kyushu	103
Hokkaido	175
Tohoku	208
Yamagata & Fukushima	245

Contents

	Caveats	vii
	Preface	ix
1.	Tokyo—The Powerhouse	1
2.	Taming the Tiger—A Shoppers' Guide	32
3.	Hakone—Tokyo's Mountain Playhouse	59
4.	Kyoto, Nara, and Osaka—of Kings and Priests	69
5.	Hiroshima and Miyajima—Heartbreak City and the Dream Village	89
6.	East Coast of Kyushu	101
7.	West Coast of Kyushu	128
8.	Villages on the Sea of Japan	146
9.	Kanazawa and Takayama—Rice Riches and an Alpine Village	160
10.	Hokkaido—The Non-Japanese Northern Island	173
11.	Tohoku—North of Tokyo	208
12.	Yamagata and Fukushima—Back-of-Beyond Prefectures	243
	Index	265
	Other Books in the Series	272

Caveats

Since the original publication in 1984, the yen has almost doubled in value.
Is traveling in Japan expensive today? Yes.
Can travel in Japan still be done at a reasonable cost? Yes. It just requires a bit more research and initiative on the part of the traveler.

So many good detailed maps are available through the Japan National Tourist Organization, including detailed maps, that the maps used in this book are intended only to give the reader an idea of the locale of the islands and cities visited.

The Japanese custom is to put the family name first which can be confusing, a custom also used in historical references. However, we have used the Western style of putting the family name last. Japanese who are accustomed to dealing with Westerners will use the Western style on their calling cards, often using a simple nickname in front. The traditional Japanese will never call you by your first name, nor would you use theirs, but the modern Japanese—will easily call you by your first name, after asking permission, and you can do the same.

Should you ask a Japanese friend or guide to give you an historical date, he will pause, count on his fingers, draw imaginary figures in the air, then give you the date. The reason is that the Japanese date events in history from the beginning of each Emperor's reign. The guide or friend has to convert the Japanese date to coincide with the Christian calendar.

> Note: Entertaining is a custom in Japanese life, both privately and commercially. You can enjoy this hospitality in Home Visit Programs and in business contact. We were guided, particularly in the northern part of Japan—Hokkaido and the "Back of Beyond" districts of Honshu—by prefectural tourism offices eager to show off tourist areas and accommodations which have long been popular with the Japanese but are relatively unknown to the overseas visitor. Such offices are also eager to assist you with itinerary planning and guide or interpreting services.

Preface

To appreciate Japan you have to forget the rumors and erase the negatives.

The crush of people, it is said, is unbearable.

True, Japan is made up of a series of relatively small islands and the limited physical area is emphasized by the large numbers of people—over 120,000,000.

During the daytime when there are 20,000,000 people at work, Tokyo is the largest city in the world. Add 5,000,000 in Osaka. A 1,500,000 in Kyoto.

How can you manage to enjoy yourself with so many people?

Easy. You learn to become part of the current and flow with it. That's part of the fun.

The language presents another barrier.

You can cope with a foreign language with the help of a dictionary and finger language . . . but Japanese! As the indignant lady said, "Japanese isn't even written in English!" Also true. Generally Japanese is written in unreadable characters. The original Chinese characters are called *kanji*. The Japanese adapted versions are *hiragana* and *katakana*. We can't tell the difference and always use the term kanji.

Even the names of the cities are impossible to memorize.

But it's a tribute to the human mind how quickly you learn to cope . . . and you do.

Then there are differences in backgrounds.

Meeting the Japanese raised in Confucian traditions, with a discipline almost martial in its shogunate obedience, with a religion combining bewildering aspects of Shintoism and Buddhism, the Western visitor feels intimidated by these people so different from his or her traditional Western background.

However, the longer one stays in Japan, taking advantage of the Home Visit Program, as one example, the more the visitor separates the individual Japanese out from the masses and discovers his warmth, sensitiveness, and surprising love of laughter.

Aided by the fact that the Japanese take three to six years of mandatory English, language barriers tend to dissolve with new acquaintances and disappear with friendships.

Little rumors become big bugaboos to a timid visitor.
"The Japanese eat nothing but raw fish."
"The country is unbelievably expensive."
"The accommodations are small, uncertain."
"Everybody takes a bath together."
Take them one at a time.

1. Menus are international as befitting a leading international country. Raw fish is optional.

2. You can travel in Japan as cheaply as in any country—or as expensively. To go on bare-bones, bottom-dollar excursions just takes more inventiveness and mental flexibility.

3. Western-style hotels have mushroomed along with everything else in the last ten years although the charming inns, *ryokan*, still remain.

4. Alas, the communal bathing has all but disappeared.

If the outsider believed the rumors, Japan would appear to be a country where one could get lost and never get found.

It is not so.

Japan has always been a most rewarding country for visitors.

The 'new' Japan is even more amazing.

Never in the history of civilization has a nation risen from ashes to a leading world economic power in such a short period of time. Just being in Japan, mingling with those 120,000,000 people, a visitor can feel their energy—in fact is almost overwhelmed by the Japanese devotion to getting a job done.

> If for no other reason, one should visit Japan to appreciate how and why this small country is apt to be the number one economic power in the world in the twenty-first century.

Artistically, Japan is most satisfying. The quiet simplicity of Japanese creativeness is singular in its appeal to the senses. Where else are artists designated as "national treasures?"

Adding to the pleasure of travelling in Japan is the knowledge that it is the safest country in the world. No pickpockets. No streetwalkers. No muggers. No camera and wallet thiefs.

Forget the rumors and barriers.

Modern Japan is an experience unlike any other.

Japan was not new to me. Travel conferences and business meetings had brought me to Tokyo on different occasions. On one such trip I went on day excursions to Nikko, then Kyoto.

On another I went with a blond teen-age daughter as far south as Takamatsu on the island of Shikoku and then across the Inland Sea to Kurashiki back on the island of Honshu.

Even now the names are confusing.

But twelve years had passed since the last trip, and tremendous growth and accompanying changes had occurred in Japan during the intervening years. I was going to see a new Japan.

Many parts of the country, aside from the standard areas visited on short tours, I had never seen.

Japan would be a completely fresh adventure.

My first inclination was to go to an immersion school to learn at least enough fundamentals of the Japanese spoken language to order breakfast and enough of the written language, kanji, as opposed to the Western alphabet in Roman letters called *romaji*, to find the men's room.

But I threw out that idea as being unfair. Against the rules. If most visitors go to Japan with no knowledge of the language, then I had to go the same way so that I would experience the same difficulties—and discover my own solutions.

I bought a small pocket dictionary.

> From my experience it is far more important that a visitor spend two weeks learning to eat with chopsticks before going to Japan than spend two weeks studying the language.

You can always point, which will get you by in a language, but without being reasonably facile with chopsticks you could starve to death, particularly out in the country. And you don't want to carry a secret fork. Gauche.

Before leaving home I went through one small geographic exercise. I drew an outline of Japan and then wrote in and memorized the names of the islands and principal cities I would be visiting.

The principal island of Honshu and the cities of Kyoto, Hiroshima to the south, Sendai, Morioka and Akita to the north.

The southern island of Kyushu and the cities of Fukuoka and Nagasaki. The northern island of Hokkaido and the city of Sapporo.

I eliminated the island of Shikoku from my itinerary.

In this manner the Japanese place names became familiar to me.

Besides my little dictionary I acquired a ton of information books: *Fisher's Japan, Japan, A Travel Survival Kit, Japan Unescorted, Footloose in Tokyo* and, most valuable, the Japanese National Tourist Organization's (JNTO) *The New Official Guide to Japan,* last published in 1975 and at this writing out of print. Search your library or second-hand book stores for a copy.

What you quickly learn, if you are going to be travelling throughout the country, is to travel as lightly as possible. In Japan you will be carrying your own bags most of the time.

Heavy guide books are a no-no.

You need to have a one-suiter with wheels, and one shoulder bag.

You will note in railroad trains how much the vacationing Japanese carry with them. Almost nothing. They know that in every hotel and inn they will receive a *yukata,* a light cotton kimono, to wear in the hotel and to bed as a nightdress. Every morning you get a clean yukata just as routinely as clean towels.

Toothbrushes and toothpaste and disposable razors are supplied in first class establishments as routinely as the yukata.

With a wardrobe of wash-and-wear shirts and blouses and undergarments, the clever Japanese are bag-free.

If you use a stewardess-type portable cart, remember that the luggage you put on it should be narrow enough to roll down a train aisle.

My first research objective was to explore Tokyo in some depth, visit the cities of western Honshu and then circle the island of Kyushu, returning to Tokyo via the Honshu coast facing the Sea of Japan.

My excursion outside of Tokyo would center around a first-class, Green Car, 21-day pass.

Introduced with great success in 1982 by Japan National Railway (JNR), the government-owned railroad system, railroad passes are offered on 7-day, 14-day, 21-day bases with optional choices of ordinary coach cars or first-class Green Cars.

The Green Pass costs one-third more than an Ordinary Pass. Either way you save about 100% over regular fares.

A coupon for the pass must be bought outside of Japan and then exchanged for the railpass itself in Tokyo. The pass doesn't start until the first day of usage.

Actually I went over my 21-day limit and had to buy separate tickets to finish my tour back to Tokyo. I could have saved money if I had bought a 7-day pass at the same time I bought the 21-day pass.

The first expedition took part in the spring season, an ideal time to travel, except that you find every school class graduating from elementary school or junior high school or high school is taking traditional group tours. Railway stations are jammed. Ordinary cars are overflowing, another reason to get a Green Car ticket.

Also, the Emperor's Birthday is celebrated on April 29, signaling the start of "Golden Week" which lasts about eight to ten days when, besides the students, the rest of Japan takes to the road. You guard your travel and hotel accommodations during this period with firm reservations.

This first phase of the Japan travel and research expeditions departed from our usual custom in that the Lady Navigator, pressed by a serious illness in her family, went to her relatives while I went to Japan alone.

Good and bad. Lovely and terrible.

The good part was that I designed, with the help of the excellent people in JNTO, an itinerary which covered twenty cities in thirty days and utilized thirty different trains.

Getting the Lady Navigator to any train or plane on time requires great skill in child psychology, brute force, and threats of physical and monetary abuse.

To be relieved of that strain for thirty days and thirty trains had an element of whipped cream in it.

Also, it meant more time for notebooks and reading. A sudden decision could be followed by instant action without discussion. Added, of course, was the potential of being wooed and won by so many incredibly beautiful, exotic, desirable Japanese ladies who appeared in Walter Mitty day-dreams—unfortunately, it was the only time they appeared.

The bad part was that the nights were so long. And the funny incidents and the glorious sights could not be shared by a companion who had the same sense of humor about the ridiculous and the same awe of the magnificent.

I was reminded of the little boy who was told that he couldn't take his dog on the Milford Sound trek and asked plaintively,

"Who do you tell your secrets to?"

The serious professional loss was the missing of a second pair of eyes, sharp feminine eyes that would glimpse things I wouldn't see, catch impressions that I would miss, recall memories I would forget.

All of this was rectified when she joined me for the second expedition which took place in the late summer and early autumn, another fine time to travel in Japan.

We started in Hokkaido, the northernmost island which is a country with a heritage separate from Honshu. The people, the architecture, the atmosphere is "non-Japanesque" and I have treated the island as a place to consider for an entirely separate trip.

From Hokkaido we returned to Honshu and worked our way south to Tokyo, criss-crossing the northern part of the island known as Tohoku. This time we had 21-day Green Car railroad passes supplemented by 7-day passes.

We stayed in every kind of accommodation. The minimum-price *minshuku,* or family owned inn, the more prestigious and expensive Japanese inn, the *ryokan,* the economic businessman's hotel, the average to luxury city hotel and resort hotel. Being past the age of youth hostels, we by-passed the hostels.

We didn't take advantage of the Japan Travel Bureau's (JTB) "Sunrise Super Saver."

A 7-day double room package is currently priced at Y79,800 and a 14-day package at Y159,600, including tax and service.

Our eating experiences were as widely varied as our accommodations.

Coffee shops, noodle shops, sushi bars, tempura, shabu-shabu, yakitori, sukiyaki, McDonald's, Kentucky Fried Chicken, French, Italian, Chinese restaurants, we did them all.

And drank barrels of excellent Japanese beer plus more than one bottle of sake.

Economically, we proved to ourselves that you can stay, eat and drink on any level that your budget is designed to handle.

And you don't have to understand the Japanese language to do it.

Mentally, you have to accept Japan for what it is. An adventure. This is not the place for a feet-up, sun-tan vacation. Japan is a place full of pleasant surprises which you will find in the cities and away from the cities.

In the country you will find more of the beauty of Japan, and find it easier to meet the people of Japan, and, perhaps, understand the reasons for Japan.

Above all you'll come home with a new admiration for Japan.

You'll find an enviable calmness in the spiritual lives of the people.

You'll enjoy the delicate sense of color and design in the artistry of their crafts. This is the old, traditional Japan.

You'll be astounded at the dedication they bring to their work, a commitment, a discipline which has vaulted the country into such an awesome production center.

Japan is prosperous. It has the soundest economic base in the world, and it is the leading power of Asia-Pacific.

This is the new Japan.

Japan is a place to go, to explore, to be surprised, to savor, to have fun.

A great adventure awaits you.

TOKYO

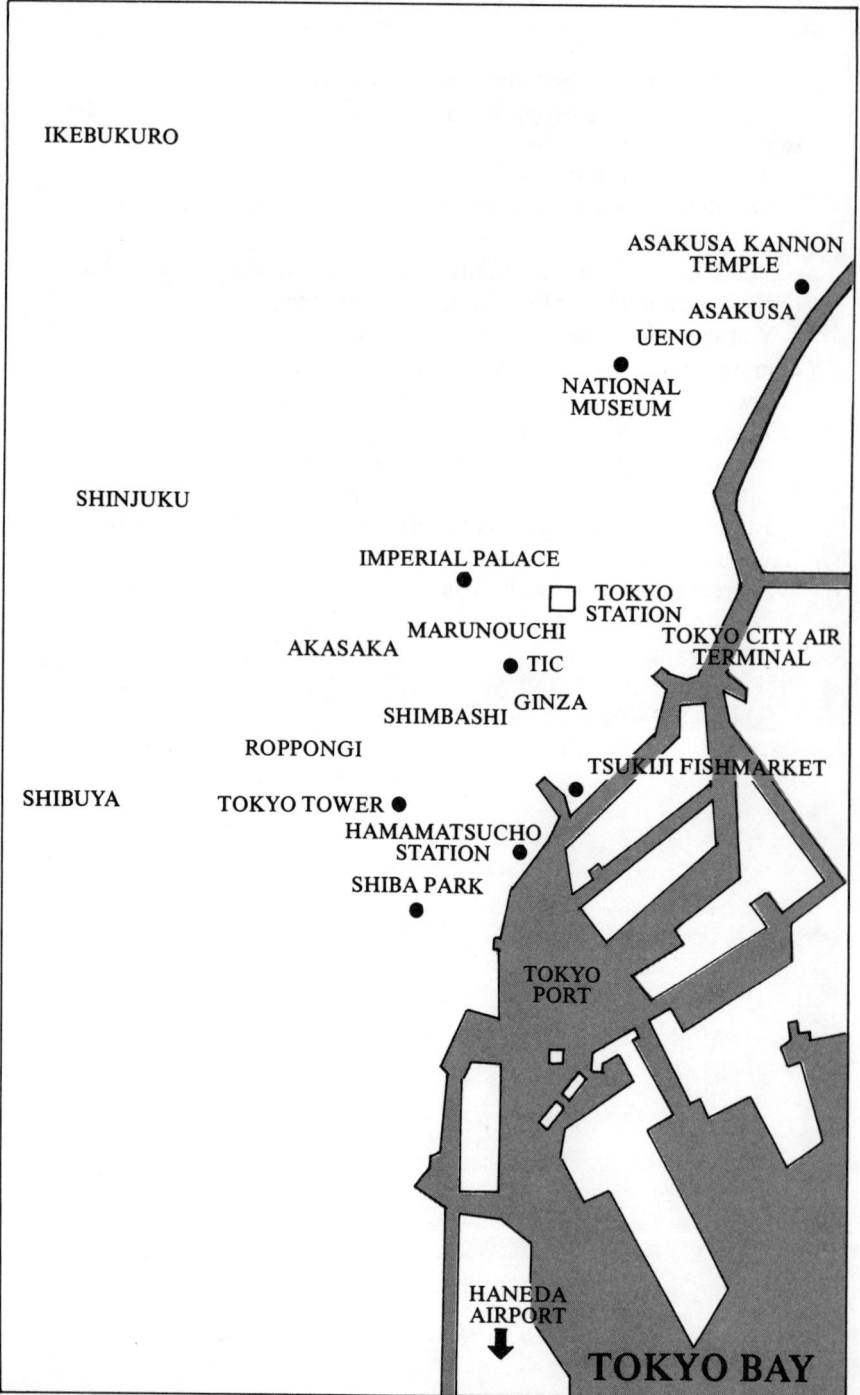

1. Tokyo—the Powerhouse

Tokyo is today the super city of the world.
It is classier than New York.
Cleaner than Paris.
Bigger than Moscow.
Safer than Sydney. Or Vatican City.
A lady from England put it in perspective. When asked why she liked living in Tokyo compared to London, she replied, "Because this is the city on the rise not the decline. Here, everything works."

I hadn't been in Tokyo for twelve years and even in that short period of time it had grown from a city stumbling towards greatness to a city which had arrived. It had become bigger, more modern, more handsome. New architecture now crowns every district.

Today Tokyo pulses with power . . . the power of money, production, distribution, transportation, communication.

Powerhouses beget playgrounds and Tokyo is crammed cheek-by-bare-cheek with all the tinsel toys of amusements including restaurants of every description, theaters, luxury department stores, sports, museums, parks and 120,000 bars.

Power is not new to Tokyo.

The capital of the Tokugawa *shoguns* (generalissimos) who ran Japan for nearly three hundred years was established here where the bay cuts deep into the Kanto Plain. It was called Edo (estuary), an ideal place for sea communications. The Emperor, a figurehead, was kept in the inland city of Kyoto.

In 1603 the first Tokugawa shogun brought to Edo 80,000 retainers. The families of the powerful lords, *daimyo,* were required to keep their families in Edo as hostages. No women were allowed out. No firearms were allowed in.

By 1787 the population had risen to 1,368,000, making Edo one of the largest cities in the world.

When the shoguns were overthrown in 1868 and the Meiji Emperor was restored to power, the Emperor moved his kingdom headquarters to Edo renaming it Tokyo, or Eastern Capital as opposed to Kyoto or Saikyo, the Western Capital.

2 How to Get Lost and Found in New Japan

With the gates open to the rest of the world, Tokyo boomed. By the time of World War II the population was well over 6,000,000.

In the world of yesterday, you stayed at the famous Imperial Hotel designed by Frank Lloyd Wright. The famous art-deco hotel withstood the devastating earthquake of 1923 which had flattened most of Tokyo. You transacted your business in the busy Marunouchi financial district next door and played and shopped in the Ginza district behind the hotel.

If you were more adventurous, perhaps you went out to the Akasaka district for nightclubing and other amusements. If you were younger, you went where the young played, to the Shinjuku or Shibuya districts.

That's all changed.

Today in Tokyo, the separate districts, in reality, have become satellite cities within the city, each with its own skyscrapers, hotels, attractions and personality. The result is that Tokyo is a multi-faceted dazzler.

Start back in the Marunouchi-Ginza District and the Imperial Hotel, still the flagship of the district and typical of what is happening throughout Tokyo.

The old Frank Lloyd Wright building was removed in 1970 and a 17-story main building took its place. In 1982 a 31-story Imperial Tower was completed next door.

The first five floors of the Tower are devoted to shops. What shops. Every internationally famous brand name is to be found on one of the floors: Gucci, Valentino, Loewe, Bally, etc.

Floors five to eighteen are offices.

The remainder of the floors are devoted to hotel rooms with bay windows—offering views over the Imperial Palace, the neon-lit Ginza, and Hibiya Park. One floor is reserved for executive apartments. Expensive but first rate. World class.

The 20th floor has saunas, massage clinics and a year-round swimming pool.

You want to jog? The Imperial has complete jogging outfits for your use at no charge.

You want to do business? There is a business center on the 2nd floor with conference space, typewriters, secretarial services, a library of international periodicals and a tax-free, tip-free bar service.

Tokyo—the Powerhouse 3

The lobby in the main building of the Imperial has a bubbling continental air about it. All types are going and coming. American tourists in jeans and running shoes. Germans in three-piece suits. Everything but monocles. Chic French. Black-suited Japanese businessmen—with white silk ties if they are going to a wedding.

You have to at least walk through the lobby of the Imperial when you visit Tokyo. It will be *the* place where you will find someone from home.

Surrounding the Imperial are banks and bars, international restaurants, department stores and airline offices and many other first class and other class hostelries with rates modest to expensive.

Note: Make sure you find the Tourist Information Center on the Imperial Palace side of the railroad lines at 6-6 Yurakucho 1-chome where publications and much good information is available.

Particularly recommended are the pale yellow, 8x12-inch brochures put out by JNTO on the cities.

Three kilometers to the west, beyond the National Diet building, where the governing bodies assemble, is the Akasaka District known for its nightlife and now a major hotel center.

The New Otani was the first hotel in Tokyo we stayed in during our return trip. We had been in the New Otani before—one tends to go back to the familiar. It has spacious grounds with a lovely garden, restaurants galore, a downstairs grocery store among the many shops and other amenities including a mailing, package-wrapping desk and two tennis courts.

I tipped the bellboy for bringing up the bags—*it was the last time I tipped in Japan.* You are charged 10% for service on your bill plus 8 to 10% for taxes. The addition of up to 20% has to be built into your mental calculator when you are quoted a room rate, but the increase is somewhat relieved by not tipping *anyone*—doormen, taxi drivers, waiters, maitres-d'. An exception is made in the ryokan when a Y1,000 note in a plain envelope can be slipped to the mama-san who takes care of you—but not in front of anyone. Poor taste.

The New Otani also has a new high-rise tower which brings its

4   *How to Get Lost and Found in New Japan*

total number of rooms to over 2,000, making it the biggest hotel in Japan.

If the Imperial bubbles, the New Otani boils.

During my spring trip the hotel was headquarters for the Young Presidents Organization's annual "university." A memorable sign. Posted on the door of the YPO convention headquarters suite was a sign:

> CHAIRMAN
> Are you here
> to solve a problem
> or to cause one?

Also moving through the hotel were many guests of spring wedding functions, banquet attendees and local and overseas visitors to view the cherry blossoms. The lobby was a large madhouse.

> Note: the young Japanese wives accompanying their dark-suited husbands to the many functions are a new breed. No longer the sunflower hat and the printed chiffon garden dress. These were smartly, expensively gowned ladies in the latest big-game, big-name fashions.

When we returned to Tokyo from our summer trip to Hokkaido and northern Honshu, we stayed at three different hotels.

The first hotel was across the street from the New Otani, the new gleaming, shimmering, V-shaped edifice of the Akasaka Prince.

The Prince chain of hotels is part of the leisure travel companies of the giant Seibu organization which has hotels, golf courses, ski resorts, spas, and employs around 40,000 people in its "family."

The Akasaka Prince, associated with Westin International Hotels, is a luxury hotel (double $125 to $250). Its 760 guest rooms and suites, designed by one of Japan's leading architects, Kenzo Tange, reflect the prosperity and sophistication of the new Japan.

The lobby is cool-on-cool. White marble and glass everywhere.

The white marble stairs in the middle of the lobby lead down to an open cafe. At the midway landing is a white piano where every evening a pretty girl, in a white dress of course, with long black hair plays tea-for-two music.

No matter where you stay you must see the lobby at the Akasaka

Prince. It looks like a stage setting for a Fred Astaire-Ginger Rogers white tie and floating chiffon dance routine.

The guest rooms are almost monochromatic in cool grays and pale blues with two desks in even the standard rooms, the best reading lights in Tokyo, refrigerators, tea-making sets. Curved glass windows give maximum outdoor light to every room.

The Akasaka Prince also has an executive business center on the third floor with secretarial services, typewriters and international communications facilities, interpreting, translating and a quick business card printing service. I ran out of cards and had a hundred *meishi* done overnight—my name in English on one side and Japanese on the other.

At the foot of the hill is the Akasaka Tokyu Hotel, 566 rooms, another major facility.

An advantage of the Akasaka location is that the subway station nearby serves four different subway lines. You are not far away from any other district.

The scattering of nightclubs and bars and restaurants of a decade ago has now become solid blocks of entertainment attractions.

Akasaka is a vibrant district.

Away from the more glamorous districts is Shiba Park and the Shiba Park Hotel, a modestly priced tourist-package hotel where we moved to for three nights.

To the west of the hotel is the sizeable Shiba Park. Within the park is the Tokyo Tower, a stop on any city tour, with a five-story Modern Science Museum at its base, and the Zojoji Temple, once the family temple of the powerful Tokugawas in the Shogunate regime, and the Tokyo Prince Hotel.

The Shiba Park Hotel is a favorite with New Zealanders, Americans and rugby players.

The New Zealand All-Blacks have stayed at Shiba Park, as have the All-France players.

When we were at the hotel, the Cambridge and Oxford rugby teams were in residence having just finished a series in Japan. The lobby was filled with walking hulks whose collegiate noses were generally bent from east to west. One had a bandage around his head.

On weekends the hotel has to turn away business when the Japanese come in from the country and from other cities to shop, play and do business.

Also—and this is true throughout Japan—autumn is a favorite travel time and the hotel is filled to capacity.

Nearby are two subway lines and the Hamamatsucho railroad station which is also the terminal for the monorail connecting Tokyo with Haneda airport, once the international but now the domestic airport.

We finished our stay in Japan at the Imperial Tower which still gets the nod for its location, so convenient to so much business or pleasure.

The Akasaka Prince has the best rooms.

The Shiba Park the best price.

The New Otani the most action.

Unfortunately we didn't test the famous Hotel Okura. After we arrived home, a close friend said, "You didn't stay at the Okura? You goofed. That is the greatest hotel in the world." Sorry.

> Note: While you are at the Tourist Information Center, get the JNTO publication *Reasonable Accommodations in Japan* which will include many clean and reliable places to stay. You don't have to pay $100 a day for a decent hotel room.
>
> A conviction we have shared in other books is applicable to Japan as elsewhere and that is a tour package—if only airfare and hotels are included—will give you substantial savings over independent bookings.

Before leaving the subject of hotels we have to relate what is happening in the district of Shinjuku.

The entire Shinjuku area is busting out all over.

Formerly an exclusive young adult, college student playground of restaurants, pachinko parlors, and small shops, it is now a city in its own right with new high-rise commercial office buildings and hotels, banks and department stores, many of which are connected with underground passages to Shinjuku Station.

You have to experience Shinjuku Station. It is mad, mad, mad.

Three railroad lines and the Marunouchi subway line use Shinjuku as a terminal.

Over one million people pass through the station *everyday*. It is

Tokyo—the Powerhouse 7

the busiest station in all of Japan.

Besides wanting to explore Shinjuku, I needed to scout the platform location of Odakyu Railway's "Romance Car" which I would take the following weekend to Hakone.

I easily found the railroad line and departure gate and felt very smug. Little did I know.

The area west of the station is the center of the new development.

Three internationally important hotel chains—Hilton, Hyatt and InterContinental—operate new hotels in Shinjuku, making the district another major visitor community in Tokyo.

The Keio Plaza InterContinental Hotel, for example, has almost 1,500 rooms... and a dazzling lobby. Nearby is the Century Hyatt with almost 800 rooms ... and another dazzling lobby.

Hilton International, no longer in Akasaka, is the new kid on the Shinjuku block with a 900-room hotel.

Next to the station are the Odakyu and Keio department stores, and on the *east* side of the tracks are the Mitsukoshi and Isetan department stores, the latter having the reputation of being the Bloomingdale's of Tokyo.

There are one million students in Tokyo who converge on Shinjuku as their favorite rendezvous area, and the shops and restaurants cater to their youthful tastes and budgets.

Two famous camera shops in the district are Sakuraya and Yodobashi. In Yodobashi the sales clerks are smartly dressed in bold, black-striped shirts and black ties and black vests. They believe in heavy oral, sales stimulation . . . the din and the hustle and the yelling have to be experienced.

Also it is said that both stores offer the best camera prices in Japan. Trade in your old one, get a new one.

Next to Sakuraya is the Takano Fruit Parlor—isn't that a great name—which used to be a fruit parlor but is now a six-story building filled with restaurants. The World Restaurant on top is recommended by James Weatherly in his good booklet, *Japan Unescorted.*

Before leaving Shinjuku Station I went into the connecting Keio Department Store basement.

Collecting department store basements, where the best foods are found in Japan, is my hobby. I have notched over one hundred on my "visited" list. Keio earned a rating of 9 plus. Excellent. I found

8   *How to Get Lost and Found in New Japan*

a 100-proof Suntory Vodka at a sensible price. Knocks the lipstick right back into your esophagus and cleans the sinuses.

Let me take you into a department store basement.

The entire basement will be devoted to food and beverages from all over the world.

Here is where you buy dried fish, Kobe beef, chocolate eclairs, Sunkist lemons, booze, *sake*. Name it. If you can drink it or eat it, you'll find it in a Japanese department store basement.

At the fruit counter you might find Taiwan or Philippine pineapple, royal in size but pale yellow in the middle. Musk melons, hothouse grown, shockingly expensive, are a favorite. Citrus from California and hot-house strawberries.

Fish is the traditional protein food in Japan. One hundred years ago no Japanese ate meat. As a Time Magazine issue on Japan stated: "It would be like eating one's tractor." So you find a lot of fresh fish. Dried fish. Big fish. Small fish. Eel, squid, cuttlefish.

(If you are really into fish, get up at dawn and take a taxi to the wholesale Tsukiji fish market, the largest in the world.)

Meat and fowl now get as much counter space as fish.

Counters display coffee beans, teas and chocolates from around the world. Counters are laden with cheese from Denmark, Germany, Holland, France, and Switzerland. Even Philadelphia Cream Cheese. I found Kewpie Berstein's Salad Dressing. (Kewpie Berstein's Salad Dressing?)

French wine, Italian vermouth, varieties of sake in large bottles, beer, soft drinks, the most expensive cognacs, Scotch whiskey, Japan-made Scotch whiskey, American whiskies, Polish vodkas, Russian vodkas, and on and on.

Did I mention doughnuts? Gold fish? (No, not to eat.) Flowers? Steak sandwiches? Roasting ears of corn? Fried chicken? Tasty dishes are made before your eyes and free sampling is common.

Upstairs the Japan department stores offer more diversification than the department stores in other countries. They are strong on good restaurants and excellent museums with world famous collections of art paintings. In the summer time, the roofs become beer gardens.

But downstairs, ah, that is where the adventure is.

For the nightlife, go to the East side of Shinjuku and just wander the streets, full of young people, restaurants, disco bars, neon signs, fast food shops.

Other prominent districts in Tokyo are equally amusing. One is Ueno bordering Asakusa. (I easily get Asakusa confused with Akasaka. Asakusa has the temple. Akasaka has the hotels.) Ueno becomes known to long-stay visitors to Tokyo because it is an important rail terminal. Near the Ueno Station is Ueno Park, the location of three art museums, the Tokyo Zoo and one of Tokyo's most important concert halls. Also the Asakusa District, site of the Asakusa Kannon Temple, an important stop of city tours where little stalls sell Japanese whatevers and candies. Three times a year Asakusa is the capital of summo wrestling but to get a ticket to one of the daily matches is difficult. Japanese companies pre-buy all of the boxes and entertain their important clients.

Another popular district is Shibuya which has also gone through a metamorphosis. I remembered it as a place where I had been taken long ago for a bit of low-life and a steak dinner. Now it is the Park Avenue of Tokyo. High-rise buildings. Embassies. Swank shops. Pricey residences. Elegant pedestrians.

We took a subway to Harajuku Station on a Sunday hoping to watch the kids in funky costumes dance to taped music in Yoyogi Park. It rained. No dancing.

Instead we had steaming noodles and cold beer in a sidewalk, hole-in-the-wall restaurant and watched the young people go by under colorful umbrellas . . . sad in their hot-to-trot dancing clothes.

Later, when the skies cleared a bit, we walked down the main avenue. On Sundays the avenue is blocked from car traffic. We window shopped and people watched. Peaceful Sunday in Tokyo.

You Must Learn the Subways and Trains

To get around Tokyo and enjoy it, you must accept the first challenge of the Japanese adventure by conquering the Tokyo subway and rail system.

Nobody runs a better system than the Japanese. They are fast, clean, efficient and safe. The only way to go.

In Tokyo there are ten different subway lines which will shunt you anywhere in the city.

With twenty million people working above ground every day, it makes sense to try and move the majority of people underground. One caveat: don't use the subways during commuting hours except for your own amazement. How do they get so many bodies into the cars?

Railways also move people within the city above the ground.

> Note: the Japanese are the epitome of politeness . . . except when it comes to getting into a railroad or subway cars or elevators. Then the bent, kimono-clad little old lady with a cane, who would ordinarily bow to you, will knock you straight on your end-zone.

Before you leave for Japan, go—or write—to JNTO, or go immediately upon arriving in Tokyo to the Tourist Information Center (TIC) and get the Color-Coded Guide Map of the Tokyo Subway System.

The map shows which lines go where, each line being color keyed and written in English, and *explains how the ticket vending machine works.*

You are charged by the number of stops you make en route to your destination. A station wall map in kanji, which I never understood, tells you the cost. Recently there has been an applaudable move to put small wall maps in English in the stations.

No matter. Buy the minimum Y100 ticket and if you owe more, the ticket-taker at the exit will point you to the fare adjustment window.

I always guessed at the fare and was never sent to the fare adjustment window.

On the station platform, signs designate the name of the station you are in and the next station in either direction. In English. This is true on railroad and subway platforms.

Yellow lines are guide marks for passengers queues during rush hours.

The rule of thumb is: always carry a map and don't be afraid to ask any intelligent looking businessman or an older school girl. We found that the Japanese people take pleasure in helping strangers.

> Note: Your Japanese friends will never walk any distance if they can get a subway. Rather than walk half a dozen blocks, they will go to a subway station, buy a ticket, go upstairs, downstairs, get in a train, go to the next station, go downstairs, upstairs and out of the station. They think this is a funny habit, too.

Tokyo—the Powerhouse

If you seek a transportation adventure and want to discover at the same time a true flavor of the city, buy Mrs. Pearce's *Foot-loose in Tokyo*. She has been a columnist for many years on the English-language daily *Japan Times*.

Included in the transportation system of Tokyo is the Yamanote Line (Yah-mah-noh-tay). The railroad circles the city in both directions with twenty-nine stops along the way.

In her book the author writes in detail about each stop and gives you a suggested, capsulized walking tour of that district.

The preface to the Pearce book offers the idea of taking a ride around the complete circuit to get a taste of Tokyo without getting off at any station. Then you can go back and explore those areas which are of particular interest.

A good suggestion.

Although the book is crammed with brightly written, esoteric information, strangely enough it doesn't describe how long it takes to make a complete round.

How would one find out how long the circuit takes? Why not test another free information service available to tourists in Japan—the "telephone aid" system?

Call 502-1461 in Tokyo and your English question will receive an English answer.

The system is available in Kyoto under a separate number (371-5649). From anywhere else in Japan, you can dial toll-free from a yellow phone or a blue phone—*not a red phone*. Put in Y10—you get it back—dial 106 and say very slowly, "Collect call, T.I.C." enunciating clearly "Tee-Aye-See." The system is made possible by donations totalling fifty million yen from private companies.

I called the Tokyo number and a young, English-speaking man answered my question that the complete circuit of the Yamanote ride would take "less than an hour and may I suggest you buy the cheapest one-stop ticket, make the complete circuit and then get off one stop beyond the place you got on." That's what I did. Cost: 20 cents. As the preface writer said, the only other competition for the cheapest ride in the world is the Staten Island Ferry.

I made one small mistake.

Foot-loose in Tokyo follows a counter-clock sequence, and I boarded a train going in a clockwise direction which meant that I read Jean Pearce from back to front which was perhaps the appropriate Japanese style.

12   How to Get Lost and Found in New Japan

You can read the book as you go but you have to be a speed reader and you also have your head down most of the time.

However, that doesn't matter because there isn't too much to see. Buildings, industrial yards, etc. Then why go? Because by going through the locations physically while reading the book you get a sense of what is there and what you might want to come back and experience on foot.

Interesting, too, is to be a spectator watching the flow of non-tourist riders. Students, giggling girls in uniform, older women in the kimono, executives in neat, dark suits. This, you feel correctly, is Tokyo.

"What do you like to do in Tokyo?" we asked one overseas resident.

"Easy. My favorite occupation is watching the people."

> Note: in subways, busses, trains, ferries, airplanes, on anything that moves, the Japanese have a talent for instant sleep. The head slumps to the side or over the chest, and, bingo. Slumberland. Are they psychologically removing themselves from the crowds around them or is it a pause from the pressures they put on themselves?
>
> Or are they staying up too late watching TV? I have seen a man—and you will too—fall asleep in a subway, standing up, hanging onto an overhead strap.

Taxis are not that expensive in Tokyo.

Rush hour traffic or rainy days slow their progress down to a turtle pace.

The taxi, for example, from the Akasaka District down to the banker's office in the Marunouchi District next to the Ginza was over Y1,000. The return on a subway cost about Y100 and took half the time.

Forget about busses. Too complicated. No English signs.

Food: the Yummy, the Yucky, and Kentucky Fried Chicken

You can find anything you want to eat in Tokyo. Gorgeous food, junk food, fast food, cheap food, exquisite and expensive food.

Name a country and its specialities and you will find it in Tokyo. German, Italian, French cuisine is common. Middle Eastern,

Indian, Singaporean restaurants are well represented.
There is even a Trader Vic's in the New Otani.

Of course there are many McDonald's, Kentucky Fried Chicken, Shakey's Pizza Parlors, et al along with their Japanese counterparts.

If in doubt about Japanese food, window shop. Realistic replicas of dishes, done in plastic, are in the restaurant windows indicating what is being served and at what price. Easy.

For example on my first night back in Tokyo I strolled into the bustling, neon-lighted Akasaka District, an area filled with a bewildering variety of restaurants, many of them upstairs but with signs downstairs in undecipherable kanji.

After wandering for an hour I finally plunged into a small restaurant with eight community tables holding six to eight people. Taking a corner chair, I was approached by a waiter who said something in Japanese. I responded with a hands-up shrug. He motioned me to follow him outside, which I did, wondering if I was being thrown out.

By the door he pointed to an illuminated, four-color poster which contained photographs of several different dishes.

"Noodles," I said desperately. He pointed at a bowl and said, "Noodles."

I pointed at another, prettier bowl. "Not noodles," he said.

I pointed back at the original bowl and said in flawless Japanese, "With beer."

Back inside, five minutes later, he brought to my table a huge, delicately colored bowl filled with lovely noodles swimming in a rich, brown broth. With chopsticks and a wooden spoon, accompanied by a large bottle of Sapporo beer, I had a delectable meal at less than Y700 and I went back to the hotel feeling as if I had conquered Tokyo.

Before leaving the restaurant I asked the waiter to write down the name of the dish and he wrote: *"ramen."*

I learned to love ramen noodles in Japan.

There are basically three kinds of noodles. Ramen is a small Chinese noodle. *Soba* is a gray noodle made from buckwheat flour and is considered lower class but is more flavorful than *udon* which is a white, fat noodle.

One of the problems in travelling is weight. The kind you put around your waist because you eat too much.

At home you have coffee, tea, a piece of fruit, a slice of toast. Enough for breakfast.

On the road you have fruit juice, fresh fruit, cornflakes sprinkled with sugar, sausage, two eggs, a sweet roll and two slices of toast slathered with butter and jam.

It's expensive on your waistline and expensive on your wallet, particularly in Japan.

A prominent Honolulu hotel executive, Japanese, confessed, "I never eat in a hotel when I am in Japan. I go to a local restaurant where there are local people and ask for the morning special. I'll get a small cup of juice, a fresh salad, a boiled egg, one cup of coffee and a slice of buttered toast which is about one inch thick. The cost will be about Y700."

I also avoid hotel breakfasts.

Almost every standard hotel room in Japan has a refrigerator in which you can put a piece of fruit. Many hotels provide a thermos of hot water from which you can make a cup of coffee if you have brought your own supply, or *o-cha*, tea, which is provided. We also carry dual-current immersion rods as Standard Operating Travel Accessories. The Japanese current is 110 but it makes no difference. Our immersion rods will handle 110 or 220.

There are excellent pastry shops everywhere in Tokyo and throughout Japan offering enticing varieties of breakfast rolls. In case of emergencies we also carry as standard equipment a package of biscuits for breakfasts or afternoon snacks. And our own mugs.

One Japanese host, knowing my pleasure of noodles, took me to Mimiu, a four-story restaurant in the Ginza District specializing in noodles.

We had *Udon-suki,* a cook-your-own noodle-soup-stew washed down with cold beer or sake.

My host was a handsome articulate travel authority who had spent four years working in New York in a prestigious post.

The Japanese like to eat and it is not their habit to interrupt this pleasure to converse while eating. My friend, however, knew I'd ask questions.

"Did you enjoy New York?"

"Yes, very much. Particularly the opera and the symphonies.

Here concerts and operas are terribly expensive."

"I would imagine that a person like yourself who makes an excellent appearance, speaks flawless English, knows the Asiatic travel business intimately, would have many offers from travel companies if he wanted to stay in New York."

"Yes, I did. But I had to come home."

"Why?"

"Because of my two children. The time had come for them to go to school, and there was no adequate educational system in New York to prepare them for a return to Japan. At some time they would have to come home, and, if they came home without the proper education, they would be severely handicapped.

"Also, our headquarters are here. We have many overseas posts but the decisions come out of Tokyo."

This represented a change of attitude from the Japan I had known before.

When I first went to the country, an assignment in America was considered an important promotion.

Now, I sensed, while the experience to speak English and the experience of an overseas assignment particularly in the United State are important, the person who is going to get ahead is the person who stays close to where the power is. Headquarters.

The decisions come out of Tokyo.

Another restaurant and another Japanese host in the Ginza area.

At the main intersection of the Ginza where the department stores Mitsukoshi and Wako face each other, go to the corner where the Nissan Gallery is located.

In the building next to the gallery is the Ginza Core Building. On the second level of the basement is the Shabusen Restaurant. Most enjoyable. The speciality is *shabu-shabu*. The same owner has another shabu-shabu restaurant on the second floor of the same building.

Three circular counters seat about twenty people each. Before every seat is a brass pot of boiling water and various sauces in pottery jars.

You will probably be the only Westerners in the restaurant but don't worry. They will give you an English menu and a set of procedural instructions.

We ordered dinner which included tissue thin slices of pork, beef, whole shrimp, salad and vegetables followed by a rice porridge and a dessert.

We followed the instructions.

"Put two spoonfulls of shabu-shabu sauce into the dish.

"Add onions to taste.

"If you want hot shabu-shabu sauce, please add a little sesame oil.

"Put the salad and vegetables in the boiling water.

"Take one or two slices of meat with your chopsticks and dip them in the boiling shabu-shabu broth until pink.

"Please cook the pork slices a little longer than the beef slices.

"For the shrimp use the regular shabu-shabu sauce or the soy sauce.

"Dip the shrimp once or twice in the shabu-shabu broth before eating." Delicious. *(O-ishi)*. It became our favorite Japanese word.

Two bastions of Western cuisine are for members only.

One is the Foreign Correspondents Club in the Marunouchi-Ginza District. Every long-time overseas resident seems to belong whether he or she has anything to do with journalism, other than writing letters home.

The second bastion is the Tokyo American Club on the fringes of Roppongi. "American" in title only, the membership includes diplomats and prominent foreign businessmen of all nations.

Mike Sano of Air New Zealand took us to the top of the building housing the Foreign Correspondents Club where a long menu included gazpacho, chili, hamburgers, steaks, etc. The cross-section of diners was more fascinating than the menu.

The Gene Sullivans took us to lunch at the Tokyo American Club, an oasis for some 2,700 international families including a representative proportion of well-heeled Japanese who helped fund the new complex which includes bars, restaurants, sports facilities, a parking garage, etc. The club sponsors cultural and pasttime events for its members to help them appreciate living in Tokyo.

It is interesting that the club, an example of Western prosperity and upper-income privileges, backs up to the U.S.S.R. Embassy whose high walls are protected by a permanent guard of Tokyo

Tokyo—the Powerhouse

police who block off the street in front of it with gray busses.

We had a fine lunch of New Zealand lambchops, and, thanks to a Honolulu country club membership with exchange privileges, obtained a guest card for a week.

Our goal during our last week in Tokyo was to eat only in non-Japanese, international restaurants to prove that everything is available.

It is available without even leaving the Roppongi District, an area known for its nightlife and international eateries.

The Sullivans gave us their Roppongi list. French: Les Choux. Indian: Moti. Singaporese: Singapore Restaurant. Italian: Gino's. Mexican: Mexico Lindo.

We tried Gino's and gave the food a "six", the restroom a ten, the service a nine. Japanese waiters in an Italian restaurant are five points better than Italian waiters in an Italian restaurant unless you speak perfect Italian or carry a gun.

We also tried Les Choux and ate on a sunny afternoon at a sidewalk table. Again the food was about a six but the service, Japanese of course, was a ten.

Roppongi also has a Greek restaurant, an American chain restaurant featuring beef, Victoria Station, an international gathering pub called Berni's and a host of others.

One exception was made in our non-Japanese restaurant experiment when Don and Doris Ferguson, residents in Tokyo for six years and frequent hosts to overseas visitors, shared one of their favorite Japanese restaurants with us, Nanbantei. There are two Nanbantei operations in Roppongi (the older one has a more authentic atmosphere) and a third one in the Little Tokyo section of Los Angeles at 123 South Weller Street.

The original restaurant is small, smokey and crowded. All of the food is cooked on sticks over an open fire, *yakitori* style. Meat, poultry and vegetables are barbecued and served in bite-sized pieces, a tradition, the restaurant claims, that embraces two cooking styles dating to the *samurai*-Edo Period and reflecting the influence of the Dutch in Nagasaki.

Ask for a 'set' and you'll receive a dozen delicious, delicately seasoned, hot-off-the-coals morsels of yummy things which you dip in a special sauce. A high protein, highly satisfactory dinner.

A solid ten.

Ask the hotel to make reservations. You need them. Justifiably popular.

In the Akasaka District we tried another Italian restaurant (five), an English-styled pub serving baked ribs (six) and a stew specialty restaurant opposite the Akasaka Tokyu Hotel called the Stew Kettle (seven).

Around the Imperial Hotel are many German restaurants. We tried a luncheon with three kinds of sausage and beer and a bit of sauerkraut. Not bad but a weak five, really.

Also just down the street from the Imperial an Indian restaurant, Marango, serving curries got another five from the Lady Navigator who specializes in curries but the *roti*, the puffed flat bread, was excellent and deserves a ten.

What our grand international food experiment proved was 1. every kind of food is available and 2. it isn't that grand.

You can't turn your back on the fact that the oriental cuisine is superior in Tokyo.

For example, a first impression of the Shiba Park area is that it is devoid of restaurants. In reality, it is surrounded by excellent Chinese restaurants.

Facing the Hamamatsucho Station is a big red sign that says simply "Chinese Restaurant." Superior.

We had almond chicken, fried rice, spring rolls, mixed vegetables, pork with cabbage and draft beer. Somewhat expensive but a solid nine.

The next night we wanted more Chinese food, one of our passions, and we went farther up the street, on the subway side of the McDonald's, to the New Asia Restaurant run by Larry Sheng and his family. Larry, a graduate of New York State University, studied for his masters degree at the University of Hawaii. We didn't eat as much as the night before but the bill was half that of the other Chinese restaurant and won a ten. Recommended.

Eating in Tokyo is a major part of the Japan adventure.
Two rules: Don't be afraid to ask. Don't be afraid to point.

What Do You Do In Tokyo?

If you are like the Lady Navigator, you shop. She found it different, challenging and rewarding. She would disappear for days at a time.

Her experiences and advice are summed up in the following chapter.

Many people like their adventures packaged.

I talked with the Japan Travel Bureau, (JTB) the principal organizer of tours for overseas visitors.

Their standard day tour of Tokyo includes a visit to Tokyo Tower, the outer grounds of the Imperial Palace, a tea ceremony demonstration, a visit to a cultured pearl shop, the Asakusa Kannon Temple and the Meiji Shrine and, to balance the tour, a visit to St. Mary's Cathedral, another architectural triumph by Kenzo Tange. A Japanese-styled barbecue lunch breaks the day.

The most popular tours however are the night tours which include a *sukiyaki* dinner, a cabaret show and a geisha house. The cost runs to about Y13,000 a person.

Popular day tours beyond Tokyo city boundaries are Kamakura, Disneyland, Kyoto, Hakone, and industrial tours. We did them all on our own except the industrial tour which you can't do on your own.

Disney by the Bay

The lobby of the Shiba Park Hotel is a fine place to eavesdrop on the conversations of overseas couples, the majority of whom are in their greying years. They all love to share their experiences. Many highs. A few lows.

What surprised me was that everyone had gone, or was going, to the new Tokyo Disneyland.

One person from Christchurch thought he was going but he wasn't because the park in the late autumn is closed on Tuesdays and it was Tuesday. "My travel agent didn't tell me," he complained.

In a government land-development project 2,000-plus hectares of land were dredged from Tokyo Bay to create a new, small city for 70,000 people with room for homes, industry and leisure-time facilities.

On 82.6 hectares of this land the Tokyo Disneyland was created. The theme park itself required 46.2 hectares of space—twice as much as the Disneyland in California. The remaining space was used for parking and maintenance facilities.

The project is entirely owned by Oriental Land Company, a partnership of Keisei Electric Railway Company and Mitsui Real

Estate Development Company.

Walt Disney Productions designed and master-planned the park, manufactured the ride and show systems and provided technical advice and assistance and on-going management direction with in-park personnel for the life of the project.

It took $600,000,000 and a workforce of 3,000 to open the doors in April, 1983. (The original Disneyland in California cost $17,000,000.)

Tokyo Disneyland is almost-but-not-quite a reproduction of the theme parks in California and Florida. You see the familiar fairyland castle dominating the grounds, an Adventureland, a Westernland, a Fantasyland and a Tomorrowland.

"Main Street", the yesteryear entrance street of the U.S.A. parks has been enlarged, covered and renamed "World Bazaar" to satisfy the enormous Japanese penchant for buying souvenirs.

Even with in-depth knowledge of buying habits, the actual revenues from the World Bazaar shops and boutiques have been *triple* the forecasts.

In the first summer rush, during a one-month period, from July 21 to August 21, the shops sold 520,000 Mickey Mouse Earcaps, 340,000 dolls and 240,000 T-shirts.

On one day in August 94,000 people entered the park. In its first 144 days, the park had reached half of its projected annual attendance of 10,000,000. One reason for the success is that the market potential immediately around metropolitan Tokyo is larger than all of California.

Tokyo Disneyland is a delight except for the drawback, shared with its American cousins, it is too popular and too crowded. The advice of park officials is to go when the park first opens—9 A.M. in summer, 10 A.M. in winter—or go in the last hours before it closes—7 P.M. in winter, 10 P.M. in summer.

Disneyland hours are subject to change without notice. If you want to call before going, the number is (03) 366-5600.

Don't go on weekends.

The cost of general admission in 1987 was Y2,700 with various prices including rides scaled up from that price.

There are some twenty-seven food facilities in the park. Avoid in peak hours. Lots of popcorn and ice cream stands to fill the void.

Because the Disney people wanted to provide a "foreign experience" in the park almost all of the food is Western; signs and songs are in English.

The hamburgers are as undistinguished as they are in California and Florida.

The Haunted House and Pirates of the Caribbean are as popular in Japan as they are in California and Florida. The thrill rides like Space Mountain are not new to the Japanese because they are to be found in other Japanese amusement parks. What the Japanese prefer are the "foreign experience" outdoor attractions: Western River Railroad, Jungle Cruise, Tom Sawyer Island Rafts, Mark Twain Riverboat, Davey Crockett Explorer Canoes.

(What I liked were the incongruous scenes. The sun-beaten, weather-lined faces of farmers wearing Mickey Mouse ears. An absolutely beautiful Japanese lady in an elegant cream-yellow kimono holding a stuffed, two-foot Mickey Mouse doll.)

Two attractions in Tokyo are not seen in other Disneylands.

"Meet the World" is a four-stage presentation of Japan's history using live actors, animation, motion pictures, and computerized, life-sized figures. The audience remains seated and the seats revolve to face each of the four stages. Also shown is a Circle Vision 3-D film presentation in a round theater.

Both of these presentations are in Japanese but the back row seats of the two theaters are equipped with head phones giving English versions.

The toilets are the cleanest public toilets in Japan.

> Note: public toilets in Japan are pretty terrible. You can often tell when you are within 100 meters of one. Why the immaculate, scrupulously clean Japanese have such horrible facilities, I don't know. Perhaps it is because this is a bodily function they would chose to pretend didn't exist.

The park employs 2,000 steady employees and peaks at 5,000 part-time employees, all of whom attend a three-day course at "Disney University" plus on-the-job training.

To reach Disneyland you have several choices.

You can buy a packaged tour including bus pick-up at your hotel, admission, rides.

You can go to Tokyo Station and find the Yaesu North Exit on the side away from the Imperial Palace. From there a bus leaves every ten minutes—every five minutes in summer—directly to Disneyland. I waited forty-five minutes just to get on a bus. The ride to Disneyland took only thirty-five minutes but the return ride back, in rainy-day traffic, took an hour and ten minutes.

Avoid busses.

The best route is to take the Tozai Subway Line to Urayasu Station and then a shuttle bus to the park.

Airport Limousine and Chiba Bus Lines both offer shuttle bus service between Narita Airport and Disneyland.

Kamakura—Ancient Capital

If I had one free day in Tokyo and the weather were half decent, I'd go back to Kamakura.

It is convenient, only an hour's train ride south to the Miura Peninsula.

Kamakura is filled with history, scenery, shrines, shops and good restaurants. A fine place for strolling, scenically and historically.

In the twelfth and thirteenth centuries Kamakura was the capital of Japan, the seat of the Shogunate government and witness to the rise to power of the Japanese military, a power retained until the return to the monarchy in 1868.

It was a time when the Hachimangu Shrines spread through Japan and the custom of the *yabusame,* the demonstration of ancient archery from horseback, became part of the shrine's annual festival in September. It still is.

The power passed from Kamakura in declining stages until it was reduced to a quiet fishing village.

Today Kamakura, surrounded on three sides by green hills and on the south by beaches facing the Pacific Ocean, is an oceanside resort and suburb of Tokyo with a population over 150,000. It retains the flavor of the power and the color of yesteryear.

It is most satisfying.

Upon arrival at Kamakura Station, take the left-hand exit and you are faced, not with a quiet fishing village, but with a maze of taxis, tour busses, souvenir shops, restaurants.

The farther you get from the station the more appealing Kamakura becomes.

We had a JNTO brochure-map on Kamakura with suggested temples and shrines circled to visit on our outing, the kind you can get at the TIC.

Our first destination was the Tsurugaoka Hachimangu Shrine, a must for tourists, reached by a ten-minute walk along the Wakamiya Oji, a most pleasant cherry-tree lined path separating the main street with one-way traffic on each side.

Wakamiya is the second street after you exit from the station.

We reached the shrine, one of the nineteen temples and shrines in Kamakura, built in 1063 by the Genji family, founders of the Kamakura Shogunate Government.

Walking back to the station I found an art gallery with original Ukiyo-e woodblock prints and hand-done copies. Ukiyo-e is an art form reflecting the style and grace of the Edo Period, highly prized among collectors of Japanesque objects. I bought two copies for $20 each, including one by Hiroshige, the original of which hangs in the Van Gogh Museum in Amsterdam.

Adjacent to the train station but on the opposite side from the main street is the local streetcar which took us to Hase, the third stop on the line. Fortunately we had the map because every sign posted was in kanji.

From the Hase Station we crossed the tracks and followed the crowds to the Kamakura Daibutsu, the main visitor destination of Kamakura. Its Great Buddha, a seated bronze figure, 11.4 meters in height, is only second in size to the Buddha in Nara, outside of Kyoto.

The Kamakura Buddha was once covered by a Great Hall as the Nara Buddha still is. The Great Hall in Kamakura was destroyed by tidal waves in 1495 and the Buddha has since been allowed to remain in the open.

The weathering has turned the placid statue into a subdued jade green. It sits in repose in an open courtyard, palms up, fingers touching, gazing solemnly through half-opened eyes at these temporary pedestrians below, taking their little snapshots, occupying the world's stage frantically, fleetingly while the Great Buddha goes peacefully on and on.

At the entry gate, a sign in Japanese and Quaker English reads:
"Stranger, whosoever thou art and whatsoever be thy creed, when thou enters this sanctuary remember thou treadest upon ground hallowed by the worship of ages.

"This is the temple of Buddha and the gate of the eternal and should therefore be entered with reverence.
By the Order of the Prior"

A five-minute walk back toward the station and then to the right—if you don't stop at an antique shop where the Lady Navigator found a forty-pound antique wooden block—is the Hasedera Temple. Go. If you are a photographer, go and stay all day.

The tallest wooden image in Japan reigns at the Hasedera Temple. The ten-meter tall, eleven-headed statue, carved from a single piece of camphor, is one of two identical figures carved from a giant camphor tree in a village called Hase near Nara.

One of the figures was enshrined in the village only to be destroyed later by fire.

The second figure was thrown into the ocean "to find its own home." It finally beached at the foot of Kamakura and a temple was built nearby and named New Hase—or Shinhase.

From a corner of the temple you can see the seacoast in front of Kamakura.

Throughout the grounds are little kannon gods, 50,000 in fact, placed to commemorate dead-born or aborted babies. With the incense and the burning candles the battalions of little images make a poignant scene.

The Glories of Nikko

A worthy competitor of Kamakura in recommendable day trips is Nikko about two hours from Tokyo by either the Tobu Railway from Asakusa Station or the JNR from Ueno.

Day tours by bus are available through JTB.

By itself the scenery is worth the trip. Waterfalls tumbling off green mountains, lakes, rivers and forests of ancient trees.

What I remembered from my first trip to Nikko were the trees. Humbling giants so tall and straight and stately. Walking up to the shrines with these towering guardians on every side was, in itself, an emotional experience.

Besides the wonder of the shrines, Nikko is the locale of many hot mineral spas, and recreational attractions such as hiking, boating, fishing.

At the time of my first visit I didn't appreciate the fact that the Toshugu Shrine is the resting place of the remains of Ieyasu Tokugawa, the founder of the Tokugawa Shogunate which was to rule Japan for almost three centuries and leave a stamp on the Japanese character which will never disappear.

Ieyasu Tokugawa, the molder of Japan.

After he died in 1616 at the age of seventy-five, his remains came to Nikko, according to his will, and by the year 1636 the elaborate shrine buildings had been completed, with lacquered vermilion beams studded with precious metals and decorated with exquisite carvings.

The entry gate is Yomeimon, or more popularly called "Twilight Gate." More than any other building in the complex of shrines, the gate is the most intricate and splenderous in its carvings, reflecting the great perfection of the early Edo period.

The sightseeing in the area centers around Lake Chuzenji reached by a fifty-minute bus trip from Nikko up the mountains in a series of hairpin curves with scenic views along the way—if you don't have your eyes closed. Two highways lead up the mountain. Irohazaka #1 and Irohazaka #2. Take #1 and you'll go by Kegon Falls which has an elevator to take you to the bottom of the gorge. The falls, when swept by wind, turn into lace and the water vapors rising from the bottom of the falls give the scene an aspect of rare beauty.

Lake Chuzenji, surrounded by mountains, is bordered with hotels and villas. The lake is a summer haven for yachts and fishing boats. A round-trip pleasure boat ride taking about fifty minutes goes the rounds of the scenic spots on the lake in the non-winter months.

A variety of packaged tours to Nikko are available at every travel desk but it is a tour you can successfully make on your own.

The Industrial Tour—
A First-Hand Look at Japanese Production

Japan's dramatic rise to the position of being the greatest producing nation in the world in automobile manufacturing, electronics, cameras and other fields is one reason for going to Japan—particularly if you can take a personal tour of some of their industrial complexes.

You can.

Sunrise Tours and JTB offer full-day industrial tours three times a week to various manufacturing companies. My tour took in Fujitsu Computer Laboratories, Canon Camera Plant and a Suntory Distillery. The current Tuesday tour includes the Tokyo Stock Exchange, the national Robot Center and Isuzu Motor Factory. The make-up of the tours will vary from year to year.

JTB can also arrange special tours for special-interest groups or seven-day and fourteen-day Techno Tours which include intensive seminars and on-site inspections.

My Tuesday tour, currently priced at Y10,000, included a hotel pick-up, excellent chicken lunch, and a monorail ride to Haneda Airport where the bus tour started.

Our group numbered about fifty—all overseas visitors including a Chinese family from Hong Kong and a contingent of French with its own interpreter.

In Japan there are four industrial centers: Tokyo, Nagoya, Kobe-Osaka and Fukuoka in northern Kyushu.

The Tokyo plants are centered around Tokyo Bay.

From Haneda, the former international airport and now the domestic airport, we went into the Chiba district and through the city of Kawasaki, the largest industrial city in Japan with a million in population. The Kawasaki Steel Works could be seen in the distance where 13,000 employees turn out eight-and-a-half-million tons of crude steel a year.

We passed Kirin Brewery. Kirin Beer has an astounding sixty percent of the Japanese market but even that pales against Suntory which we would visit later in the day. Suntory has over ninety percent of the whiskey market—and contrary to their reputation for drinking only sake, the Japanese drink a lot of whiskey.

Speaking of market shares, Toyota dominates the car manufacturing industry with forty percent, followed by Nissan (Datsun) with thirty percent.

Some six million cars are exported annually.

In Japan a small car sells for four to five thousand dollars.

We passed a plant of Fuji Electric which was the parent company of Fujitsu until 1935 when the company, now the largest computer manufacturer in Japan, was spun off. Today Fujitsu employs 50,000 workers in twelve factories. The plant where we were headed was mostly involved in research and development and for the training of overseas engineers.

In 1954 the company produced its first computer and now ranks first in Japan and second internationally, trailing only IBM. Computers are only part of Fujitsu's manufacturing menu. Telecommunications systems and equipment, a major producer of semiconductors, the manufacturing of advanced eletronic components are also part of its operations.

Tokyo—the Powerhouse

The electronic business is extremely competitive and daily breakthroughs are common. Tomorrow's success can depend on knowing more than the next company which led to an international espionage scandal involving Japanese companies trying to steal IBM research information. Fujitsu was not involved.

I was surprised that a tour was permitted to go through such sensitive areas but our guide inferred that only non-Japanese could take the tour and that "we wouldn't see much."

After passing through guarded gates, we were driven to a two-story white building where an automatic underfoot doormat sucks the dirt off the bottom of shoes as feet walk over it.

Inside we were escorted to an auditorium, given a pack of literature and showed a film concerning some of the electronic wonders of today and tomorrow.

The film opened on a shot of a robot writing computerized kanji on a grain of rice. That got the audience's attention.

Then the screen split into two scenes: a street corner nightlighted by a lamp post as seen by the naked eye and, on the left hand screen, the same scene filmed by night optic equipment. The viewer could make out in the distance the forms of a runner and a dog coming toward the camera. On and on they came. Finally, only when they reached the street corner, did the naked eye pick up a girl and a dog rounding the corner in the right-hand screen.

Scenes were shown of machines interpreting voice dictation and converting the oral words to printed words. Other machines converted written Japanese to written English.

New methods, new materials, new components are part of the daily research in the push to produce more sophisticated equipment.

It is a fierce race with high stakes and the plant we visited operates twenty-four hours a day.

Fujitsu with an international network of companies has annual sales of $3.2 billion and it is an excellent example of a Japanese high-tech company on a steady climb upward.

Lunch at a nearby restaurant consisted of mushroom soup, salad, grilled chicken with baked potato and coffee. And knives and forks and spoons.

On the way to lunch we passed a driver training school which you

28   *How to Get Lost and Found in New Japan*

see throughout Japan. Simulated streets, lights, curbs, lanes, the works.

"The driving schools are licensed by the government," said Robin, our guide. "Do you know how much it costs to get a driver's license in Japan? About $1,200."

We next visited Canon factory making Canon cameras. "No pictures, please," requested Robin.

Canon is the world's largest manufacturer of single-lens reflex cameras but even its camera sales are surpassed by Canon copying machines.

Today the company with $3.5 billion in sales is divided into cameras, business machines and optical products.

Canon owes its success to excellence in technology, an example being the famous Canon AE-1, the first camera on the market with an electronic, microprocessing "brain" which automatically determined exposure and flash settings. The revolutionary camera sold almost a million units a year for its first five years.

The newest in Canon cameras is the successful "Snappy" series with features including automatic winding, rewinding, loading, focusing and exposure. It does everything but hire models.

The plant we visited was primarily a research and development facility making prototype cameras and employing about 1,000 people.

We saw casings and components automatically stamped and drilled by computerized machines. However, a sophisticated camera has over one hundred parts requiring the human touch and we passed through floors of assembly sections where workers, mostly women, were engaged in putting together the minute parts by hand.

The concentration and the intensity demanded by the work is relieved by frequent work breaks. On a post I saw a cartoon series of suggested exercises and, sure enough, during a work break most of the workers were stretching muscles according to the routine suggested by the cartoons.

Some time ago, our Canon guide said, the company introduced a suggestion system. It is now mandatory for each employee to make 48 suggestions a year. One employee, she said, made 532.

Monetary rewards are passed out according to the value of the suggestions. Fifty thousand yen down to five thousand yen. The annual President's Prize is three hundred thousand yen but the top prize is a two week overseas trip for two.

Our last visit was to a Suntory bottling plant with vast tanks and casks where a variety of products are bottled and distributed. We saw the usual film and toured the bottling lines. Suntory Whiskey is very popular and its squat bottle of "Old" can be seen on the shelves of many restaurants where the guest buys a bottle, drinks from it as much as he wants. The bottle is then labeled and reserved for his next visit.

Suntory makes dozens of products: rum, vodka of various strengths, gin, wines, liquors and even beer, although it has no sizeable portion of the beer market.

In addition, it imports the most prestigious spirits from around the world including Haig & Haig, Jack Daniels, Campari, Harvey sherries, among others.

We ended the plant tour in the hospitality room where we were offered free drinks and given a miniature souvenir bottle of "Old."

Tsukuba—Science City

Japan is outgrowing its 'copycat' reputation with the rise of new Japanese originated technology, particularly in electronic equipment and in robots.

The Japanese are creating their own frontiers.

The use of robots in Japan industry, I was told, totalled 47,000 compared to 5,000 in the United States. Later I was cautioned to beware of such statistics because the term 'robot' can depend upon definition. For example, the ability of a machine to put and place is called a robot in Japan but not in the United States.

The latest statistics I found, quoting Joseph Engelberger, "father of robotics" according to a newspaper report, was Japan 18,000, the U.S. 7,000 and all of Europe 9,000.

Sixty kilometers northeast of Tokyo is a vast complex of government and private research centers called Tsukuba Science City where 7,000 engineers are investigating new areas of agriculture, physics, weather and other sciences in fifty research centers.

One set of buildings is devoted to the Mechanical Engineering Laboratories, including a research facility for robotics.

Through friends in the JNTO, I was able to visit the robot center where two engineers, Nobuki Yajima and Satoshi Hashino, showed me films of work in progress and conducted me on a walk-through of the working laboratories.

I saw under development "Mel-Dog", a seeing-eye robot for the blind. It looked like a streamlined vacuum cleaner.

At present Mel-Dog, with sensors attached to the operator's arm, can perform most of the operations of a seeing-eye dog—sensing, seeing, remembering, making decisions based on simple commands, provided the operator is in a controlled environment with limited space, and on flat terrain.

Safety and reliability are the key factors for a seeing-eye robot. The ability to operate in an uneven terrain is a problem yet to be solved.

Cost is another problem. A seeing-eye dog costs about $4,000 and there are only 400 in the country with a blind population of 450,000. The present seeing-eye robot would cost about $40,000.

Mel-Dog shared his kennel with a sophisticated six-legged machine, operating on a small battery, capable of walking.

In another laboratory a giant arm could perform seven arm functions, operating hydraulically. The first such arm created weighed 100 kilos and could lift only three kilos. The new arm weighed 50 kilos and could lift ten kilos.

Adjacent to the arm was a mechnical "nurse." The machine could lift a heavy patient in a fork-lift fashion, safer than a human nurse, and transport the patient from one place to another even in confined quarters.

We encountered a research engineer experimenting with a robot which had the ability to insert a precise part into another part through a sense of touch—just as if you were given two parts to join together, you would do it not by seeing but by feeling the areas of least resistance.

In other rooms I saw heavy drilling machines manufactured of plastic and fibers and metal to reduce vibration.

Fascinating place.

Two hundred and twenty research engineers work in the Mechanical Engineering Laboratories in basic research, applied research and special projects, with an annual budget of $12 million, a small part of the $600 million being spent in Tsukuba.

My guides thought it highly amusing that a travel writer was interested in their work.

"We have had lots of journalists through here," they told me as they took my picture, "but you are the first travel writer."

Currently, the Expo site is being converted into a high-tech industrial park.

RING-AROUND-THE-PALACE SHOPPERS MAP

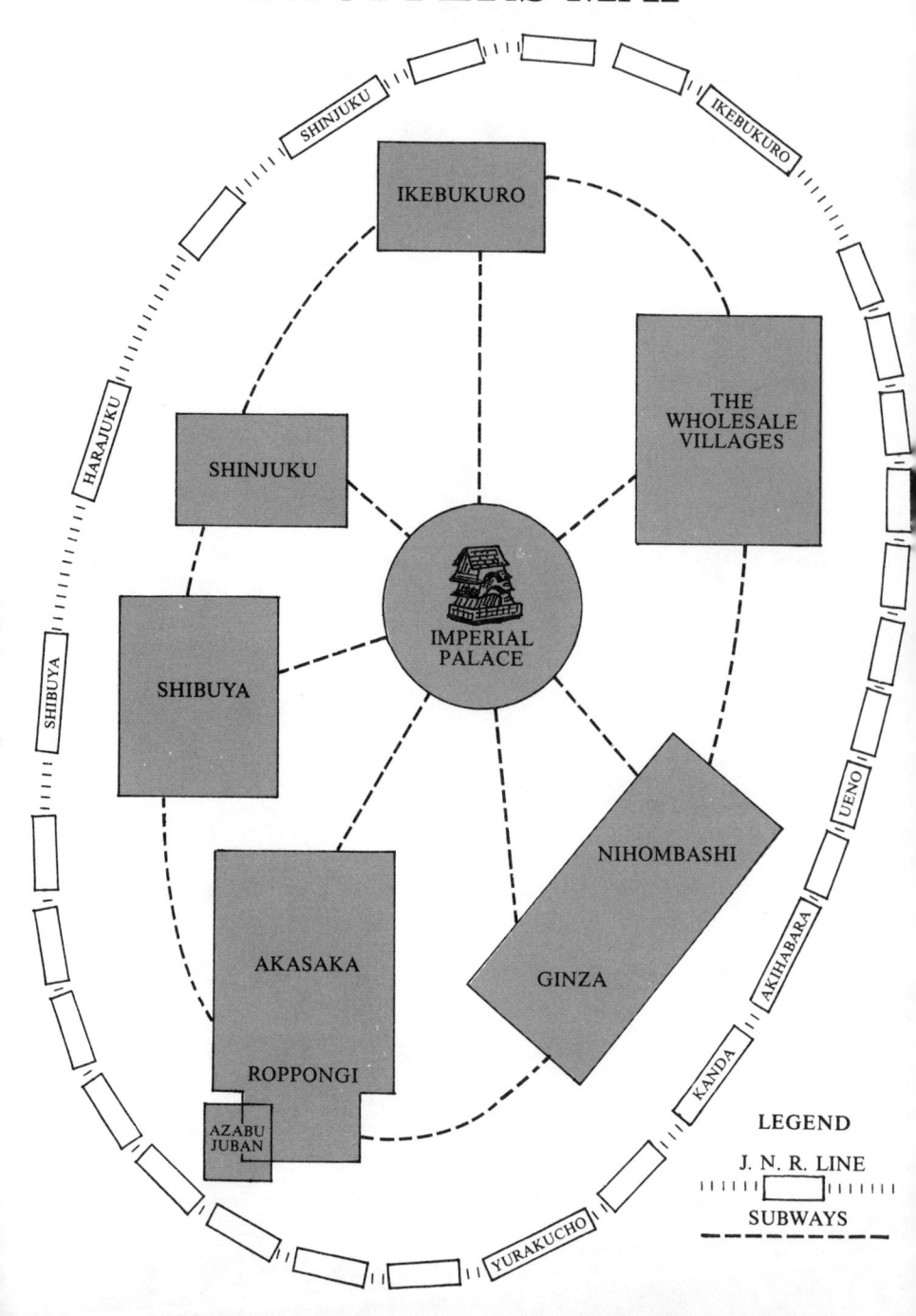

2. Taming the Tiger
The Lady Navigator's Shopping Guide

"There are no bargains in Japan today."
Balderdash.
So many people said it so often I almost believed it.
There are bargains if you know where to look for them.
There are bargains in the street markets and in the second-hand stores and at department store sales.
There are bargains, also, in the sense that you have a greater selection of the better quality items manufactured in Japan such as contemporary Noritake china, delicate Hoya crystal, or ancient Imari.
There are bargains in the Japanese *mingei,* the utilitarian handcrafted items in daily use, not to be confused with the factory-produced folk art souvenirs sold everywhere.
There are phenomenal bargains in second-hand Japanese kimono because no self-respecting Japanese will wear a hand-me-down.
The ersatz lacquerware you've possibly admired in Japanese restaurants undoubtedly came from Kappabashi, the wholesale hotel/restaurant supply district. Not only is it hard to distinguish from the real, it is a fraction of the price—and just as beneficial—some of it is dishwashable.
There are bargains in cameras, in electronic gadgets, in jewels.
Some bargains are bargains because Japan is the only place you can find them.

You begin the search for bargains in Tokyo because, most probably, that's where you will enter the country. There is no denying that tackling Tokyo takes verve.
Tokyo is a tiger of a town, capable of scaring the daylights out of the first time visitor.
Yet, she can be a pussycat.
The adoption of four simple precepts will take a lot of the ferocity out of the tiger but leave unharmed her vitality and mag-

nificence for you to marvel at and thoroughly enjoy.

One: think of Tokyo as a series of small, unterrifying villages . . . which, indeed, once it was.

Two: entrap those villages in a "safety" web to give you protection while you examine small parts of the beast from its nose to its tail, at your leisure. That web exists. It is the Tokyo rapid transit system, a transportation network unrivaled in the world: clean, fast, efficient and cheap.

Three: substitute, as the hub of each village, the rail or subway station instead of the customary City Hall. Town Center of each of Tokyo's villages has grown up around "The Station."

Four is the biggy: communicate with the Tiger. You don't speak his language and he doesn't speak yours. It's his territory, so he's cool. You're the one who must exert the effort to understand him.

Start by demystifying the exotic street and district names found on the "English" city map. Prefixs and suffixs like these recur with great regularity: *shi, ku, cho, chome, dori, bashi.* If you know that shi means city, ku is ward, cho is precinct, chome is block, dori is street, and bashi is bridge, it helps.

Thus, subway or train stations names like Bakurocho and Jimbocho are more easily remembered as being in the precinct of Bakuro or Jimbo, or Kappabashi is near the bridge of Kappa.

Never mind the redundancy of English map labeling "Chuo-dori Ave" (translation: Chuo-avenue Avenue). The zoo keeper is just trying to be helpful.

Before setting off on a field test, let's review a few common denominators of each village and pack an emergency kit which you may never need but, should you, could prevent frustration.

Addresses in Tigerland are like Treasure Hunt maps: they give you a sense of the right direction but they are imprecise enough to remain a challenge. Zoning, as we know it, doesn't exist. The house or shop number refers to the chronology of its construction, not the juxtaposition to its next door neighbor. For example, a house bearing #34 as an address could very possibly be next door to a shop whose address is #2.

Therefore, the custom of the illustrated meishi (business card) is practiced widely. Even personal calling cards carry simple maps denoting the exact location within a well-known area as an aid to taxi driver or chauffeur.

Tokyo taxi drivers, unlike London cabbies, do not pride themselves on knowing every street, block and address number. There simply is no way they could! You are much better advised to take a subway or train to "The Village" of your choice, then a taxi to the shop, if it is not within walking distance. In the predictable event that the taxi driver does not know where the street is, don't panic. Look around for the Police Box—there's one at most major rail/subway stations. Get the on-duty officer to draw you another imprecise map, but in kanji, to give to your next taxi driver, who, almost predictably, will know *exactly* where the address is without your map! It happens all of the time.

Now for the emergency kit. Stop by the hotel Information Desk to get a card with the hotel's address written in kanji (most hotels have meishi for this purpose). Have them translate into kanji also the names pertinent to your destination: the district, street and address of the specific shop. Few Japanese taxi drivers speak enough English for clear communications purposes. These "cue cards" are vital.

Do not leave your hotel without a map of the city, subway and train maps, your sunglasses and an umbrella, and a supply of Kleenex. No matter what the weather is when you leave, it changes throughout the day. The Kleenex? Few toilets in Japan dispense tissue, and most are likely to be the Japanese-style which requires a bit more agility and a lot more accuracy than their Western counterpart. Remember to face the flushing handle.

(If it is any consolation, the Japanese have trouble adjusting to the Western style *loo* too. You'll see cartoon placards on Western toilets depicting what to do with the hinged seat.)

An optional item for your kit: soft-soled walking shoes. It's what the ladies who live in Tokyo wear. On one occasion when I was being chauffeured on a shopping excursion, I dressed up—high heels, silk dress, you know, the *right* look for a limousine exit from the Imperial Hotel. My hostess was dressed to the nines in a chic layered ensemble that would peel off throughout the day . . . chic except for her old reliable scuffy loafers with that Have-I-Tracked-Down-A-Few-Bargains-In-My-Day comfortable look. Barbara Sullivan saw my expression of disbelief, smothered an amused smile and explained "I dress to kill from the knees up, hoping no one will look at my feet. We'll do a lot of walking in spite of having a

GINZA/NIHOMBASHI

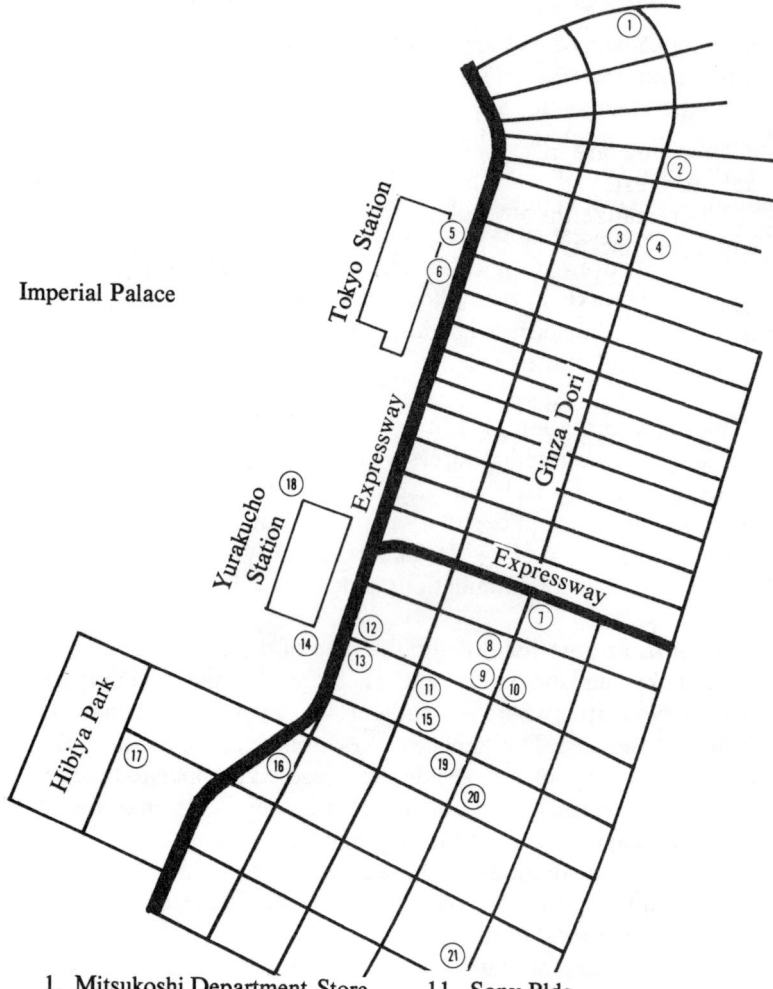

1. Mitsukoshi Department Store
2. Tokyu Department Store
3. Maruzen Book Store
4. Takashimaya Department Store
5. Perfectural Tourist Offices
6. Daimaru Department Store (above Tokyo Station)
7. Matsuya Department Store
8. Mikimoto Pearls
9. Wako (fashion specialty store)
10. Mitsukoshi Department Store
11. Sony Bldg.
12. Sukiyabashi Shopping Center
13. Hankyu Department Store
14. Tourist Information Center
15. Kinokuniya Book Store
16. International Arcade
17. Imperial Hotel
18. Sogo Department Store
19. Komatsu Department Store
20. Matsuzakaya Department Store

driver." I quickly changed to the clod-hoppers I had worn throughout Japan.

Now you are ready for the Take-The-Tube-Then-The-Taxi field-trip test.

To dramatize the location of each Shopping Village, we have created a Ring-Around-The-Palace Shopper's Map of Tokyo." It deliberately diminishes the importance of those "villages" not included in this Chapter: Marunouchi, for all of its business clout; Asakusa, known to locals as "downtown" but, in translation, more literally meaning "old city;" Ueno Park, a cultural/amusement center and many, many others. The Asakusa Kannon Temple may be one of Japan's finest Buddhist temples and a landmark of the city, but the gaudy, gay Nakamise shopping street leading to it does not make most shoppers' Top Ten list.

This deliberate omission is still another attempt to tame the Tiger.

Ginza/Nihombashi

Say Tokyo and think Ginza. They really do go together like ham n'eggs. Next door neighbor Nihombashi (spelled Nihonbashi on the maps) adds a dash of Old World seasoning. As a matter of historical record, the Ginza/Nihombashi district is both the font for the mercantile trade in Tokyo and the point of origin from which all official mileage distances are measured. That tradition began in 1604, one year after the construction of the bashi (bridge) in Nihombashi, when a stone marker was erected. From this marker, on five main roads radiating out to all parts of Japan, official mileage originated. It was from this bridge that public announcements were made and that feudal lords passed over on their mandatory biannual trips to the capital.

Being a realist on limited time, I ignored the stone marker—the original has been replaced on the north side of the bridge—in preference to the department stores, boutiques, art galleries, restaurants, museums and bookstores. I barely scratched the surface.

These side-by-side "villages" are convenient for the overseas shopper. Nine of the fourteen department stores in Tokyo are located within their walkable boundaries. Many of their salespersons speak some English, or will find someone who does. They accept credit cards, wrap, package and mail purchases, cash travelers checks, sponsor outstanding art exhibitions and craft shows.

Thirty years ago Matsuya imported the first Impressionist art show which proved so popular with the masses that today the department stores play a continuous Can-You-Top-This-Art-Show game in what appears to be a national insatiable appetite for modern art. When we were there recently Takashimaya had imported a Phillips Museum (Washington DC) Collection of 190 Impressionists, including Renoir's famous "Luncheon of the Boating Party", the first time, we understand, the collection ever went on tour.

In one or another department store, most any time, there will be some kind of a sale in progress. The "sales" area is the top merchandising floor—not to be confused with the elaborate playground rooftops where you'll encounter hundreds of over-indulged moppets riding miniature roller coasters or Ferris wheels, mechanical cars or eyeing an animal in a miniature zoo . . . and, almost certainly, eating.

The sales event may be a bargain offer, like that I encountered one autumn when Takashimaya sold off its rental bridal gowns and kimono stock at incredible prices beginning at Y1,000 (about $4). A Tokyo resident friend bought four petite—and lovely—formal Western bridesmaids gowns for her nine-year-old daughter and friends to play "dress up" in. Ornate, elaborately embroidered kimono—the kind people mount as wall hangings—sold for Y15,000 (about $62.50).

Or the sale might be accompanied by an artist or craftsman demonstration. The number of such attractions is extensive. You must decide priorities among the multitude of choices weekly, a listing of which you will find in one of the English-language periodicals.

Name a haute-couture fashion label. You'll find it in one of these Ginza/Nihombashi stores. They have them all, whether the designer is American or Parisian or British or Italian or Japanese. Many of the international brands are made in Japan. They are not "knock-offs" (copies) but legitimate franchises granted by their designers not solely for sizing or economic reasons. To be sure, requirements for sizing run smaller in Japan but the surprise is, although the Japanese are addicted to prestigious imported brands, they find fault with the quality of workmanship. In a 1983 governmental survey, women complained that foreign clothes shrank or lost color when washed. Many called for "greater efforts to adjust foreign products to Japanese local conditions."

Which is the best department store in Tokyo? Ask ten people, get ten answers. Among the top three in the Ginza/Nihombashi area, you'll usually find these three.

Mitsukoshi, with 310-years practice in building a loyal clientele, is wearing a crooked halo these days since the head of the store was caught in a scheme of buying merchandise for the nationwide chain through his mistress. Still, the hotel concierge will commend Mitsukoshi to you as a #1 priority shopping stop.

You also learn that a gift from a Mitsukoshi store carries a lot of weight with a Japanese hostess. For goodness sakes, leave the wrapping paper on the gift. It's as important as the gift itself—a barometer of the amount of respect you hold for the recipient and an indicator of your own status! The main Mitsukoshi store is in Nihombashi; a smaller branch store in Ginza.

Takashimaya is ranked as the "Harrod's" of Japan and certainly stands at the front of the class. Its Japanese wares are top quality.

Wako, which is owned by the Mikimoto pearl organization, is an exquisite store. Small and classy, it's like an I. Magnin or Saks Fifth Avenue. Everything in the store tends to be imported.

Tokyo vibrates with shopping every day of the week, from 10 A.M. to 6 P.M. (6:30 on Saturdays and Sundays), but not every store is open every day. The large department stores each close on a different day—sensible—but they all seem to be open on Tuesday, Friday and Saturdays. I wonder why?

The best time to shop is 10:00 A.M. until 11:30 A.M. before the crowds begin to swell. At ten o'clock, when the store opens, the uniformed staff line up from the entrance to "bow in" the first hundred or so shoppers, a tradition that makes you feel warm all over and a lot happier about parting with your money. Another touch of class mastered by the Japanese.

Good times to avoid department stores are weekends and during the traditional "gift-giving" seasons *(ochugen* and *oseibo)* in July and December. Entire sales floors are converted to special ordering rooms for the convenience of buyers in selecting just the right gift at just the right price for their extensive list of obligatory recipients. In stores, gift catalogs are categorized by price, rather than type. The sales floors will be filled to the rafters with proven popular items of exchange: boxes of fancy soaps, whiskey, sake, elaborate imported food packages (Fauchon, and Fortnum and Mason edibles are so common you'll think you're in Paris or London).

Why not weekends? Because the natives flock to their department stores like Americans to their country clubs and Australians to their beaches and bays. Every department store has its special "draw": Mitsukoshi has two live theaters, Seibu a gymnasium, Hankyu twin rooftop beer gardens, Odakyu (in Shinjuku) even has a driving range or a dental clinic, take your pick.

It is a classic case of adopt-and-adapt for which the Japanese are famous. They adopted the American model *departo* around the turn of the century and adapted it to their standard of service ("sahvees"), a commodity for which they are equally famous.

If we're honest, we have to admit that we've been one-upped.

Tip: unless you have a lot of time, don't eat in a department store restaurant despite the temptations and inordinate opportunity. It seems to take a lot longer than necessary unless you have a Japanese friend along.

Tip: deposit your wet umbrella in a free lockable umbrella stand at the entrance to the giant emporiums. Either the umbrella grates or a hostess dispensing plastic covers will be at the door. They think of every service.

Alongside these elegant retail giants you'll find a host of tiny, single item stores, many of which have been making the same traditional speciality item for three hundred or so years. Fifty such family-owned stores are documented in a charming and sensitive book, *Kites, Crackers and Craftsmen,* by Camy Condon and Kimiko Nagasawa (Sixth printing, 1983). If you have the uncommitted time, browse their book first then go "window shopping" into Japanese history with two dedicated traditionalists who guide you to specific shops.

One of the craziest shopping arcades you'll encounter is the International Arcade, a number of hole-in-the-wall shops built *under* the elevated railway that sidles up to the posh Imperial Hotel. Shop entrances are on both sides of the street—or rather train tracks—and many stores offer tax-free items on presentation of a passport.

A Shoppers' Guide 41

Our expatriate friends living in Tokyo tell us they get the best prices for watches from a minuscule shop called Sundry Trading Co. in the Arcade. So good are the prices that one Hawaiian bank buys its corporate and employee Christmas gifts there instead of through more normal channels.

While you are this close to the Imperial Hotel, experience real elegance; roam the unhurried corridors of the shops in the main building Arcade (basement) and in the adjoining Tower. Heads of state and international celebrities do. If you must buy pearls in Tokyo (they are cheaper in Hong Kong, but just probably of better quality in Japan), check out K. Uyeda Jeweller in the Imperial's Arcade. Of all the pearl stores shopped in the Ginza, including the swank Mikimoto (whose five-floor store near Wako is a treat just to look at), Uyeda was the only jeweller willing to restring an older strand, matching new pearls to it. As a result of their cooperation and voluntary discount policy, Uyeda has more than a few satisfied pearl customers.

A block north of the Imperial Hotel is still another good reason for beginning your shopping adventure in the Ginza: the TIC (Tourist Information Center). Ask one of the representatives to recommend the absolutely best place(s) in town for buying whatever item you seek. Never, in all of our travels, have I experienced such candor from government employees. It is so refreshing to get a straight answer, isn't it, instead of a lot of politically motivated mumbo-jumbo? Better still, their information proved to be right on target.

At TIC also pick up, free of charge, their Tourist Map of Tokyo and a copy of *Tour Companion,* the English-speaking community's "bible" for keeping posted on what's happening in Tokyo. It also is a font of practical information, like overseas mailing rates, metric conversions, English-spoken radio or TV casts. *Tokyo Weekender,* also free, is more directed to the residential foreign community's interest, but still worth reading.

If you plan to be in the city more than a couple of days and have unstructured plans, you should also read *Tokyo Journal* and *Joyful Tokyo.* The *Journal* is a monthly tabloid full of information about cultural activities, including the exhibitions—and sales—at the department stores. *Joyful,* a slick cover little magazine, is a bit thin—but adds a layer of fact to the knowledge pool.

TIC can direct you to Maruzen (opposite Takashimaya Department Store) where these publications and any reference book about Japan you've ever wanted probably can be found. To the right of the elevator on the English language floor is a superb, if small, selection of quality crafts, some traditional, some contemporary.

Three other recommendables in the area, if you are interested in the crafts or antiques of Japan, are Takumi Craft Shop at 8-4-2 Ginza Chuo-ku, Sukiyabashi Shopping Center with eighty-four shops on two floors (the second floor is especially interesting) and the offices of Japan's prefectures, located on the ninth floor of Daimaru Department Store and the Kokusai Kanko Building near Tokyo Station. Each prefecture displays the crafts of its region. Those items that are for sale are at bargain prices.

You could spend your entire time budget shopping in the Ginza/Nihombashi villages and never regret it. But your pocketbook might. Neither village has a reputation for frugality. There are better buys to be had elsewhere, but more importantly, new adventures await you in any one of the other villages.

Spread open a map of Tokyo. Take a pin. Blindfold your eyes. Now stick the pin into the map, look at the destination targeted and find the nearest tram station. Go there. Trust me, you'll have an absorbing encounter whether it is a mega or a mini-village . . . although mini-villages are hard to find in Tigertown.

Most probably, you'll find another whole city around The Station: huge department stores, office buildings, theaters and restaurants, specialty stores of all kinds. But in the narrower streets intermingled with the broader ones, you are apt to find the neighborhood rice or kimono store, the inevitable *sento* (public bath) or a tatami mat maker. You are bound to see small specialty stores that sell a single product: chicken—any part of it—tobacco, umbrellas, *osenbei* (rice crackers), fish, pork, to name but a few. There will be sushi bars, mom'n'pop green grocers, the local record rental shop (big business in Tokyo).

If you do not subscribe to the Pin-Your-Fate-On-A-Map theory, perhaps you would take the advice of the shopping pros who live in Tokyo? We have friends who live or have lived in Tokyo for years, who, in turn, introduced us to other top resources for ferreting out the best places to shop. From the shopping guides compiled by the Tokyo American Club and the Tokyo Union Church for their members, and from the experiences of our friends, we offer thumbnail sketches of a few of the more fascinating shopping districts.

Akasaka/Roppongi

Akasaka—not to be confused with Asakusa—is a "Hotel Village" with an international transient population. Roppongi is an "Embassy Village" with a cosmopolitan well-heeled community. Both are famous for their nightlife.

So where does the shopping come into focus?

In Akasaka, the best shopping exists in hotel arcades such as the New Otani, Akasaka Prince, Hotel Okura where sales clerks are accustomed to the foreigner, and usually can speak English. Even better, they can package and post your parcels and accept just about any kind of payment you prefer to offer. Not all bad. You may pay a slight premium for the convenience, but not much. Prices are high because of the kinds of goods sold in space-limited hotel arcade shops, but you'll find some of the best antiques and hand-crafted items there. Why? Shopkeepers are attracted by the constant turnover of potential buyers.

Roppongi, on the other hand, is a neighborhood village grown big. It's shops are mostly boutiques and specialty stores with heavy emphasis on antiques. You will want to make sure that the antique you buy can be taken out of the country. Japan, like so many enlightened countries, has rather strict laws about the export of its old art objects. You may need a license. Certainly, you'll want reassurance that none is required.

Among the notable antique dealers in the area are: Antiques Fuso (Sendai tansu), Edo Antiques (tansu, hibachi, pottery and porcelains), The Gallery (furniture, Imari, jewelry, lamps, accessories), Harumi (furnishings, ceramics, baskets, tansu), Honma (Imari), Kurofune (Northern Japan antiques), Michael Dunn Oriental Art (scrolls and screens) and Nakabon (Imari). Also, try the shops in the Okura Hotel.

A couple of interesting craft stores are Tsukamoto Pottery (Mashiko pottery) and Washikobo (traditional handcrafted paper items).

Interestingly, the only Flea Market of two day duration is held in posh Roppongi. The affluent are usually good bargain hunters.

I loved it. Silk kimono at outrageously low prices, the highest being $45, the lowest $4.15. And obi, wonderful silk gifts to be used

ROPPONGI

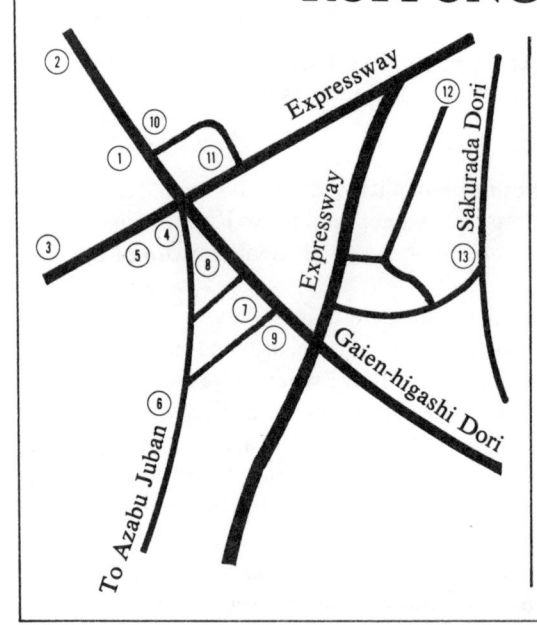

1. Fuso Antiques
2. Kurofune
3. Washikobo Paperware
4. Almond Coffee Shop (Favorite meeting place)
5. Roppongi Crossing Station (Subway)
6. Sweden Center
7. Roi Building (Flea Market Site)
8. Andre Bernard
9. Michael Dunn
10. Japan Defense Agency
11. Tsukamoto Pottery
12. Hotel Okura Shops
13. Japan Tax Free Center

AZABU JUBAN

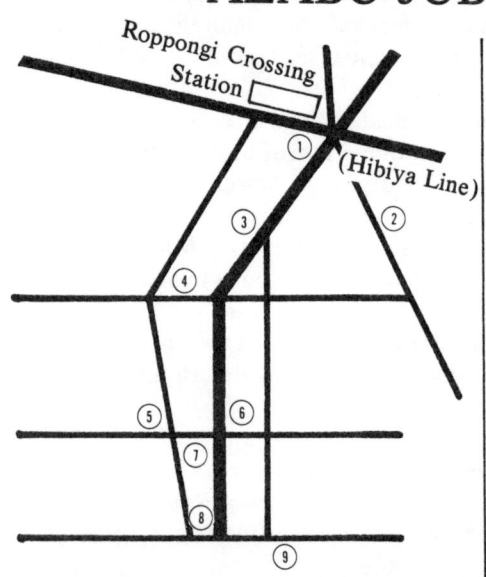

1. Almond Coffee Shop
2. Roi Building
3. Sweden Center
4. Public Bath
5. Blue and White Shop
6. Hasebe-ya (antiques)
7. Kimono shop
8. Wendy's Hamburgers
9. Police Box

as table runners or to be re-fashioned into glamorous vests or jackets.

Azabu Juban

Down the hill and two waggles away from Roppongi Crossing is a neighborhood shopping area dating back to the Edo period that, until the foreign community "discovered" it, was traditional in every sense of the word. Today, it is still traditional but "tarted up" to meet the expectations of its new neighbors, primarily the diplomatic crowd from the surrounding embassies. The streets connecting the two hundred or so shops are festooned with colorful street pendants and—for goodness sakes—on the south end of Juban dori there's a new Wendy's hamburgers!

Needless to say, prices have risen in direct proportion with the streets' facelift but they are still considerably lower than those in Roppongi and Akasaka. One one-of-a-kind store in the area is the Blue and White Shop, owned by an American woman married to a Japanese businessman, which specializes in clothing, accessories and gift items made of *yukata* and *aizome,* the hand-dyed Indigo blue-and-white classic fabrics from which the summer kimono and peasant work clothes are made. I spent a small fortune in the shop because its merchandise blends the heritage of Japan with the requirements of the West—like sizes to fit the "queen-sized" figure and paper products using English language copy, for instance. Five stars.

Take time to browse other shops there. You'll find mostly residents, shopping the human-scaled shops, sipping coffee or snacking in the intimate bars and cafes. I found another tansu antique store here, Hasebe-ya. Prices seemed very fair. Don't go Tuesdays. Most of the stores take the day off.

Shibuya: Harajuku To Omotesando

If you are young and fashion trendy, you'll want to be seen walking down Omotesando Dori from Yoyogi Park to Aoyama Dori any day, especially Sunday when most of the tree-shaded avenue is reserved for pedestrian traffic.

Even if you are not young and trendy, go and goggle.

Even in the rain, it's a sight.

Even on the parallel side street, narrow and crowded with soba and sushi shops, small cafes and coffee bars, His-Her-And-Their

SHIBUYA

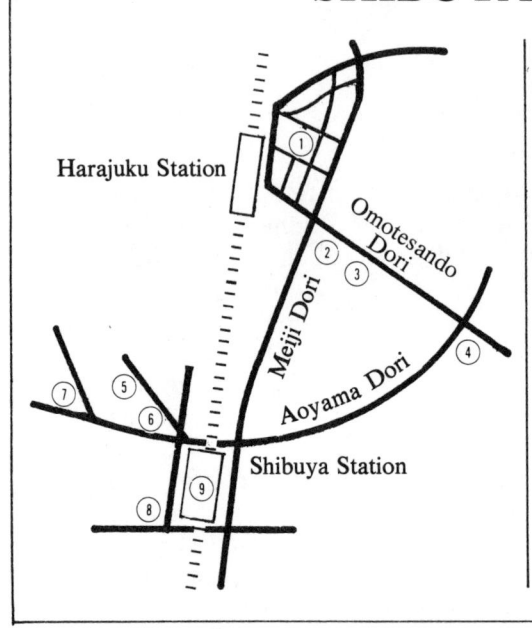

1. "Trendy" Town
2. Oriental Bazaar
3. Hanae Mori
4. Issey Miyake
5. Parco Department Store
6. Seibu Department Store
7. Tokyu Department Store (Main Store)
8. Tokyu Plaza
9. Tokyu Department Store (Over Station)

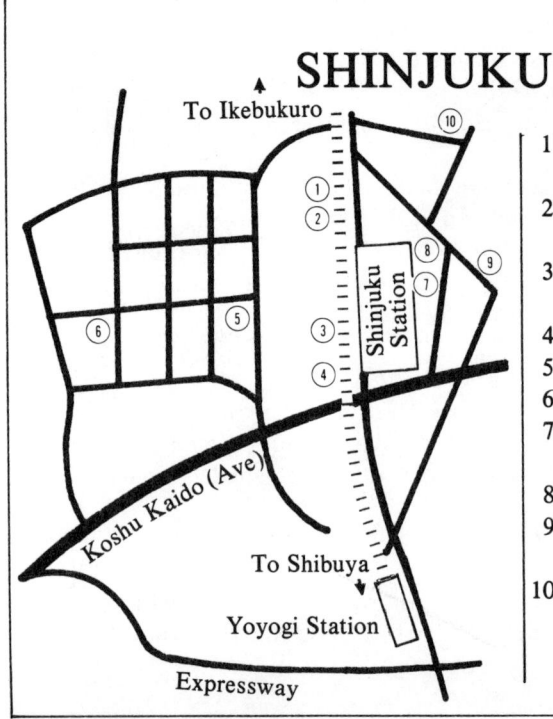

SHINJUKU

1. Odakyu Department Store
2. Odakyu Department Store
3. Keio Department Store
4. Yodobashi Camera
5. Keio Plaza Hotel
6. Century Hyatt Hotel
7. Mitsukoshi Department Store
8. Camera Sakuraya
9. Isetan Department Store
10. Bingoya Craft Shop

clothing boutiques, there's a sense that the purpose of being is being seen.

"Being seen" may even be the motivation behind the Sunday special attraction for which Yoyogi Park is known: dance fever. This isn't of the Travolta gender—way before his time. More like Elvis Presley or the Big Band era. Teen-agers in dress vintage, mostly of the Fifties, dance to recorded music.

Midway between Harajuku Station and Omotesando Station on the street residents call Tokyo's "Champs-Elysees" is a pagoda-roofed building that resembles a shrine. The foreign community in Tokyo and overseas visitors make frequent pilgrimages to this commercial shrine.

Throughout my research, I asked friends who had lived in Japan and those who still live there "If you could shop at just one store in Tokyo, which one would it be?" I fully expected answers to be Mitsukoshi, Takashimaya, Seibu or any one of the full-service department stores.

Do you know the singular answer I got? Never a deviation. Never a long, meditating pause. Snappy and decisive, the answer was "The Oriental Bazaar."

I had to know why personally. The Oriental Bazaar stocks old and new crafts including a large selection of Imari-ware, screens, chests, old and new silk and brocade kimono, cotton yukata—but sized to fit Western bodies and at half the price you'll pay in most department stores—plus hundreds of souvenir, household and kitchen items. A kind of a one-stop shopping center for things Japanese.

"The slightly higher price you pay for some of the quality antiques, including Imari, is more than compensated for by the lack of frustration of trying to find it elsewhere," a banker's wife said. She also confided that the better buys are downstairs. Seems that the shop is operated by two concessionaires.

The Oriental Bazaar makes converts daily . . . like our friends who bought a tea chest but didn't want to ship it home or lug it with them on the rest of their Japan tour. Management promised airport delivery on their day of departure, despite a nervous-making one-hour connecting flight schedule. That's service, and confidence.

A block and a half away towards Omotesando Station is the sleek and silvered headquarters of Hanae Mori, dean of Japan's fashion designers. Not of the "new wave" Madam Mori, with her classic silhouettes aflutter with gay butterflies, but, nonetheless, the respected leader of the pack. Her small emporium offers antiques in the basement—a lot of which are European. Boutique collections and an upmarket coffee lounge occupy the first floor, and her couture fashions—pricey they are—are on the second floor.

For the freshest approach to fashion, shop the Issey Miyake boutique two blocks beyond Omotesando Station on the same street, the same side. The acknowledged frontrunner of the "counter-couture new wave", Miyake's clothes are easy-to-wear separates in fabulous fabrics. "My concept of fashion is the wearing of fabric—not clothes," he was quoted in a newspaper. In addition to his own shops, you'll find the Miyake label in many of the "departos."

Ikebukuro

On a clear day you can see forever from the observation floor of the Sunshine 60 Building, Tigertown's tallest. That is, if you can find your way out of the Seibu Department Store that envelops Ikebukuro Station. You get the impression, upon disembarking from the train, that the Seibu store *is* The Station.

The behemoth, larger than Macy's Manhattan store, is one of the new breed of "subway stores" founded after World War II by private railway companies in mass-transit suburban terminals. What started as a series of platform kiosks has emerged as sophisticated shopping emporiums on multiple floors. (In a sense, they still are platform kiosks. At the Shibuya Station, for example, tram tracks run down the third, fourth and fifth floors of the Tokyu Department Store.)

Sunshine City, also developed by Seibu, is a five minute walk from Ikebukuro Station. It claims the nation's tallest hotel, Sunshine City Prince, the first laserium, US and British Trade Centers and a variety of shopping opportunities: Alpa Building with about two hundred shops, and Mitsukoshi Plaza, in the World Import Mart, which has over a hundred shops specializing in quality imported items.

I never saw Sunshine City because (1) it was raining too hard for me to enjoy the sport of exploring, and (2) I never found my way out of the Seibu store at the Ikebukuro Station.

Talk about full-service; Seibu's non-retailing facilities include experimental theaters, a museum, sports clinic centers, and—for goodness sakes—a community college. The store has a reputation for a good selection of Japanese made "queen" sizes which simply means anything over size 9. Whether you are a size 9, 10, 12, or 14 start by trying on size 9 first.

Jimbocho

Jimbocho Station is closest to one of the highest touted antique and crafts centers in Tokyo, the Tokyo Komingu Kotto-Kan (Japan Old Folk Craft and Antique Centre). It is also in the second-hand and English language rare book district known as Kanda, a fascinating place to browse.

After searching dozens of antique and other craft stores, I turned to TIC for help in finding a *dai-za,* a ceiling hook made from a tree trunk and formerly used in traditional farm houses to hold the bamboo *jizai* (hook) which held the kettle over the fire. TIC called the Centre to find out if any of the fifty-five shops occupying four floors had a dai-za.

Of course! Chalk up another star for TIC.

The shops in the small six-story building look like rats' nests and, often, the merchandise is dusty to dirty but the prices are fair and the dealers cooperative. They accept credit cards, will deliver heavy objects to your hotel or ship your purchases. They go out of their way to help you find any object you desire. Look for the association's red banners outside an unimposing grey building.

On the 3rd, 14th and 24th of each month auctions are held for dealers only, on the sixth floor. You need to speak Japanese.

Shinjuku

Shinjuku might be Tokyo's prime candidate for the psychiatrist's couch. Once the sanctuary for radicals, hippies and the "folksong guerrillas", it became the target of "big money" corporations who found its fertile fields ideal for constructing skyscrapers.

Today west of The Station, Shinjuku is slick and modern; east, it's still cheap restaurants, gawdy neon lighting, huge department stores and tiny boutiques . . . like it use to be, only more of it. Shinjuku is the front door to the western suburbs, one of the busiest train/subway terminals and Tokyo's second largest shopping district.

It is chaotic . . . and a kick.

Political theater in the street, a bicyclist "surfing" on his tummy among the night throngs in a Look-Ma-No-Feet-Or-Hands position, neon signs that make Las Vegas look subdued, loud speakers and megaphones blaring out messages for the masses.

There are two particular shopping reasons to go to Shinjuku. Crafts and cameras. Quality crafts. Bargain-priced cameras.

Bingoya Folk Craft Shop is a splendid reason to meet the challenge of Shinjuku if you, like me, agree with the author of *Mingei, Japan's Enduring Folk Arts,* Amaury Saint-Gilles, "Whenever and wherever I visit another culture, I find it is folk art and handmade crafts that fill my suitcases to overflowing. Perhaps it is merely their lack of pretensions but I think also their attraction has to do with the obvious care with which they have been crafted."

Bingoya is credited with having provided much of the background for this bibliography of folk art, and many of the 116 depicted items are for sale in the small but well organized store. I confess to preferring the old mingei over much of the newer folk souvenirs Bingoya stocks. There seems to be something more honest—and more artistic—in an item that has function as well as decor value.

I also confess bewilderment over Bingoya's high inventory of India products; it strains their claim as purveyor of "the best traditional handicrafts manufactured in Japan."

Take a taxi from The Station. (Short cut the inevitable: go directly to the Police Box in The Station and ask for a map in kanji to give to the taxi driver.)

The lowest camera prices in Japan are to be found in Shinjuku at two well established stores, Yodobashi and Sakuraya—one east, one west of The Station. We compared Sakuraya's prices for a Canon A1 against Mitsukoshi's tax-free center, Auckland's Duty Free Shop, and our favorite Honolulu camera store. Sakuraya's price won hands down over all but the Honolulu store which had a special close-out sale on that model.

Incidentally, it is always wise to check that all is in good working order before leaving Tokyo.

There's one other reason for going to Shinjuku: Isetan departo, formerly thought as being strictly for the young, has changed its merchandise and its image. Friends now refer to it as the "Bloomingdale's" of Tokyo.

"I Can Get It For You Wholesale"
Akihabara, The Electronic Village

The least "Japanese" place we encountered was Akihabara, its air filled with every conceivable functioning electronic device—loud speakers, blaring stereos and TVs, hawking salesmen, each trying to top the next one's discount claim.

That part is in character; it's the bargaining that is different. This is the only place in Japan that expects you to haggle—but just a little.

So unusual do the Japanese find Akihabara that city sightseeing brochures list it as one of Tokyo's "Seven Wonders" and tours make stops on Chuo Dori Avenue to permit their passengers to shop.

If you plan to shop for things electronic in Tokyo, do your homework first. Know the precise model you seek. Know the price you would pay for it at home. Then compare. Akihabara, with roughly six hundred stores, is geared for the Japanese customer. Dealer discounts are restricted by their manufacturer. While prices are twenty to thirty per cent lower than in the rest of Tokyo—the lowest in all of Japan—overseas visitors most probably can get better deals back home through discount retail stores, annual sales at department stores or friends with wholesale or manufacturing connections.

We priced Sony Betamax models in several Akihabara stores, and when I observed that the "domestic" price was lower than the "tax free" price for the same model, the salesman explained that charges for modification are added, *then* taxes deducted. These modifications are necessary to convert the appliance's voltage and cycles to the overseas buyer's requirements. Confronted with my persistent questioning, he suggested that it may be more advantageous to buy at home, especially for the "aftersale" service.

It was also cheaper, by about thirty per cent.

"Take", my Japanese companion who is an electronics buff, explained that Sony and Yamaha allow the smallest discounts of all the Japanese manufacturers. Many of the other brands—National (Panasonic), Sanyo, Sharp, JVC, Hitachi—are of equal "or better" quality, and permit the dealers more leeway in price negotiation.

"Once," he said, "Sony and Yamaha were superior products, but the competition is so keen, technology so advanced now, that you can buy any Japanese brand with confidence."

He feels that the dedicated electronic do-it-yourselfer can get real bargains in Akihabara . . . but for the rest of us, the option should be closely examined.

Two of the main stores in Akihabara are Hirose and Laox. Between them, they have seven stores on the main intersection.

Bakurocho

"I can have the driver and car on Thursday if you'd like to go shop the wholesale districts." The lilting voice on the telephone belonged to my friend Barbara.

I'm not above a little luxury in spite of my firm conviction that Tokyo's subways or trains are faster. Besides, it provided transportation for the loot bought in "the name of research."

En route to Asakusabashi, the paper goods and party decorations district, Barbara reported that Komoda-San, her driver, told of a wholesale clothes district where he bought his wardrobe. "It's on the way. I've never been there so I don't know if it's worthwhile."

It's worthwhile.

It doesn't resemble any of the wholesale districts I've ever shopped. As a matter of fact, it looks a lot like other *retail* shopping streets in Tokyo: stores with display windows and staffs to serve the drop-in trade.

Komoda-San dropped us off on Edobori Avenue, just down the street from Bakuro Yokoyama subway station, and in front of a store named Sanyo Fashion, which is, I found out later, licensee in Japan for Burberry, Bill Blass and Liz Claiborne and is, additionally, an internationally established brand label in its own right. It was one of the few stores that contained a placard both in English and kanji "Wholesale Only. No Sightseeing Allowed."

Elsewhere, however, accessories and apparel are available in abundance, inside and outside of stores. In an umbrella store—the pocket-sized folding ones make good packable presents—a most helpful non-English-speaking clerk dramatized the incredible effect that a designer label has on price. She opened up a butterfly printed umbrella; unmistakenly Hanae Mori. Price: Y5,000. Then she showed us the *same* umbrella sans butterflies but with the "HM" on the handle. Cost Y2,500. Finally, out came the plain, unsigned version: Y1,800. A couple of days later, in Mitsukoshi's, I priced it again, complete with "HM," butterflies and *departo* markup: Y10,000.

THE WHOLESALE VILLAGES

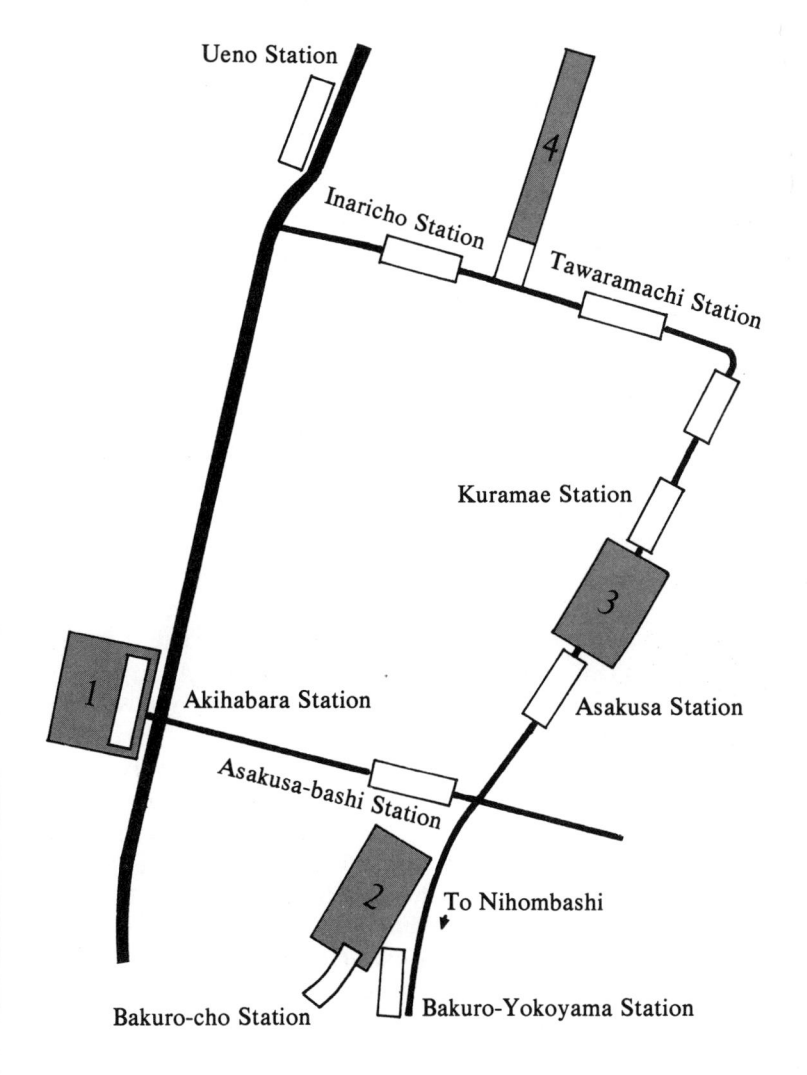

1. Akihabara: Electronic Village
2. Kodemma-Cho: Garment Village
3. Asakusabashi: Paper Village
4. Kappabashi: Housewares Village

"I'm coming back to this goldmine," announced Barbara as we crossed Asakusabashi and entered the wholesale paper district.

Note: you'll probably not find the "new wave" couture designers in Bakurocho, but you might find Renown (licensee for Perry Ellis and Norma Kamali) or Studio V, Alpha Cubic, Ichiju, Kashiyama, Micalady, Tsubame, or World, all well known manufacturers in Japan producing quality apparel for women.

Asakusabashi

Everything you ever wanted or needed in paper crafts or wares is carried in some store in the area between Asakusabashi Station and Kuramae Station, or just beyond. Shops line both sides of the street and wrap around the corners.

Decorative wrapping papers, floral supplies including fabric and paper flowers, ribbons, tapes, foil papers, party decorations. It's here.

Asakusabashi has, in addition to paper goods, fabrics and trimmings, inexpensive pocket-sized toys, traditional handmade Japanese kites in every size and design, and small department stores filled with all kinds of items for hobbists with which to "make things." (A "recommendable" fabric/trimmings shop is around the block from Kuramae Station. Look for Aichiya.)

From late October, traditional Christmas ornaments begin to appear in the stores and most of the year you can find the lustrous and vibrantly toned thread balls, *ito-mari,* made in every prefecture of Japan. They make attractive Christmas decorations too.

Some of the stores, as in the garment district, do not sell to the general public. But, you'll know this the moment you walk—or try to walk—into the store, in spite of any language barrier. One popular store with the foreign community in Tokyo is Takahashi Company which specializes in tea canisters covered with Japanese paper. One recent report was that they have placed the "Wholesale Only" placard in the window, yet did not deny the privilege of buying to the overseas shoppers. Who knows? Try if you like and report back. Location: from the exit at Kuramae Station, turn left.

I bought Christmas and general-use wrapping paper in wonderful colors and patterns—one hundred sheets for Y1,000 was average—and collapsible shiny gift boxes and assorted tapes and ribbons.

Heavy to cart back to Honolulu, but what a buy.

Kappabashi

If you are a kitchen freak, head for Kappabashi-dori Avenue. Do not shop the department stores. Do not pass "Go." Do not collect $100. You won't need to. You'll save that much or more.

"The Station", in this case, is Tawaramachi Station or Inaricho Station. It is about a five-minute walk from either to Kappabashi-dori Avenue.

Technically, it is a restaurant supply wholesale district and you will find shops that sell only uniforms, or plastic bottles, dixie cups or aluminumware; several places specialize in plastic food models—those replicas displayed in restaurant show windows denoting what-you-see-is-what-you-get.

But you'll also find traditional bambooware utensils, specialty pots and pans used both for show and for utilitarian purposes in restaurants, china, pottery, cutlery, and plastic lacquerware that looks good, has a respectable weight and is more durable than the real.

The prices are half that in the department stores.

And there wasn't a "Wholesale Only" sign to be seen.

Flea Markets

Always on Sundays and once monthly on Thursdays, Fridays and Saturdays, Tokyoites participate in lively flea markets. If there is a "best" trash-or-treasure operation, it probably is the two-day Spring (April) and Fall (September) Fair of folk crafts and antiques held at Heiwajima Tokyo Ryutsu Center, near Haneda, the domestic airline town. It's the granddaddy of the fleas; over two hundred dealers from throughout Japan bring their wares to the city to sell.

The rest of the year, it is business as usual with dealers from the city, all members of the flea market association, selling their wares at most of the weekly affairs.

I spent an hour at the Roi Building market (Roppongi) and blew Y18,000 on eight kimono, ten obi, and an enchanting piece of sculpture which I knew had to be mingei but I hadn't a clue what it was or how it functioned.

I scored that hour a "ten."

A telephone interview with the kimono vendor, an exporter,

couldn't even dampen my enthusiasm when he contended that dealers take only the "bottom pile" to flea markets and that, at the Fleas, the average price per kimono is Y1,000 but if you buy a few you can get them for Y300 each! Yipes, I blew Y12,000.

It's all a matter of perspective: the same garments in a store could run into the millions. Of course, in yen. The kimono, in Westerners' lives, will be worn in the privacy of a home or to a costume party, mounted on a wall or re-fashioned into a Western styled garment. I got some beauties, and according to my dressmaker in Hawaii, some had never been worn, all had been freshly cleaned.

How did she know that?

By the white basting threads in them. When a silk kimono is cleaned it is taken apart, each piece washed separately by hand, then re-sewn. Why? Because washing shrinks silk and each piece has to be trimmed and rematched. After it is reassembled—or assembled originally—the seamstress runs a thread along the finished seams.

And I thought the basting threads meant I would have to re-sew all the seams.

The obi cost more than a kimono, even at the Fleas. It is to the Japanese dress what a jewel is to Western dress. Its width, fabric and texture indicates its value.

The mingei piece? An amused pair of hotel maids made me understand through pantomime that it is a ink-pot used by carpenters for drawing straight lines. I found out later that it is a *sumitsubo*. Made of zelkova wood, it is beautiful.

The monthly action takes place at these locations:

1st Sunday:	Arai Yakushi Temple Arai Yakushi Station in Shinjuku (Seibu Shinjuku Line)
2nd Sunday:	Nogi Shrine Nogizaka Station in Akasaka (Subway Chiyoda Line)
3rd Saturday & Sunday:	Sunshine City, Alpa Shopping Arcade B1, Ikebukuro Station (Seibu Shinjuku Line)

4th Thursday: & Friday:	Roi Building Roppongi Station (Subway: Hibiya Line)
1st & 4th Sundays:	Togo Shrine Meiji Jingumae Station Subway Chiyoda Line or Harajuku Station Yamanote Line

Omiyage

Our Japan shopping experience started at home, in Honolulu. Yours should too if you plan to see Japanese friends because omiyage—gifts for family, business associates and friends—is a Japanese custom.

For a new father, I bought a baby's T-shirt/diaper ensemble with an "Hawaii" inscription because, if the Japanese are mad for T-shirts with English titles, they are even madder for Things Hawaiian.

Duty-free scotch, champagne, brandy and cigars—all good brands because the Japanese are name-brand conscious—were for our Tokyo business associates and friends. Designer accessories—names like Gucci, Hermes, Cartier—go over very big with the sophisticated.

Chocolate-covered macadamia nuts, small cans of salted macadamias, and copies of our other HOW TO GET LOST AND FOUND travel books were intended for our "Home Visit" hosts and people who showed us courtesies along our routes.

Tipping is an embarrassment to most Japanese but the person who goes out of his way to help you will treasure forever a cigarette lighter, ballpoint pen, insignia golf cap or some other souvenir imprinted with an English logo.

Omiyage is not mandatory for the foreigner in Japan, nor even expected, but it will be greatly appreciated as the social grace it is.

Between Japanese, however, omiyage is a deeply-rooted tradition, often a burden to both giver and receiver. In its simpliest interpretation, the custom means "I would like to establish an on-going friendship with you."

"On-going relationships" can become expensive if, as the custom seems to be, everytime you go on a trip *anywhere* you must return bearing gifts for all of your friends and family. Wherever we went to Japan—cities, villages, parks, visitor attractions, shrines or temples—it was the Japanese who crushed around souvenir stands, buying for the folks back home.

What do they buy? The local food specialties are very popular. Folk toys. Curios. The local handicrafts. Cheap lighters, pens, miniature flashlights, amulets . . . items in the Y250 to Y2,500 ($1 to $10) range. Little "diddlies" that you shake your head in disbelief over.

But a truism is that once you separate a diddlie from the pack of look-alikes, it becomes something special. I turned my nose up at painted wooden jewelry of the symbolic "North Fox" on sale throughout Hokkaido only to have a pin presented to me upon departure from a ryokan. It became a staple to my travel wardrobe; a warm memory-jogger in my jewelry box.

3. Hakone
Tokyo's Mountain Playground

I took a taxi to Shinjuku Station to catch the Odakyu Limited Express "Romance Car" to Hakone. (The taxi was equipped with a miniature TV set activated by a Y100 coin.)

Having scouted Shinjuku, I was feeling sure of my bearings on arriving at the station and I stepped confidently into the building carrying my two bags. I looked around—and didn't recognize anything.

I was lost.

The time was between 8:30 and 9:00 A.M. and the bulk of over one million people who transit the station every day surrounded me in giant, engulfing human waves moving in all directions.

I looked at my ticket trying to establish a relationship between the kanji characters and the overhead directional signs. No clue.

As desperation set in I was approached by a disheveled old man who, by sign language, indicated he wanted to look at my ticket. He wore a baseball cap askew on his head. A cigarette was tucked behind his ear. In one pocket of a slovenly jacket an old, rolled up newspaper stuck out and from the other pocket hung a towel. He carried a box of crackers and an umbrella.

The town nut.

I tried to ignore him, setting off resolutely in a direction he had indicated, getting away from him as fast as I possibly could. No use. It was soon apparent out of the corner of my eye that he was still with me. Embarrassing. I really didn't want to be picked up by a character who either had some sort of mental disorder or a very strange tailor.

We came to a ticket taker, my companion said something to the person on duty who looked at my ticket and passed me through but let my new, self-appointed friend through without a ticket. We came to another barrier and another ticket taker and the same thing happened.

My guide now pointed to stairs leading up, and, not having any better solution, I followed him. At the top of the stairs he motioned to the right and I went to the right and—*voila*—there was the

Odakyu line! Another ticket taker, in a friendly fashion, permitted my companion to go through with me. Once on the platform, he looked at my ticket again, took me to my designated car and put me on board, waved goodbye, turned and walked away.

No tip expected. No thanks expected. Just a good Samaritan in a funny cap.

I felt very small, very humble.

When I told this story to other overseas visitors, which I did a dozen times, they always replied, "Wait! Wait until you hear what happened to us."

And they would have heart warming tales of being rescued in Japan.

Hakone is a mountain and lake playground for the millions of people who live in and around Tokyo, a long-time favorite of the foreign community, and a day-trip out of Tokyo for many visitors.

Its scenery attracts the outdoor lovers who enjoy the space of nature after the crowded cities. The romantic atmosphere attracts the indoor lovers.

Golfing brings many businessmen who desire prestigious recreation. Hiking, fishing, boating, sight-seeing, steam baths bring hordes of others.

In the lake area there are ten hotels, eight spas with mineral baths, eight golf courses.

Hakone is easily accessible. My "Romance Car" ride in a comfortable first-class carriage took less than one and a half hours.

The district itself lies in the remains of a giant volcano in which rests a large lake, forty kilometers in circumference, properly called Lake Ashi but most often referred to as Lake Hakone.

The train stops at the Hakone-Yumoto station.

Yumoto is a center of tourism in itself with surrounding hotels and tourist-oriented shops.

My destination was Miyanoshita, half an hour's taxi ride into the mountains, following a curved road along a running stream, to the venerable (1878) Fujiya Hotel, an inn famous for its famous clientele.

The Fujiya looked absolutely proper for a Japanese mountain hotel. Big-timbered buildings with curled up eaves framed by cherry trees in bloom. A light rain was falling. A tree-covered mountain was barely visible through the veil of soft mist. It was

CENTRAL JAPAN

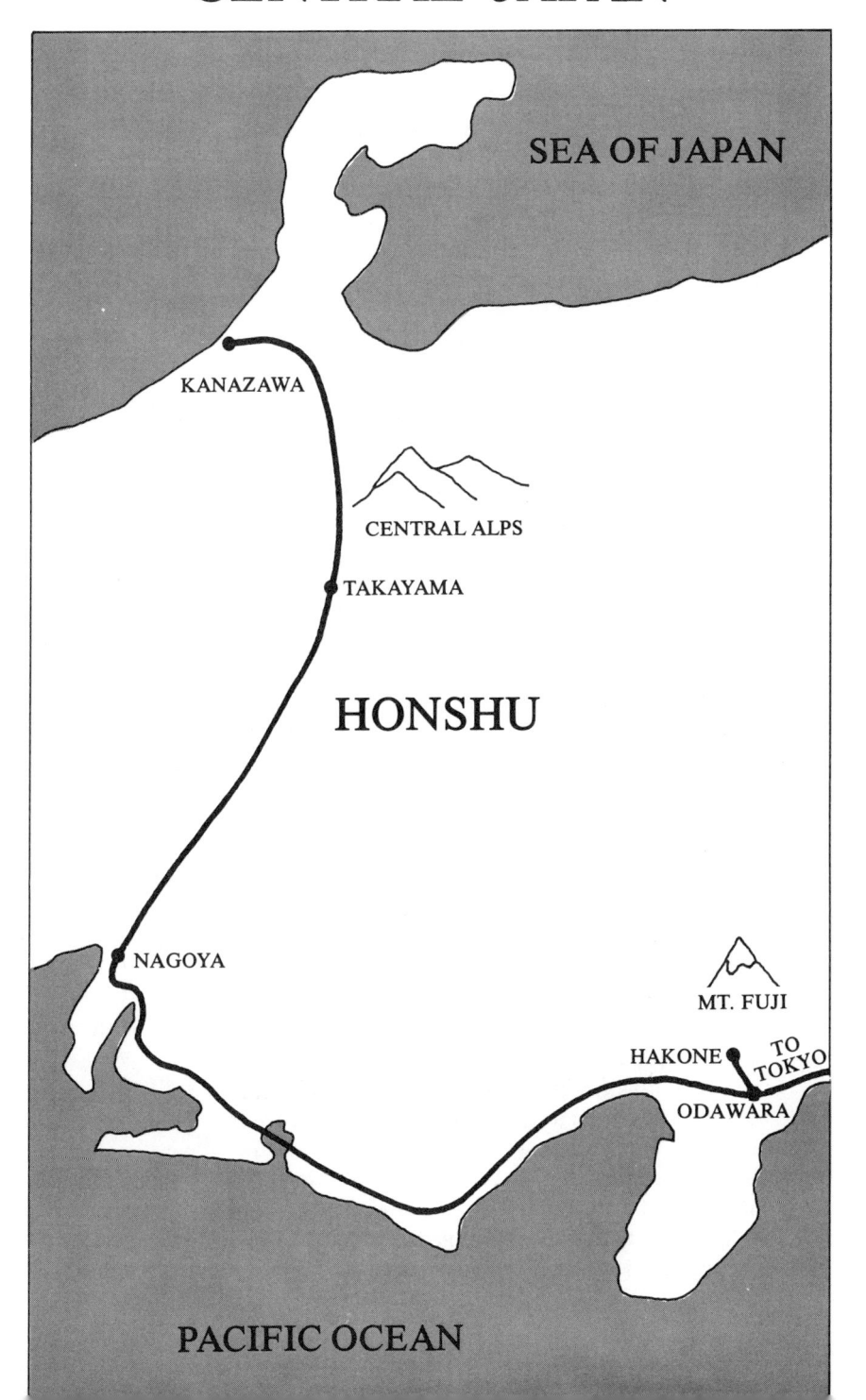

very satisfyingly Japanesque.

I was early. The room was not ready. (I soon realized that JNTO almost always had me travelling during the noon period so that a room would be ready when I arrived and I could wash, unpack and begin to explore.)

At the entrance my bags disappeared and I was bowed into a large room with overstuffed leather chairs and couches. The manager came and introduced himself. Mr. Takayasu Akiyama.

As the East comes West and the West comes East, an interesting change of customs is occurring.

The traditional Japanese bow. The inferior one bows lower than the superior one. In commerce the businessmen exchange cards. There is no shaking of hands, no touching.

The Western custom is to shake hands. Close friends clap each other on the shoulder, and in some countries even exchange bear hugs and cheek kisses.

Today what you often witness is that the Japanese, wise in Western ways, is the first to extend his hand while the Westerner, also pre-trained, is bowing from the waist and reaching for his card. There follows a confusion of bowing and hand-shaking and card-exchanging.

Funny.

Mr. Akiyama, a slight, bespectacled gentleman with an innate kindness about him, ordered coffee and sat for a few minutes before moving over to a conference with local officials.

"Tell me about the hotel."

"Fujiya was started in 1878 as a small inn and then became a hotel in 1884," he said.

"In those days people came by palanquin, hand-carried litters. Food stuffs were also transported on foot from Yokohama.

"One of the buildings still in use was built in 1891 and is the oldest hotel building in Japan."

"You've always been known for your foreign clientele?"

"Yes. The hotel has always been a favorite to the foreigners who came to enjoy the flowers in the spring and the leaves in the autumn. People from Tokyo came because they wanted to escape the heat of the summer. All of our rooms are Western style.

"We built one of the first golf courses in Japan in 1917. It had only seven holes. In 1935 the golf course was enlarged to 18 holes.

The Emperor played the course when he was the Crown Prince. "Generals MacArthur, Eisenhower, Secretary of State Dulles, prime ministers, members of European royal families . . . they have all stayed with us."

He put down his coffee cup and stood and bowed.

"Now I have a young lady standing by to show you the hotel. When you finish the tour, your room should be ready. Tomorrow I'll arrange for a car to take you around the district."

Takae Susuki, a recent graduate of Nihon University, was my petite Madamoiselle Butterfly guide, with black-on-black hair, black-on-black eyes and a pink-on-pink complexion. She probably brushed five feet, a sort of doll you'd like to take home with you—if you had a most understanding wife.

We toured the green house, the banquet room, the main dining room—it has alpine flowers painted on the ceiling and a prominent poem written by Emperor Meiji, founder of the Meiji dynasty:

"O that I could show people from afar across the seas our scenery of mountains and streams."

We toured the grill room, the main bar, the indoor swimming pool filled with natural, hot, mineral water, the Japanese style baths, the game room.

Due to the rain, we skipped the gardens behind the hotel but could see a waterfall in the garden gushing into a small pool just off the lobby making a lovely Japanese vista through the floor-to-ceiling windows.

The two wings of the hotel are the new wing, the Chrysanthemum Building, and the old wing, the Flower Palace.

My room, now ready, was in the old wing. It was big, handsome and named "Lily of the Valley." All the rooms in the Flower Palace wing have names. Down the hall was "Thistle", maybe for couples not getting along.

I had two large twin beds, a separate sitting area with sofa, television set and a desk. The bathroom was tiled and the closet-dressing room was larger than many rooms I would be staying in during the rest of the trip.

Lunch in the dining room was served on immaculate white table linen with matching linen napkins. The service was impeccable . . . even finger bowls after the meal.

And it rained. An ideal afternoon for reading. I curled up in my suite with the large windows looking out over the misty landscape and read about Japanese tourism. Fascinating figures.

Item: with a population of 120,000,000, 5,500,000 Japanese go over seas every year.

Item: 83% for pleasure.

Item: twice as many males go abroad as females.

Item: 3,000,000 go to Asian countries.

Item: the others go everywhere in the world: 1,750,000 to North America, 850,000 to Hawaii. Listen to this: almost 300,000 go to Switzerland.

Over 2,000,000 foreign visitors came to Japan in 1986 but the visitors were down 11% because of the higher priced yen; it almost doubled in two years. The Taiwanese, freed from money restrictions, were an important part of the market.

Over half of the overseas visitors came from Asian countries.

Visitors from Europe totalled 415,000 in 1985 but, of that figure, 182,000 came from the United Kingdom, distorted by the British passports from Hong Kong.

About 558,000 visitors came from the U.S.A.

Japanese going abroad spent $4,814,000,000.

Visitors coming to Japan spent $1,137,000,000.

Tourism resulted in a $3,677,000,000 deficit for Japan.

Foreign visitors spend 30% of their in-Japan budget on shopping!

Perhaps the figure is distorted by Taiwanese and Hong Kong Chinese who come to Japan to buy medicines and major appliances, usually pre-arranged with a wholesale discounted price.

Western-style hotel rooms in Japan increased in ten years from 47,000 to 190,000.

In January and February when the wind comes from Russia, the eastern side of Japan, facing the Pacific Ocean, is protected by the mountains and the skies are clean. It is one of the nicest times of the year.

In May the weather is stable.

The summers are muggy and hot.

October weather is stable again and showtime comes in the first two weeks of November when the trees change their leaves in a spectacular, muted rainbow of reds and rusts and yellows and golds and tans and browns.

Cherry blossom season in April can be cloudy and bring, what I was experiencing in Hakone, a "mustard rain"—so called because of the blossoming of mustard plants covering fields with blankets of yellow.

It was still raining the next morning. At the entrance to the hotel to see me off was the hotel manager, waiting beside a gleaming large car with a righthand drive, a chauffeur, and Takae-san who would act as interpreter guide. Mr. Aoki, the driver, spoke no English.

We drove up the mountain through the nearby resort of Kowakidani, towards the lookout at Owakudani where, on a clear day, it is possible to take a cable car over the boiling thermal pools and mud pots in Owakudani Valley and down to Lake Hakone.

The bad weather had shut down the cablecars. Nothing was running so we settled for a visit to the Owakudani Natural Museum with its exhibits of wildlife in the area: black bear, fox, deer, wild boar and Japanese monkeys. Also picture exhibits of the flora, fauna, and fish: black bass, brown trout, rainbow trout.

Not to be missed in the museum is a simulated giant lizard, a dimetrodon, living in a recreated cave. It moves and emits fierce roaring sounds.

Our next stop was another museum—The Matsuda Porsche Museum. I had seen the sign in passing and insisted on going back. What was a Porsche Museum doing in the middle of Hakone? I never did find out but, like all car buffs, was grateful for the chance to admire an unusually fine collection of automobiles.

In a single large room, thirty-two vintage cars were assembled including the winning car of the 1981 Le Mans, the most renowned of French racing classics. Every famous Porsche model was on the floor.

On an elevated space above the showroom was a spectator area with chairs. When we entered, there must have been a half a dozen young men sitting there just staring—mesmerized—at the cars as if they were works of art . . . which they are.

Our next stop was the Sengokuhara Golf Course. If Porsche racing cars make up one world of fantasy, welcome to the crazy world of golf in Japan.

Golf in Japan is more than a game. It is "face." To play golf is a signal of success, of affluency, of having arrived.

Therefore, golf is the rage. Go into a sports section of a Japanese department store and look at the number of men inspecting golf clubs.

(Fortunes have been made in Hawaii by shops selling America-made golf equipment to visiting Japanese. When Isao Aoki, Japan's top touring golf professional, became the first Japanese to win a PGA tournament, The Hawaii Open, by sinking a 128-yard chip shot on the final hole at Waialae Country Club, every visiting golfer from Japan wanted to play Waialae Country Club. Because I am a member at Waialae and witnessed the shot, I was very popular among golfers in Japan.)

Japan golfers who belong to private clubs are members of the elite. Land is so precious that creating a golf club is exorbitantly expensive and in turn so are the memberships. Ten thousand to $100,000 will be the membership fee.

The Sengokuhara Golf Course belongs to the same company that owns the Fujiya Hotel. It is a 72-par course, just over 6,000 yards, and in season, on weekends, costs $100 a round.

When we visited the golf course, it was high season, a Saturday, i.e. Y28,000 a round. The rain and fog had settled around the course reducing the visibility to a maximum of fifty yards.

Yet, the manager said, there were one hundred golfers out on the course! At Y28,000 a round.

I asked Takae-san as we awaited our car, "What is the word for crazy?"

She wrote in my notebook "ki-chi-gai" but said, "It is not a polite word. Use it only with your friends."

We were going to the Five Lakes District for lunch, according to Takae-san, about an hour and a half drive away. Saying that, she took me back into the clubhouse, spoke softly to the manager who, in turn, motioned me to follow him. To the men's room. Takae-san, the complete guide, didn't want her charge uncomfortable during the drive.

Our destination was Lake Kawaguchi and the Fujiview Hotel and as we drove westward the skies began to clear.

We passed Lake Yamanaka and the town of the same name, obviously a vacation-oriented playground by its number of hotels.

At Lake Kawaguchi the wooden Fujiview Hotel looked to be of the same vintage as the Fujiya. The dining room featured massive timbers supporting a ceiling of intricately woven strips of wood. A beautiful room.

The Fujiview Hotel was destined to be torn down because of new fire codes. But another large hotel would be built in its place within a year. Only a year's construction time? A year. Typically Japanese. A similar project in Hawaii would take over two years.

I had delicious lake trout for lunch but Takae-san confided that she never ordered fish. A Japanese who never ate fish?

As we talked during lunch I learned that her father owned a fishcake factory. The smell of fish turned her green.

She was a delightful luncheon companion. Stumbling, hesitant in English, she brought a pausing charm to the language as she would stop and search for a word.

She had had the hotel job for just sixteen days, having graduated recently from Nihon University, a mammoth institution with many campuses and a total enrollment of 100,000 students. Her major was in international relations and one summer she spent six weeks in Anjou, a pretty French town in the Loire valley, famous for its chateau and its rose wine.

"The sun never went down until after ten. We couldn't sleep at night so we slept during the day. Then we went shopping. Made trips. I failed the course."

Very un-Japanese, I thought. Some weeks later I would learn that while the competition to get into university is most intense, once gained, the students play more than work.

Takae-san made a "study" visit to Rome, Geneva, Paris, London—and did just what an oversea student is supposed to do.

"I drank rose wine every night."

We retraced our route, stopping at the Yamanakako Hotel overlooking Lake Yamanaka and Mt. Fuji for after-lunch coffee. The seventy-room hotel is fully booked in July and August at rates around Y28,000 a day.

The best known scenic drive in the area is the Ashinoko Skyline Drive with many viewing areas looking down on Lake Hakone (Lake Ashi) on the east side of the highway and the towering magnificence of Mt. Fuji to the west. It is a winding, stomach-churning drive—I thought for a while my lake trout was going to come off the hook—but, on a good day, worth the time.

The highway descended to the lake and the resort city of Hakone-machi where fishing boats are available for rent and cruising boats designed like giant Oriental pirate ships take passengers across to the north end of the lake to the cable car which goes up to Owakudani. Except when it is raining.

Hakone-machi is an historically famous village because it was on the Tokaido Road from Kyoto, residence of the monarchy, to Edo (Tokyo), headquarters of the Tokugawa Shogunate.

The *Fifty-three Stages of Tokaido* was made famous in prints and on stage. The road was traversed by the feudal lords who went to Edo to spend their alloted time serving the shogun. An important daiymo could have a retinue of two thousand.

Because no women were allowed out of Edo and no firearms were allowed in, *The Barrier* was built in Hakone-machi to inspect all travellers. A replica of the guardhouse still exists just north of the village. Four hundred giant cedar trees still mark the lane of the old road.

Nearby is the Hakone Shrine, a major attraction at the lake, with red lacquered portal gates in a spacious forest setting and steps leading a hundred yards up to the shrine itself.

In front of the shrine are two stone lion guardians, one with its mouth open and one with its mouth closed, as is traditional with shrine guardians. Piled up around the lions are small pebbles placed by visitors who believe that if their stone remains, their wishes will come true.

A giant cedar near the shrine and another at the bottom of the steps leading to the shrine are sashed with giant ropes. I wondered why and Takae-san couldn't tell me.

The Hakone Shrine is surrounded with a forest-calm atmosphere, and the red lacquered gates, the trees, the stone lions tempt the most fumble-fingered photographer.

It had been a full day but before dinner I walked alone along the single street of Miyanoshita and window shopped and looked at pearls, antiques, crafts, curios . . . and kicked pebbles.

Hakone is a place to weekend with a very close friend. And let it rain.

4. Kyoto, Nara, and Osaka Of Kings and Priests

Kyoto is a favorite visitor city. For ten centuries it was the center of Japan's royal court, the fountainhead of creative arts, a traditional focal point for learning, the seat of the Buddhist religion. So many splendid palaces and gardens, libraries and schools, shrines and temples filled Kyoto that it was declared an open city during World War II and was spared the destruction of bombing. It remains a city where the culture of the past is most faithfully preserved.

To reach Kyoto from Hakone, I taxied down the mountain to the town of Odawara on the mainline of the JR to catch the *Shinkansen* (Bullet Train). There are two types of Bullet Trains. The *Hikari* is the fastest, making the fewest stops. The *Kodama* makes more stops such as the one on Odawara.

Being early, as usual, I had a half hour wait so I went to a telephone, put in a ten-yen coin and dialed 106.

When the operator came on I said very slowly, "Collect call to tee-aye-see." It didn't work. There followed a profusion of Japanese words and finally a dead line.

Tried it again. This time I had an English-speaking girl on the other end.

"Tell me. At the entrance to a shrine there are always two guardian-statues. One of the guardians will have a mouth open. The other will have the mouth closed. Why is this?"

Silence. "I don't know. Call back in a half an hour and I'll have the answer."

"I can't. I'm calling from the Odawara Station and in a half an hour I'll be on a train. Try this one. At the Hakone Shrine two tall cedar trees were wrapped with giant ropes. Could you tell me why?"

"Oh, I know that one!" was my party's gushing reply. "The tree has a spirit, you see. And the rope is a symbol of purification. This is called *shimenawa*. According to Shinto beliefs, evil cannot pass beyond the line of trees so decorated."

On the platform for Kyoto, I went to a post marked #12. The

70 How to Get Lost and Found in New Japan

number was painted on the ground between two white lines indicating where I was to enter car #12.

The train was to arrive at 10:19 A.M. At precisely 10:19 Kodama 227 stopped at the platform, its door to car #12 precisely between the white lines.

In catching thirty trains in the next thirty days this perfection was never—*never*—marred.

While waiting for the train, I saw a man buy a little plastic jug from a platform food stand. In "point" language, I indicated that I would like one of those. The lady behind the counter filled the plastic jug with hot water and gave it to me.

"Tea?"

"Hai," she said and pointed to an envelope on the side. From a handful of coins offered to her, she took a Y100 coin.

With ten minutes to train time I retreated to a corner, popped the tea bag in the hot water, waited a few minutes and then poured hot tea into the tiny plastic cup which capped the jug. On a cold station platform I had a warming spot of tea for forty cents. *Ichi ban!* First class.

On board I had another problem. Lunch. The Hikari Bullet Trains carry a dining car and a buffet car. The Kodama has neither. I would be travelling for two hours through the lunch period. The solution seemed to lie in the frequent attendants who kept rushing by selling colored boxes, but with what inside I didn't have a clue. The attendants also sold soft drinks, beer, oranges, candy, etc.

By one o'clock my empty stomach was demanding a decision. A young man opposite me was munching nice looking sandwiches from a red box. Good enough.

The next attendant was stopped and I secured a box.

The box was hot. What kind of sandwiches were these?

One look revealed two filets of cooked fish and a large portion of rice, a tiny plastic jug of soy sauce and small slices of sweet pickles, a paper napkin and chopsticks. Poured soy sauce over the fish, over the rice, not the pickles and devoured it all.

> Note: it is considered polite to dispose of your debris in a receptacle at the front of the car.
> Also in the front of the cars on Bullet Trains are the

KYOTO

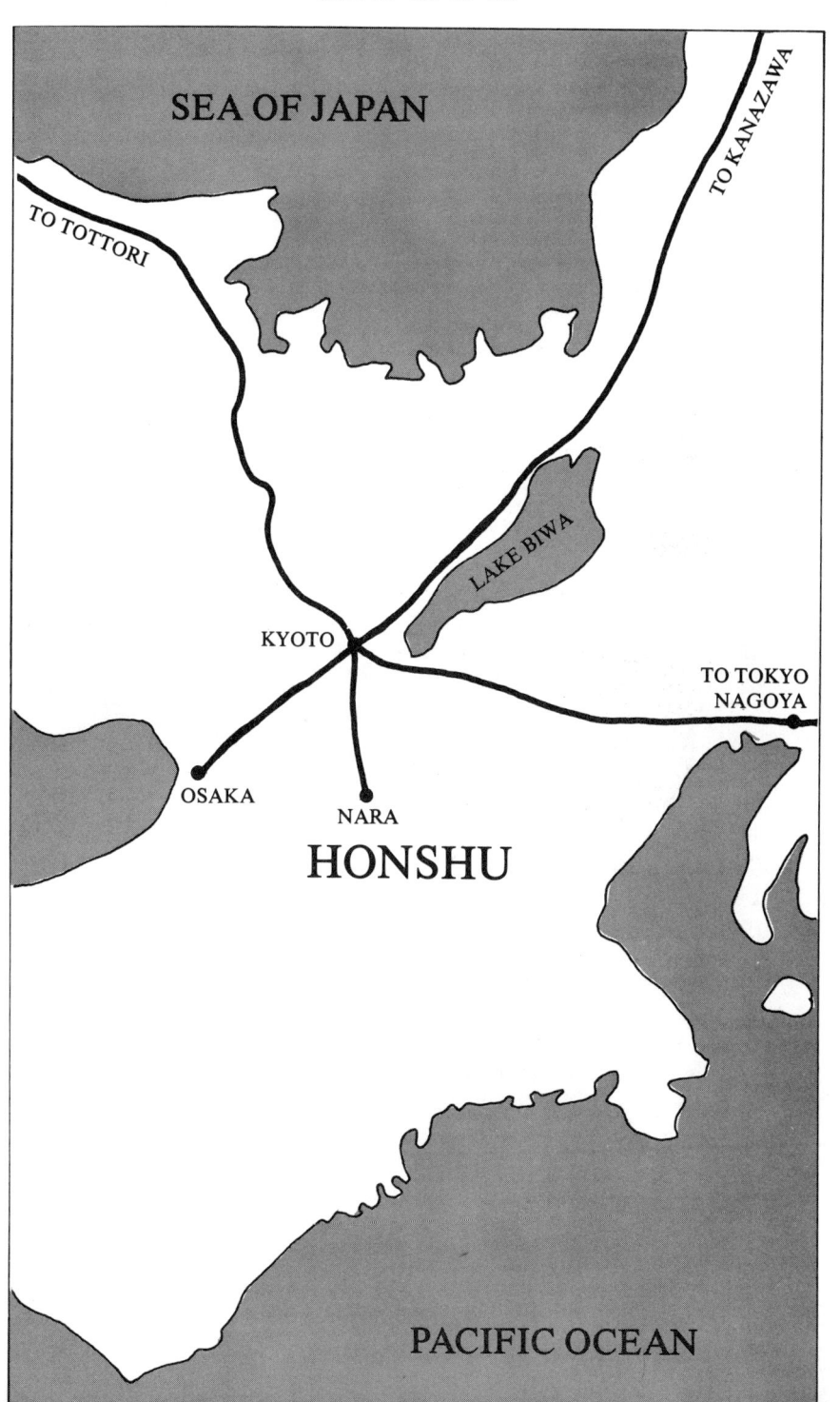

toilets. One toilet is labeled "Western Toilet" and another "Japanese Toilet." On the other side of the aisle is another tiny room with a glass portal. It contains a urinal.

Washbasins are in open partitions nearby.

Also Bullet Trains are numbered starting from the Tokyo direction. The number one car is a non-smoking car and it will always be on the Tokyo side of the train. The only non-smoking car. The Green Cars have no non-smoking sections and men in Japan are heavy, heavy smokers.

You realize when you pull through the high-rise buildings around the station of Kyoto, for all of its cultural reputation, this is not a quaint little university town or a preserved village. On the contrary, it is a pulsing city with a million and a half people. In addition to the classic industries of silk weaving and dyeing, doll making and printing, lacquerware and porcelain manufacturing, there is also major machinery manufacturing, and industries in metal, foodstuffs and chemicals.

The Bullet Trains run on special gauge tracks and have their own modern terminals. In Kyoto the Bullet Trains stop on the east side of the station while the principal part of the city lies on the west side together with the depot for the local trains, busses and the one-line subway which shoots about two miles straight through the heart of the city.

Underneath the Kyoto Station is another city of shops and restaurants.

One of the pleasant problems facing the first-time visitor to Kyoto is how to divide one's time.

Besides the palaces and parks and castles there are 200 Shinto shrines and 1,500 Buddhist temples!

Make a list of the "must sees."

You should visit the Kinkakuji (Golden Pavilion) and the Ginkakuji (Silver Pavilion), the Heian Shrine and the Sajusangendo, Hall of a Thousand Buddhas, all with different faces. If you find one that looks like you, make a donation.

Visit the Nijo Castle, founded by Ieyasu Tokugawa, the founding shogunate whose shrine you visited in Nikko.

Put on your list the Kiyomizu Temple hanging over a cliff, the Daitokuji Temple and the Kokedera (Moss Temple). Two Imperial households, the Katsura Imperial Villa and the Kyoto Imperial Palace, both require written passes. For fuller information go to the TIC office across the street from the railroad station on the ground floor of the Tower Hotel. Pick up a "Walking Tour Courses of Kyoto" while you are there.

> Note: I think it is important to remember that you can't do everything. Sometimes it is more memorable to stand on a street corner and watch the people go by than it is to force yourself to visit another temple, shrine or museum. The recall of an unusual street scene will be in your mental scrapbook longer than that of another statue.

This was not my first visit to Kyoto. Previously I had toured the Imperial Palace and the Nijo Castle. I had visited the Golden Pavilion in the autumn when the last leaves were falling. The deserted, quiet garden surrounded by bushes and water ponds seemed to epitomize nature just before it went to sleep in the winter.

Another time, in the spring, I had stayed at the old Miyako Hotel, one of the best known hotels in Japan, when a freak snowfall sent large flakes down from the heavens, matching the size of the cherry blossoms on the trees.

On this visit, travelling alone, I sought a different experience. I was booked into my first ryokan, and my first tour would be conducted by a student guide.

The taxi wound through back streets of Kyoto and finally left me at the front of an old traditionally-wooden Japanese inn, the Matsukichi Ryokan, its entry from a small courtyard set back from the street.

I was greeted by an ancient, kimono-clad lady, gold of tooth and broad of smile, who greeted me effusively in Japanese. A small, age-bowed retainer took over my bags and disappeared.

Behind them, in sharp contrast, a bright-eyed college girl bounced out of the inn dressed in jeans and blouse and announced perkily, "Mr. McDermott, I'm your student guide. Where would you like to go? What would you like to do?"

First, I had to inspect my quarters, recalling all the advice of good manners when staying in a ryokan.

You shed your shoes at the door. Put on slippers provided by the inn. Slipper-slide, because the slippers are always too small for Western male feet, down the wooden corridors to room. Doff slippers. Enter soft-matted *tatami* floored entry room with place for luggage, a tray containing a silk robe for lounging, a short coat *(haori)* for added warmth, a cotton kimono *(yukata)* for sleeping.

Sliding *shoji* doors opened onto a spacious second room, bare except for a massive, red-lacquered, ankle-high table in the middle of the room, an electric heater, an air-conditioner, a television set and a telephone. Against one wall was an ornamental alcove, a *tokonoma*.

Another set of shoji doors opened on a side room with two western bamboo chairs and a table. Floor-to-ceiling sliding glass doors looked out onto a small, classic Japanese garden of artistically arranged stones and delicate trees. Perfect.

Across from the entry hall, as part of the suite, were three small rooms: a room with a bidet, a room with a western toilet with slippers outside—you always wear the special slippers into the bathroom—and the third room with a tiled floor and a *furo*, a deep, deep wooden tub. A little sitting stool was level with wall spigots where, with the help of a wooden bucket and a bar of soap, one must, *de rigueur*, wash thoroughly before stepping into the wooden lobster pot to be boiled before dinner.

The mind turned to luxurious thoughts of end-of-the-day abolutions. Not yet. First the tour.

I returned to my student guide.

Her name was Nafumi Tamura, an immediately likable, pretty, soft-faced creature, bubbling with personality—no Japanese reticence here—who was a sophomore at Doshisha University, a private institution renown for its English courses.

We sat on the front step of the inn and established an easy rapport over a happy, prolonged, getting-to-know-you chat.

As a high school senior she had taken part in a student exchange program and had spent ten months with a family in St. Michael, Minnesota, an hour's drive from Minneapolis, attending St. Michael and Alberville High School.

Her English was excellent.

To answer her question of where we should go, we scanned JNTO's publication "Walking Tour Courses in Kyoto."

One such walk outlined in the brochure, "Along the Old Canal", sold us because the cherry blossoms were still in bloom and also because of its subtitle, "The Path of Philosophy", so named because a famous scholar once walked its banks while cogitating. Hard to resist.

First we walked half an hour to the Eikando Temple, a temple surrounded with restaurants featuring a famous Kyoto dish, boiled *tofu* or *yu-tofu*.

Tofu is a white, custard-textured food, a curd made out of soy beans that has recently become an international health-food fad.

"You Americans put ketchup on your tofu!" hooted this graduate of the St. Michael and Alberville High School.

Along the shady banks of the canal, cherry blossoms were raining into the water. On this sunny Sunday, the whole world was out: school children in uniform, families en masse, the elders, the youngsters. It was a day for schoolgirl giggling, familiy reunions and a time for lovers to hold hands.

Nafumi-san and I talked of her family—her father was a former newspaper editor—of my travels and books and my two daughters and my only son, "Charley", a $10,000 electronic word processor, and especially of her high school days in Minnesota.

"Did you have trouble being accepted by the other students into St. Michael?"

"No. A couple of girls came up to me first thing and said that they would be my friends. Also the father of my St. Michael family was a counselor for the school, and that helped.

"I had slides of Kyoto and Japan which I showed and that raised lots of questions and led to other conversations and subjects."

"Are you Buddhist?"

"Yes."

"Did you find explaining Buddhism difficult?"

"Yes. This was a strong Catholic and Protestant community. They all went to church every Sunday. In Buddhism we don't have a weekly service, and for younger people, like myself, religion is less important to our lives than it is to our parents and their parents. At *obon* time in August, when the dead return to the earth, we go with our parents to the temples and the graves, but, for us, it is more of a family habit than a ritual of beliefs."

"Tell me, how difficult was it for you to get into university and how hard do you study now?"

"In junior high school and high school I worked very, very hard—much harder than in the American high school where one learns to make furniture and chocolate chip cookies and writes current-event essays based on weekly reprints from Time Magazine and Newsweek.

"But once we get into university, I think we work less hard than university students of other countries."

We had reached the end of the Old Canal walk. Crowds were pouring uphill to visit the Ginkakuji Temple, more popularly known as the Silver Pavilion.

Built as a villa at the end of the fourteenth century, it is known as an example of Muromachi architecture. The builder intended to cover the villa with silver but his demise ended the ambition and the buildings became a temple. The gardens are among the finest in Kyoto, particularly the sculptured sand garden at the entrance. On the way back to the Ryokan, I asked Nafumi-san about the student guided tours.

"The idea was started over twenty-one years ago by students from Kyoto University. Other students now take part in the program which operates out of a club headquarters. I do about one tour a month during school periods and twice a month in vacation times. I've led people around Kyoto from all over the world—but you are the first one to have a word processor for a son!"

A humorous young lady given to infectious outbursts of laughter, Nafumi Tamura provided a delightful re-introduction to Kyoto.

That night in my spacious quarters, after having washed and rinsed all parts of my body while sitting on the tiny wooden stool, and after having a deep, bone-melting soak in my wooden tub, I dressed in my yukata and put on the short coat.

Promptly at six—you eat early in Japan—mama-san with the gold teeth brought my dinner which I ate in solitary splendor at the lacquered table sitting cross-legged on the floor. (My legs would have gone numb if it had not been for the circulation provided by two procelain flasks of sake.)

Course after course after course. I counted twelve separate dishes. Including the raw fish which, dipped in sauce, was quite tasty.

After dinner, flushed with sake, I worked on notes until mama-san returned, pushed my table aside and laid out covered sleeping cushions (futons) directly on the tatami mats where, shortly thereafter, I curled up and had one of the best nights sleep in Japan.

Unfortunately, in my eagerness to try everything, I said forthrightly, "Japanese" when asked if I wanted a Japanese or Western breakfast.

Breakfast consisted of *seven* dishes including miso and seaweed soup—delicious—little potatoes, two kinds of noodles, cold spinach, a fried egg, a huge pot of rice, something I couldn't identify and o-cha, the Japanese tea.

When the mama-san came in I pointed at the unidentifiable dish with two oval things in it and, in sign language, asked, "What is that?"

She flapped her wings like a chicken.

Chicken eggs? Terribly small chickens.

Later I was told they were quail eggs.

Much, much, too much food.

Before catching a train to Hiroshima, I visited the TIC office on the ground floor of the Tower Hotel and talked to Mrs. Tamai, a walking encyclopedia of Japan. Here is where you write to request a student guide. Give TIC a month's lead time if possible.

"Mrs. Tamai," I asked, "in front of the temples there are always two guardians. Why does one have its mouth open and one have its mouth shut?"

It was embarrassing. She didn't know.

"When you return next month, I will have the answer for you," she said.

"When I return, I was promised another student guide to take me to Nara. Would it also be possible to take the guide to lunch in Kyoto at a restaurant featuring boiled tofu?" I asked. It was promised.

En route to the train, I stopped by a bakery to buy a sack full of various neatly-wrapped sandwiches to eat instead of fish and rice.

I left Kyoto to explore the southeastern end of Honshu, moving on to make a complete circuit of Kyushu and to visit the coastal villages and towns off the usual tourist circuit facing the Sea of

Japan. Many times I would be the only foreigner in the hotel or inn and sometimes in the entire village.

The return to Kyoto was like coming home. Familiar landmarks. Many English-speaking people. Lots of *gaijin* (guy-gin), foreigners like myself.

My first call was to the TIC, to Mrs. Tamai. She was ready for me. Without my asking the question, she said, "Here is your answer" and handed me a paper.

Why does one guardian at a shrine or temple have the mouth open and the other guardian have the mouth closed?

The paper said: "The one on the left (from the temple) with its mouth opened to pronounce the Sanskrit vowel of 'ah' is a positive image, which invites every good to come in, while the other, on the right, with its mouth closed to pronounce 'um' is a negative image for shutting evil out."

Elsewhere I had read that the open-mouthed guardian represents life and the closed-mouth guardian represents death and that when a pilgrim walks between the two guardians the person is reminded how short a time there is of life on earth.

The Buddhist temple guardians will be Deva-kings.

The Shinto shrine guardians will be animals, usually a lion on the left and a dog on the right, but today they are difficult to tell apart.

The return to Kyoto called for a revisit to the Nijo Castle if only to put into perspective two men whose strengths and talents were critical in an important formative period of Japan at the turn of the seventeenth century.

The first was Ieyasu Tokugawa, the first Tokugawa shogun, who after defeating his enemies was appointed the generalissimo of Japan. He set up his *bakufu*, headquarters, in Edo (Tokyo) and built Nijo as a visiting castle in Kyoto in 1603.

Earlier he had adopted William Adams, an Englishman from a Dutch trading vessel, as part of his entourage. Adams became the central figure in the popular historical novel, *Shogun*.

Ieaysu Tokugawa initiated the social structure of the Edo Period including the division of the country into domains ruled by two hundred and seventy daiymo, feudal lords. The lords controlled the merchants and the farmers within their fiefdoms thereby establishing the feudal system which would dominate Japan for nearly three hundred years.

The second character preceeded the first and laid the foundation for the unification of Japan. His name was Toyotomi Hideyoshi, a very tough warrior, a general, the son of a poor farmer, who became the country's military ruler.

For a hundred years preceeding his rule, the country had been torn apart by internecine wars until Nobunaga Oda started bringing the country together by force of arms. When Oda was assassinated by another general, General Hideyoshi stepped in to complete the job of unification—and to become the ruler of Japan for sixteen years.

Hideyoshi created a memorial to his own prowess by building a colossal castle to which every feudal lord contributed.

The daily work force in the three years of construction averaged thirty thousand laborers. As the project neared completion the work force was increased to one hundred thousand.

Massive stones dominated the construction. One stone alone contributed by one of his generals was as big as a room and can still be seen it in the fortress walls. You are reminded of the pyramids.

The castle is in Osaka and is one of the sights of Japan.

My first inclination had been to skip Osaka altogether but Osaka is only thirty minutes away from Kyoto and not to see the castle was unthinkable.

Also another magnet in Osaka was a new development at the Osaka Station, ACTY, a major complex including a giant department store, a combination office building, restaurants and hotel.

A morning trip to Osaka with a student guide familiar with the city returning to Kyoto for a boiled tofu lunch was scheduled. The following day the same guide would take me to Nara.

In contrast to the old-world ryokan the month before I stayed on the return visit in the new, modern Kyoto Century Hotel.

At precisely the appointed hour—not a minute early, not a minute late—the phone rang. The guide was downstairs.

Naomi Nishimura was waiting demurely in a lobby chair. Her bobbed black hair and gay, black eyes had the characteristics of a bright, vivacious Japanese kokeshi doll, but this doll was dressed in white slacks and T-shirt.

Like Nafumi, my first Kyoto guide, Naomi had been a senior high school exchange student spending ten months at Shell Lake, Wisconsin at the Shell Lake High School where the total student body enrollment was two hundred.

How a delicate Japanese flower not only survived but thrived in an American rural high school student body of two hundred is a lesson in human flexibility.

The principal interest of the girls was boys and the common ambition was to get married *now,* Naomi said. Yes, they had a football team and had won the state Class "C" championship the year she was there.

She learned to eat peanut butter and jelly sandwiches but her favorite American dish was lasagna made by her "mother", Mrs. Glenn Hite.

During winter vacation the family took her to Florida and to Disney World which she visited from early morning until it closed at night, and the memory of the day was still such an emotional experience for her that she choked up just talking about it. Touching.

So was the emotional problem of parting eventually with the Hites. They were her family.

We talked on the train to Osaka about many things Japanese. One subject in the news was most un-Japanese.

The scandal was the frequency of incidents of violence in junior high schools even including physical attacks on teachers. Unthinkable to me, a foreigner. It was even more unthinkable in the eyes of the Japanese. Not at all in character.

Naomi said these occurrences had begun since she had left junior high school, only six years earlier.

She felt the reason for the violence sometimes rested with teachers who ignored students who didn't hold up the class grade average. A lower class grade average was a loss of face to the teacher. Instead of working with the slower pupil, the teacher ignored him.

Also, she said, parents often put too much pressure on the boys to get top marks.

The combined frustrating factors resulted in physical eruptions, mostly against teachers. Shocking.

It is a strange break in a characteristic that has been a backbone of the Japanese way of life since the thirteenth century when *bushido,* the discipline of the hero *samurai,* became the mental and physical role model for Japanese youth.

Is this part of the new Japan?

Osaka and the Castle

Osaka on a May morning was surprisingly pleasant.

"Why didn't you plan on coming to Osaka until now," Naomi wanted to know.

"Because the last time I was in the area, we had a car and a driver who took us from Kyoto to Nara and on to Kobe, and we by-passed Osaka which lay under a grey cloud of pollution as if it were in the grip of a hand of a dark giant called greed. But today it is beautiful. Is it my imagination or has the air pollution problem been solved?"

"It is much better," confirmed Naomi. "When I was in elementary school in Kyoto, there was an air-pollution meter and sometimes it registered so high that we couldn't go outside at recess time. The pollution blew in from Osaka and was trapped in the hills surrounding Kyoto and just stayed. It's not like that any more. What time of year were you here?"

"About this time...May...or late April. It was cherry blossom time. I was told then that the ladies were wearing blossom motifs on their kimono and that they change the motifs according to the season."

"Yes, it is considered quite correct to wear the cherry blossom pattern just before the cherry blossoms come out."

"What do the ladies wear in other seasons?"

"In summer something that looks cool, a water or sky motif. In the autumn perhaps a maple leaf or a color scheme suggesting the multi-colored leaves. In the winter a chrysanthemum or a design inspired by a snowflake. Then comes the plum blossom and then back to the cherry blossom.

"The news of the seasons is very important to us. We have daily ski reports in winter and then we have daily plum blossom reports followed by daily cherry blossom reports.

"The blossoming moves from south to north at about one hundred kilometers a day."

Although it was too late in the year for cherry blossoms, the spring sun made Osaka Castle camera-perfect.

The castle was under siege, adding to the picture.

Invaders were not new to the fortifications. When General Hideyoshi died, the Tokugawas came to power and reduced the castle to rubble. Then, to establish their own prestige, the

Tokugawas rebuilt it again.

Later in the civil wars, at the time of the Meiji take-over in the nineteenth century, the castle was again destroyed.

In 1931 the citizens of Osaka donated funds for the re-creation of the massive, seven-story *donjon,* or main tower.

The invaders on the day of our visit were mostly under eight years old, dressed in yellow safety helmets, wearing yellow rain slickers and standing in straight lines, holding each other's hands.

> Note: when visiting any famous garden, castle, shrine or temple, the best childless viewing is first thing in the morning or the last thing in the afternoon.

Visiting Osaka Castle's donjon is made easier by an elevator which takes you to the top and you then walk down five flights of stairs. Each floor is a separate museum. Armor, screens depicting stories, mostly battle stories, models of castles, weapons, and much more are displayed in exhibits.

On one floor there's a reproduction of the Golden Tea Room, a symbol, Naomi thought, of Hideyoshi's insecurity of being the son of the poor farmer.

The walls were panelled in gold. The tatami mats were fringed with gold brocade. The tea set was solid gold.

"When he died," Naomi said, "it all disappeared."

From the castle we taxied to ACTY, the new twenty-seven floor complex built over the Osaka main station.

The first sixteen floors belong to the Daimaru Department Store—a glittering showcase; the next ten floors are guest rooms of the Terminal Hotel. Topping the building on the twenty-seventh floor is a complex of restaurants.

Osaka can afford it. The port city is a center of financial power, the second largest city in Japan with 5,000,000 people, and a reputation for an abundance of excellent, reasonably priced restaurants.

Turning our backs on Osaka cuisine, we returned to Kyoto for the famous hot tofu which we found, after much wandering, in a restaurant near the Eikando Temple.

Outdoors on a raised platform covered with tatami mats and cushions, we sat at a low table cross-legged which the Japanese find easy to do but I soon find my legs going numb and have to stretch out on either side or I may never walk again.

Bamboo trees sheltered the setting and off to one side was a willow-shaded pond.

Delightful atmosphere enhanced by having one of my best meals in Japan.

A gracious kimono-clad waitress brought a soup made of shredded yams, then a dish of tempura vegetables, mushrooms, pumpkin, taro, parsley, dipped in a light batter and deep-fried with a sweet sauce on the side, then a dish with six barbecued pieces of tofu covered with a miso paste. Everything was so delicately flavored and so delicious.

Another dish was presented of cold tofu, green, made with sesame seeds.

The fire was lighted in a clay pot in the middle of the table and a container of boiling water in which tofu was floating was placed over the charcoal fire. The waitress poured hot soy sauce adding red pepper and shaved leek. The hot tofu was then ladled, piece by piece, into the bowls of soy and eaten with chopsticks.

A bowl of rice, tea and beer completed the meal.

Luncheon for two cost about Y7,500.

Several hot tofu restaurants are in the same area. Our lucky choice happened to be the Okutan, telephone number 771-8709, located between the Nanzenji Temple and the Eikando Temple, a short taxi ride from Kyoto Station.

The Okutan is open from 10:30 A.M. to 5:30 P.M. and is closed on Thursdays.

You find the best tofu, Naomi said, around temples because Buddhist priests' menus prohibit meat and the bean-curd tofu, high in protein content, is the priests' principal food.

That evening I had an educational experience touring the Kyoto Century Hotel which is adjacent to the west entrance of Kyoto Station.

Mr. Tak Hashimoto, a manager of the hotel, Hilton-trained, gave me a walk through.

First, the lobby.

"The objective we gave the architect," said Mr. Hashimoto, "was to create a lobby in which a woman will appear to be more beautiful than she is."

How sensitive . . . and how smart.

The result is a softly muted lobby that rises five floors to the ceiling. The carpet is of small wool squares in different shades of brown. In one corner are several connected white-latticed gazebos furnished with tables where one stops for refreshments.

A tour of the public function rooms presented an insight into a most important Japanese custom: weddings.

It was the wedding season, a major income source for Japanese hotels, and at the Kyoto Century there were three weddings in progress.

Hashimoto-san showed me the Shinto shrine in the hotel where the weddings take place—the hotel does everything—and the complete photographer's studio where the bride and groom are photographed in as many as four different costumes and where the families and attendants are also immortalized on film, the reception room where refreshments are served and the banquet room where elaborate wedding feasts are held.

No expenses are spared. Guests even take home sacks of gifts.

"How much does it cost to stage an average wedding per guest?"

"About Y30,000 for each guest," he said. ($200!) "There is a slight trend among couples to take the money and go to Europe or take some other grand tour. But it is not serious. You have to remember that it is not just the bride and the groom being married. Their families are also getting married.

Later I was told that the wedding guest also leaves, at the registration table, a white envelope containing a substantial amount of money. The closer the relationship to the bride or groom, the larger the contribution.

The Century has a unique feature unmatched anywhere in the world: The Shelter.

The basement parking garage is equipped so that it can be converted into a nuclear bomb shelter able to sleep, water and feed three thousand people for three weeks!

Massive metal doors, ventilation systems, sanitation facilities have been carefully engineered and installed.

Two other Century items: The hotel is connected with an English-language cable television channel. Also the hotel offers overnight film developing service. I left three roles of color print film at the desk before 8 P.M. and picked up the developed prints the next morning before breakfast. The charge was on my bill.

Nara and the Deer and the Buddha

The next morning Naomi was in the lobby prompt as a Bullet Train and we were off to Nara on an ordinary train, thirty-five minutes away from Kyoto . . . but hundreds of years away in time frame.

From 710 to 784 A.D. Nara was the capital of Japan.

It was a time of flourishing Buddhism and political reform and a country-to-country interchange with the Tang Dynasty in China.

During this period the most famous image of Buddha in Japan was cast—the Great Buddha or Daibutsu—an immense bronze statue 16.2 meters (53.1 feet) in height, weighing 452 tons.

In order to see as much as possible in one day, Naomi and I rented bicycles—smart move—and for five hours pedalled around Nara.

First we pedalled five blocks up hill, past the Sarusawa Pond, known for its postcard visual of the Five Story Pagoda reflected in its waters on a moonlight night, then on to Nara Park, better known as "Deer Park."

Here among the giant Japanese cedar and oak trees are one thousand deer looking for a handout. Nearby vendors will sell you the proper food. The deer bows to you. You bow to the deer. They are sacred messengers. You feed them. They are hungry messengers.

On a Spring Sunday when all the families are out, the ratio is one deer for every five children.

We visited the Kofukuji Temple (Happiness Producing Temple) filled with national treasures, then the Todaiji Temple (Great Eastern Temple) which includes the world's largest wooden building, The Hall of the Great Buddha, containing the bronze Daibatsu cast in 749.

We walked—no bikes allowed—past some of the 1800 stone lanterns that lead to the Kasuga Shrine, founded in 768, one of the most revered Shinto shrines in the country.

A sign reads: "Have your fortune in English—Y100." It was an offer too tempting to refuse. I paid 100 yen and was given a wooden box to shake, then turn upside down until a wooden peg emerged from a small hole in the bottom. The peg had a number on it. Four. From a pigeon hole marked four I was then given a piece of paper on which was inscribed my fortune:

"When spring comes, the bare trees of winter blossom forth with flowers, and when the black clouds of midnight part, the moon shines brightly. In like manner your lot will improve and your happiness increase."

We visited the local museum with many gold figures and scrolls and screens. One screen depicted the "heaven" of Buddha and on the other side of the river was "hell" where, at a table, a terrible figure was holding court.

"You know who that is and what he is doing?" asked Naomi. "That is Satan, and he is having a trial for people brought before him. If the person has told lies in his life, his tongue is pulled out.

"My grandmother used to tell me 'Don't tell a lie or your tongue will be pulled out'."

We pedalled back down the hill into Nara and found a sukiyaki restaurant and had a pleasant lunch before going to the other side of Nara to see the Toshodaiji Temple.

After the crowds of Nara Park—the thousands of children, the deer, the Sunday-at-the-zoo atmosphere—the quiet atmosphere, the attractive buildings, the woods and gardens of Toshodaiji made a serene, spiritual, peaceful, welcome change.

"I like this temple," said Naomi. I agreed.

Early in the eighth century an illustrious Chinese abbot, Ganjin, of the Tang Dynasty was invited by the Emperor in Nara to come to Japan and teach the concepts of Buddhism.

Five times, over twelve years, Ganjin tried to cross the turbulent Sea of Japan. He was finally successful. The effort left him blind. Here at Nara he established his temple and was a force in making Japan a Buddhist country. Ganjin died in 763 at the temple he founded and is buried in a quiet corner of the temple grounds.

The many structures in the temple are considered to be the most valuable buildings in Nara, reflecting the style and harmony of the period.

By this time I was over-shrined and over-templed.

"Home," I pleaded to my leader.

Back to the center of Nara we pedalled towards the train station.

"Do you remember where to go," asked I of little faith.

"Trust me," said my leader turning south. The train, it turned out, was north. We made it by two minutes.

The train back to Nara had the conformation of a subway with long seat-benches running the length of the car. My seat companion was all of four years old. The moppet would have made an ideal laboratory study for a time-and-motion research engineer. He never stopped moving or talking. He bounced. He stood up on the seat. He pulled the window up and down, then the window shade up and down. He slugged the little boy next to him. He babbled incessantly.

Five minutes before Kyoto, he and his classmates stood up and lined up to get off the train.

"Goodbye, you little monster," I said softly. "I'm going to miss you."

"Satan is going to pull your tongue out," said Naomi.

It wasn't a gay goodbye when we parted at the train station. It wasn't Satan. It was sadness. I hated to see her go and kissed her on the cheek, Hawaiian-fashion, very un-Japanese, perhaps even impolite. She didn't seem to mind. I waved and turned away from a very neat young lady.

HIROSHIMA
and Western Towns

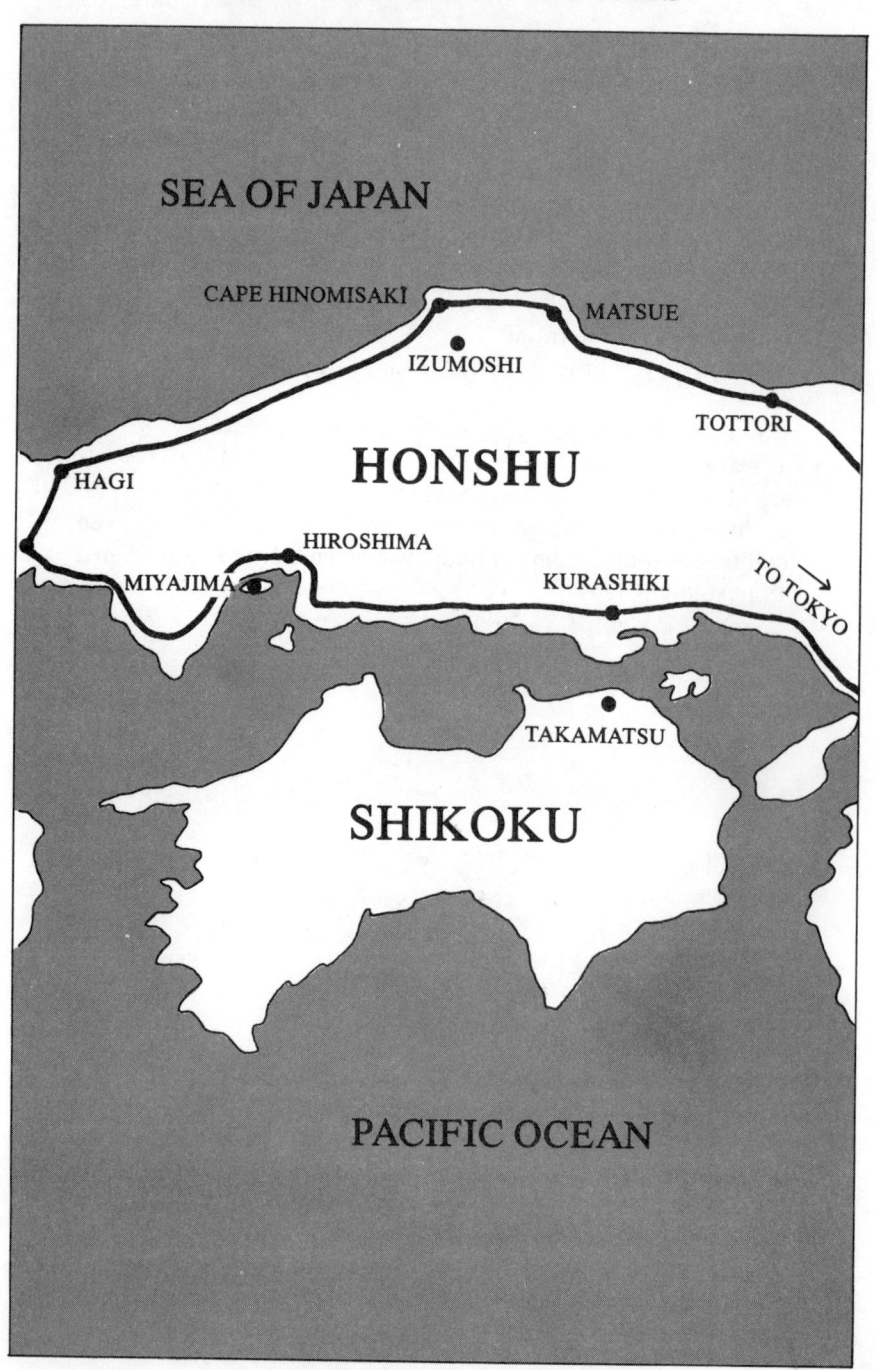

5. Hiroshima and Miyajima Heartbreak City and the Dream Village

On the zip-trip to Hiroshima from Kyoto on the Bullet Train, an attractive, intelligent looking young couple, obviously honeymooners, sat reading comic books.

Curious.

At Hiroshima I took a taxi to my accommodations. Riding through the street, past modern shops, high-rise buildings, well-dressed people busily hurrying back and forth, it was difficult to believe that this was the city destroyed by the first atom bomb.

I had now stayed at a luxury resort hotel, a traditional ryokan and a modern city hotel. In Hiroshima, I was booked into a family-run inn. Such family-operated inns are called *minshuku*. They are clean, neat and economical—most charging less than Y5,000 a day, thereby avoiding the standard ten percent room-tax.

The Minshuku Ikedaya was a good example.

Mr. Ikedaya and his wife operate the ten-room facility along with a six-room annex for students who don't mind sharing a room—like six to a room.

My single room was a six-tatami-mat size—or about one hundred square feet. The sleeping mattress, futon, was already laid out, along with a standard quilt and woolen blanket. A clean yukata kimono was placed on top. In the middle of the room was a low table with a back-supported cushion on the floor. In one corner was a small, red television set and in the other corner, a coin-operated air-conditioning unit.

Never a private bath in a minshuku.

Down the hall were two toilets with plastic toilet slippers facing the doors. One was a urinal and the other a Japanese toilet. A Japanese toilet consists of an oblong, oval, ceramic bowl set flush in the floor over which you assume the fetal position. Sometimes there is a metal bar for you to hang on to. (It is said that the Japanese toilet is more natural and healthier for you. It also takes a second round of toilet training.)

Squatting is an easy comfortable position for the Japanese. You'll see thousands of Japanese students waiting in railroad stations on class tours, not sitting in chairs but resting by squatting on their haunches. Laborers on work-breaks or lunch-breaks do the same.

The first experience in a Japanese toilet, unless you have been taking aerobic exercises, is liable to be a short one. It's not a place where you'll go and read the Sunday newspaper.

Another lesson, quickly learned, is that it is better to go to the toilet wearing a kimono, especially for men where the hitching, releasing, tucking of trousers is frustrating and potentially dangerous. In addition to the indignity of the whole thing, the chance of dropping loose change out of pants pockets could lead to hilarious, disaster problems.

The second time is, of course, twice as easy as the first, and the third time—well, you wouldn't say it was a piece of cake—but at least you will have become operational.

Downstairs at Minshuku Ikedaya were two baths; one room for showering, the other for the usual deep furo.

That evening I didn't want a large dinner. Ikeda-san directed me to the corner noodle shop. The noodles in rich broth enriched by a large beer was just right—and inexpensive.

Over dinner in the noodle shop I watched other customers select reading material from a stack of magazines. The magazines were, in fact, comic books.

Curious.

The next morning, I declined the Japanese breakfast offered at the minshuku for two dollars and went to the coffee shop opposite the noodle restaurant and, again instructed by Ikeda-san, said in English on entering: "Morning special, please."

A light salad, juice, a cup of black coffee, a hard-boiled egg, two gigantic golden slices of hot, tasty, buttered toast an inch and a half thick were placed before me. After devouring it all, I was served a mug of green tea.

Totalling my food bill for the last twenty-four hours, including the sandwiches from the Kyoto pastry shop to eat on the train, I reached the grand sum of $12 and, throwing in my minshuku bill and the taxi rides, my entire day had cost less than $50.

The economy of the minshuku can be enjoyed in most corners of

Hiroshima and Miyajima 91

Japan. Some of them have banded together as the Japanese Inn Group. For further information inquire at the head office c/o Hiraiwa Ryokan, 314, Hayao-cho, Kaminoguchi-agaru, Ninomiya-cho-dori, Shimogyo-ku, Kyoto 600. Or contact the Tokyo liaison office through the Sawanoya Ryokan.

In previous visits to Japan I had avoided Hiroshima because I didn't know if I could handle it emotionally. Having been through one war, having looked at the burned-out heart of London, having seen so many German cities flattened from outskirt to outskirt, having seen enough of sunken ships and charred frames of airplanes, having stood heavy hearted on the deck of the Arizona Memorial in Pearl Harbor where, underfoot, 1,177 American sailors were still entombed in the battleship, who needed to go to Hiroshima for another emotional kick in the head?

At first in walking around Hiroshima, seeing the new buildings and the people bustling about like they were in Tokyo, I thought it was going to be easy. Here was a real phoenix risen from the ashes.

My first appointment was at the Rest House which borders the Peace Memorial Park in the middle of the city where I rendezvoused with Akiko Omotu, coordinator of the home visit program. An arrangement had been made for me to call on a Japanese family that evening and I had to fill out a form giving my age, occupation, hobbies, and show my passport. In turn I was given a similar form detailing the facts about the family I was to visit together with a map of instructions telling me how to reach their apartment.

Being at the Peace Memorial Park, an area a block wide and two blocks long, the focal point of the atom bomb tragedy, I decided now was the time to walk it from end to end.

On August 6, 1945 a B-29 bomber, *Enola Gay,* opened its bomb doors and released the first atom bomb over Hiroshima.

Forty-three seconds later at a height of about 580 meters the bomb exploded. The time was 8:15:17 in the morning.

The resultant fireball, shockwaves and radiation annihilated Hiroshima in a matter of seconds.

Almost directly under the "hypocenter" of the bomb was the Industrial Promotion Hall. Its shattered concrete walls and the skeletal iron framework of the dome are the only physical remains of that dreadful morning. Now known as the A-Bomb Dome, it is a permanent memorial.

The Dome stands opposite the apex of the Peace Memorial Park which is an island created by two rivers flowing by on each side before they empty into nearby Hiroshima Bay.

Near the head of the island the Hiroshima Lions Club has built a clock tower. At quarter past eight every morning, the mortal moment of the 1945 fireball, the clock chimes a prayer for perpetual peace.

Nearby, the Bell for Peace built by another civic group urges viewers to "step forward and toll the bell for peace."

Farther on is a statue of a young boy with his arms raised in supplication. The base of the statue is covered with flowers donated by "The Students and Pupils for Peace."

Continuing down the park, I came to an eternal flame reflected in a broad pool of water held by two symbolic, concrete cupped hands. Just beyond is the Memorial Cenotaph, a vaulted concrete hood covering a marble tomb containing a scroll of 103,777 names, people lost in the disaster.

Near the end of the park is the elevated Memorial Park Museum and next to it a theater for the showing of two films, *Hiroshima* and *Hiroshima and Nagasaki*.

Fronting the park is a flower clock, a fountain, and a statue. I was fairly emotionally stable until I saw the statue.

A mother holds her infant to her breast, her body bent horizontally to shield the baby from the terror above while her small boy scrambles in panic to reach the safety of her back. The mother reaches behind her with the other arm in a desperate attempt to touch the child.

Oh, God. Why can't the leaders of the world meet in a tent right here?

I left the park and walked toward the center of the city, a bustling, modern, alive city. I walked through a covered arcade for half a mile window-shopping the stores on each side. Fashionable clothes, international designers, fast food shops, noodle shops, expensive restaurants, book stores selling piles of thick comic books. Back on the main street I found Sogo's, a high-rise department store, and I immediately dived into the basement's food department (a good eight-plus) and bought a box of chocolates for the family I was to visit that evening as my omiyage, the gift one

brings to a host, to relatives, to co-workers.
Hiroshima had just inaugurated a Home Visit Program and I was to be one of the first visitors.

My "family" was a dentist, Dr. Yoshiaki Okamoto, thirty years old, and his wife, Mihoko. The instructions for reaching their apartment were not needed because they would pick me up at the Minshuku Ikedaya at 8 P.M.

At 7:50, just after I had returned from my noodle dinner, a pretty young lady with a laughing countenance put her head through the door and asked, "Mr. McDermott?" It was Mihoko. She led me outside to her slender, boyish-looking dentist husband who was standing beside a new car. After introducing ourselves we drove off to their apartment.

It was a case of instant friendship. They loved to laugh, were given to gentle teasing, shared a bubbling sense of humor. I was becoming more aware that joking and teasing and laughing are common Japanese traits.

Yoshiaki was a research dentist in the Department of Operative Dentistry at Hiroshima University and had just applied to Harvard for acceptance into their dental research program. He had a whimsical touch of the absent-minded professor about him.

Mihoko was anything but a reticent Japanese housewife-servant. She could have graduated from Vassar and captained the soccer team. She held a master's degree from the Elizabeth University of Music and gave piano lessons.

Although she apologized for the small, one bedroom apartment, it was still large enough to hold an upright piano on which she gave lessons half of her time. The other half she taught at her parent's house where there was a grand piano.

Our meeting, although it was their first experience as hosts in the Home Visit Program, and mine as a guest, was devoid of any apprehensiveness because we had so many questions to ask each other.

Over beer and later chocolate cake and tea, we exchanged questions and family histories.

Why had they taken part in the visitor program?

Besides meeting overseas people, they said, it gave them a chance to expand their English. "Yosh" had been taking English conversation for a little more than a year but, although fumbling in conversation, he would always come up with the proper word when she hesitated.

My objective was to learn more about Japanese customs and I soon realized that the most important event in Japanese lives is the time of the wedding. I looked at their three-year-old wedding pictures—it was a Christian wedding—where, during the dinner, they changed dress three times. Customary.

From a white tie and tails wedding costume, he changed into a grand samurai regalia and then into a formal white suit.

She changed from a lovely Western-styled wedding dress into the traditional kimono, complete with traditional wig, then into a modern travel ensemble which she had designed.

They showed me their honeymoon pictures of Europe—it was her second trip—pictures of London and Paris and Geneva and Rome.

They liked to read. They liked movies. He cried watching "E.T."

Conversation never stopped.

Later they drove me to the top of a hill overlooking the lights of Hiroshima's port and a Mazda automobile assembly plant that employs 50,000 people.

I felt close enough to my new friends by now to ask a delicate question.

"The impression one could get from visiting Hiroshima is that the war is forgotten, the A-bomb is a thing of the past, and the people are pushing forward into today's world only looking to the future. Is this true?"

It was a sobering moment.

"No," said Yosh, "We never forget the heritage we lost, part of our culture we never can replace. Not just shrines or temples but think about the books. Hiroshima has always been a center of learning, and we lost hundreds of thousands of books, historical scrolls, paintings. And lives, particularly the young lives. No, it is something we'll not forget."

At parting, Mihoko gave me a small package. "Open it!" she said.

Inside was a petite enamel pen and, on top, attached with a gold chain, was a tiny gold cross.

"My wife will appropriate it the minute she sees it," I told them. And she did.

Marvelous time with bright young people.

The next morning in the rain I met Akiko Omotu in front of the Memorial Park Museum. She was to be my interpreter and guide at the museum.

She took me first to the museum's administration quarters where we were bowed into a private office and served tea.

We were soon joined by Yoshitaka Kawamoto, a smiling, amiable member of the staff. He looked younger than fifty, black hair, not much over five feet tall, dressed in a neat blue suit, with a blue-striped shirt and blue-striped tie. Very correctly Japanese.

I was hoping to interview someone who had been in Hiroshima on August 6, 1945 but, instead, I got an administrator and, therefore, I asked adminstrative questions.

Attendance last year was 1,300,000 of which 70,000 came from overseas, up from 26,000 ten years ago.

The Y50 admittance fee supplied enough money to make the museum self-supporting.

In the give-and-take of Akiko's translation I sensed that Mr. Kawamoto was speaking about a personal experience that hadn't anything to do with the museum.

He was becoming more animated and Akiko was now on the edge of her chair asking questions.

"Wait, wait," I interrupted. "Tell me what he is saying."

"Mr. Kawamoto was in a school only eight hundred meters from the hypocenter when the A-bomb went off."

What!

"He was one of two children in his class of fifty to live."

He continued with his story to Akiko, his voice edged with excitment, and words coming faster and faster as he recalled the events of the day. Akiko, on my pleading, would get him to stop only with difficulty and quickly translate the story.

In the summer of 1945 the entire Japanese nation, including schoolchildren and housewives, were engaged in the war effort. There were no holidays. Every possible resource was committed, especially in Hiroshima, a military-industrial city subject to air raids. Fires from the bombings could be more devastating than the bombs themselves.

Part of the school effort called for students to assist in the demolition of buildings to create fircbreaks along designed open-spaced lanes.

Mr. Kawamoto's elementary school class was working in shifts. One hour outside. One hour inside. He was inside and he remembers a boy at the window say, "There is a B-29."

That's all he remembers except for a subsequent blue-white flash. No noise. No earth movement. Just a blinding blue-white flash and the ceiling of the one-story building collapsing.

Mr. Kawamoto was knocked down between two desks. A ceiling beam fell across the two desks providing him protective cover.

His schoolmates outside died instantly as did all but one inside.

His arm was badly gashed, an artery severed. He lay under the beam for over an hour calling for help.

The heat intensity of the fireball was measured in millions of degrees. Fires broke out across the city, but, fortunately, didn't reach the schoolroom from which he was eventually pulled to safety by a sub-master.

Drilled to handle emergencies, Kawamoto and the sub-master helped rescue several others from nearby buildings before going to a fire-free playground near the school.

Fires were everywhere and he was told by an adult, "Run into the wind."

He remembers picking up a hand of dirt, throwing it in the air to get the wind direction, and fleeing south.

Unknowingly, he not only ran away from the direction a fire would normally take but he also escaped the fallout direction of "black rain", the radioactive particles which would later result in horrible deaths for thousands.

He ran about a mile before reaching a river. It was full of corpses. Nevertheless he pushed to the river's edge and handcupped water into his parched mouth to slake the thirst—then collapsed, unconscious.

He was found and thought to be dead.

Two trucks were by then in operation. One for the living, another for the dead, bodies layered over one another to be hauled away.

The boy was thrown on the truck for the dead. He fell off.

They were about to throw him back on again when a soldier, said, "Wait. I think this one is alive." They felt his pulse and said, "He can still be useful." They then put him in the truck for the living.

He was moved first to Miyajima and then to Saka during which time he received only one medical treatment. Mercurochrome was poured on the wound which was then plugged with gauze and wrapped in old rags.

In the meantime his mother had chartered a boat to search for him along the seaside medical camps, going from camp to camp. Five days later they were reunited.

Eventually he returned home with a hugely swollen arm which one surgeon wanted to amputate. Another said, "No, he has a future."

Then he started to bleed from the nose, a bleeding that went on twenty-four hours at a time. A bedside basin was filled with blood.

"There is no hope," the doctors said.

Relatives supplied blood transfusions. He continued to live.

Three months later his hair fell out. It was another six months before it started to grow again.

"Through it all," said Mr. Kawamoto "the doctors kept saying I didn't have a chance." He shrugged, pulled back his coat sleeve and unbuttoned the shirt cuff and pulled back the shirt sleeve to reveal two deep scars in the left arm above the wrist.

"I never talked about my experience except once about twelve years ago. Up until last month I worked for the city as an omnibusman and then I was transferred to the museum. Now, I feel, telling my story is part of my job.

"I don't want sympathy. To remember, to tell others, maybe it helps peace."

For a moment all was silent in the office.

"Does the memory of that moment, of that day, and the following days haunt you in any way?"

For the first time Mr. Kawamoto's eyes went somber and he looked down at his feet through a layer of tears.

"The heartbreak of remembering is that it means recalling dead classmates. I am alive. I'm living a good life. And they are dead.

"Every August sixth I pray for the friends I can't forget."

Mr. Kawamoto then lead Akiko and myself on a tour of the museum. I followed along reluctantly. After his story I didn't need any more lumps in the throat.

At a three-dimensional topographical layout in the center of the

98   *How to Get Lost and Found in New Japan*

first room with a red ball suspended over the city at the height that the A-bomb was activated, Mr. Kawamoto pointed to the location of his school, so near the hypocenter.

He indicated the southerly direction in which he ran and the spot at the riverbank where he passed out.

Circles in the map outlined the devastation. Of the seventy-two square kilometer land area containing Hiroshima it is estimated that thirteen square kilometers were immediately decimated and 55,000 people died instantly.

Another thirty square kilometers were affected by the bomb including the deadly radioactive black rain, resulting in another 50,000 deaths soon afterwards.

Many more were to follow.

One exhibit shows a piece of white wooden wall streaked with black rain.

Black rain fell as far as two miles north of the hypocenter.

Patches of clothing remains are shown, charred, shredded, pathetic.

Keloids—cancerous growths that resemble animal claw marks caused by exposure to radiation—were explained in a series of photographs which turns your stomach.

An iron safe-deposit box is exhibited—its contents incinerated.

At the time of the holocaust a person was sitting on the steps of the Sugimoto Bank. The bomb went off and the person simply vanished, leaving a shadow on the steps of the bank. *Nothing but a shadow.*

The steps of the bank had been donated to the museum.

That was it—all I could stand.

There was much more in the museum but I packed it in and fled to the beauty and tranquility of Miyajima.

A visit to the calmness and beauty of Miyajima is almost a required catharsis to the madness remembered at the Hiroshima Museum.

Miyajima is famous for its red torii—a shrine portal—seeming to float on the water. It is a subject of a million postcards and as many posters. It "says" Japan and is listed by JNTO as one of the three most memorable sights in the country.

The portal leads from the sea or, more properly, Hiroshima Bay to the Itsukushima Shrine whose wide corridors and galleries stretch out into the bay, and, at high tide, like the torii, are adrift on the waters.

The streets of the resort town are overrun with tame deer and tame school children and Japanese tour groups led by guides with hand-held electronic loud speakers.

A cable car takes you to the island's view-top mountain, and back down to a museum, an aquarium, a five-story pagoda and a thousand candy shops.

You reach Miyajima-guchi Station in a thirty-minute train ride from Hiroshima. The ferry crossing to the island of Miyajima takes ten minutes. The entire tour can be done from Hiroshima comfortably in a day, even a half day.

Unfortunately, I didn't take a day-trip from Hiroshima but stayed the night on the island which meant struggling with luggage to station, luggage to platform, luggage to ferry, luggage to my accommodations at the Ryokan Kamefuku, which is not a nice, low-lying Japanese inn with Kyoto elegance but a multi-storied hotel, and not recommended.

Nobody drew my bath. Nobody asked me what time I wanted to be served dinner in my room. In addition, I couldn't check in until three and had to be out the following morning before ten. Hotel No-No.

At the minshuku in Hiroshima I picked up a political economics professor from Dayton, Ohio, Arthur Oster and his wife, Judith. He was bald of head but bold of mustache, fierce nosed with a resonant, deep, professional speaking voice.

I admired him instantly because he had the fine quality of forthrightness in asking directions. In that booming, attention-grabbing voice, he would ask startled candy-shop girls, firemen, ticket-takers—and any pedestrian—for directions. In English, of course.

He always came back with an answer. Always. Often it was an incorrect answer, he admitted, but any answer is better than none. At least you knew something.

Oh, yes, another lesson.

I had been told that in Japan you can leave your wallet, your wife, your watch unattended. "But never, *never* leave your umbrella."

On a misty afternoon, Mr. and Mrs. Oster and I were several hundred yards away from a museum we had just visited when an attendant caught up with us on a bicycle—and handed me my forgotten umbrella.

The only thing stolen that day was a map of the area. A deer took it out of Judith Oster's hand and stood there and ate it.

6. The East Coast of the Island of Kyushu and Cities of Hot Springs

The English lady at the next table at the Suginoi Hotel overlooking the city of Beppu said to a lady at an adjoining table, "Well, I am going to do the mud pots and the monkey park but my husband refuses to go to the monkeys. He hates monkeys."

"I'm going to the mud pots, too, but only after I have taken the baths. Have you taken your bath yet?"

"No, I'm going to take my bath tonight before dinner."

They both nodded at having completed a satisfactory conversation, as though bathing was a common topic during breakfast at home.

But this is Beppu, one of the most popular hot-springs resorts in Japan where many hot springs hotels make such conversations commonplace.

If you have a healthy allotment of imagination, you can dream that Japan is shaped like a dragon. The island of Hokkaido in the north is the head of the dragon and Honshu in the middle is the body of the dragon and Kyushu in the south is the detached tail.

Kyushu is an island of semi-tropical beauty. Here you can see palm trees and exotic flowers. The country is more open, less populated and greener than industrialized Honshu.

Volcanic action has created springs and spas, famous mineral baths and cures for everything from athlete's foot to dandruff.

Beppu, on the east coast of Kyushu, boasts of almost 4,000 hot springs producing thousands of gallons of mineral water with miraculously curative powers in which, it is assumed, you will dunk yourself ritually at least once a day.

In the area are eight "hells" or mud pots, plopping, bubbling holes of melted earth giving off sulphuric odors such as you see—and smell—around Lake Rotorua in New Zealand. One of the more different "hells", and also the largest, is the Umi Jigoku which is the color of the sea and goes to a depth of 120 meters.

The other scenic attraction is the Takasakiyama Natural Zoo where a couple of thousand monkeys live in a primeval forest on the slopes of Takasakiyama Hill.

I didn't do mud baths or monkeys, opting to stay indoors on a rainy day to nurse a bad, bad cold.

The hotel room facing the mountains was not a bit glamorous. One, there was no place to store clothes. None. Secondly, there was no place to send laundry. No place. Is it because the Japanese don't travel with enough clothes to get dirty?

The room wallpaper was stained.

My cold didn't help my attitude.

Later, however, as I started to explore the interior of the Suginoi Hotel I began to realize how huge it was, how unique in so many ways, and what an unusual variety of diversions it offered the visitor. It was a combination hotel, theater, amusement park, bathhouse, garden and museum.

After my initial late afternoon look-around and return to the room, I was accosted by the roommaid waving a slip of paper. "Dinner," she said in English and motioned me to follow her.

"No," I said. "No dinner. Bad cold. Bed. Sleep."

She was stunned. I wasn't obeying.

I put the "Do Not Disturb" sign on the doorknob and prepared for bed.

The phone rang.

A young girl's voice asked, "Have you had dinner?"

"No," I said. "I don't *want* dinner."

"No dinner?"

"No."

A half an hour passed and then there was a knock on the door. So much for "Do Not Disturb" signs. It was the roommaid with fresh towels.

Another half an hour went by, another knock.

I ignored it. A key rattled in the lock. The door opened only to be halted by the safety chain. With head stuffed and joints aching, feeling feverish, I went to the door, yanked it open to find roommaid number three staring at me and I shook the "Do Not Disturb" card in her honest, open, startled face and bellowed, "What the hell does that mean?" She fled in terror, waving criss-crossed hands in front of her face.

I was guilty of bad form. One does not lose one's temper in Japan. When I checked out of the hotel, I left a bottle of perfume as a gesture of apology.

KYUSHU

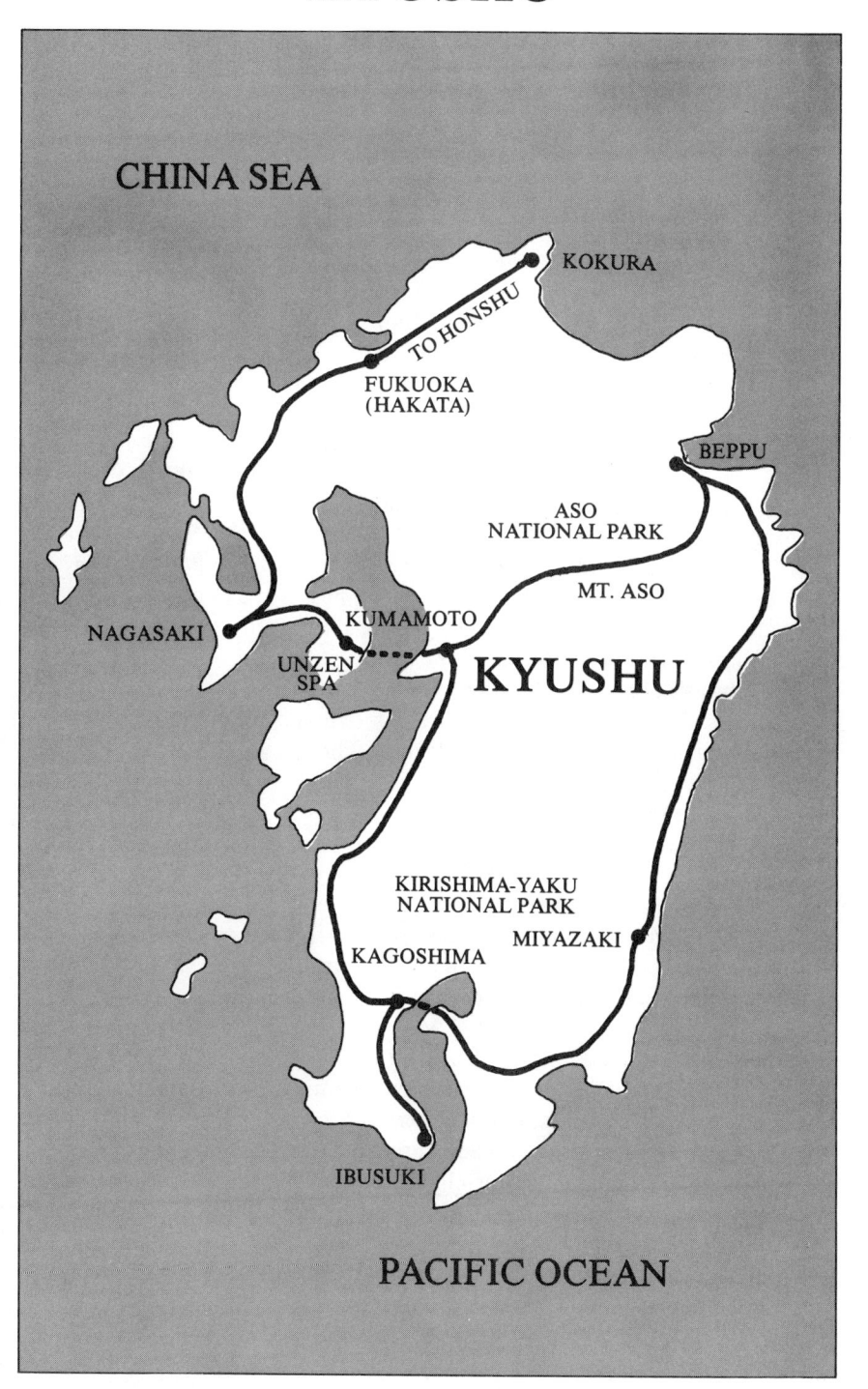

I stayed tense for another hour waiting for another knock, another ring—but all was still and I slipped into a nine-hour sleep.

The next morning I found a slip of paper underneath the door. It was a coupon for breakfast.

Late that afternoon the telephone rang and the same young girl's voice asked, "What time would you like dinner? We have a Japanese buffet and a Western buffet." A pause, then again: "What time would you like dinner?"

All I wanted was a hot bowl of noodles and a hot pot of tea, but I gave up.

"Western," I mumbled. "Seven o'clock."

"Western," confirmed the relieved voice. "Seven o'clock. Wait in your room. The roommaid will come by to lead you to the club for dinner."

Once, a long time ago, on my first day in a Tokyo hotel after a long pan-Pacific flight and needing a full morning's nap to recover, I hung a "Don't Disturb" sign on the door and went through a similar multiple knock-ring Marx Brothers routine, culminating in two boys vacuuming the room while I clutched a pillow over my head and repeated the commandment "Thou shall not kill."

Amazing, the Japanese persistence. The job will be done.

Back to the Suginoi Hotel.

One twelve-story tower contained Japanese-style rooms next to a fourteen-story tower with Western-style rooms.

That was just the base of the complex.

The next morning after a breakfast of cornflakes, poached eggs, juice, ham, coffee, I explored the Suginoi trailing, most of the time, two older ladies who were looking for the greenhouse.

One lady was from the Isle of Man in the middle of the Irish Sea, the other from the Isle of Wight off the south coast of England. When I asked them how they found themselves in Beppu, they answered, "Doing Japan, donchaknow."

We passed a shopping arcade, three restaurants, a bowling alley, a huge electronic-games-for-children area. We passed an empty swimming pool (ice-skating rink in winter) and a show theater that seats 1,700 and advertises "100 girls waiting for you." My companions had seen the show the night before and reported it excellent.

Finally, mounting another flight of stairs we were in an open garden complex with waterfalls, lawns, playgrounds, a small restaurant, more games for children and, not one, but two greenhouses.

One greenhouse was exquisitely Japanese with bonsai azalea plants in blossom, orchids and an artistic gurgling stream.

The other greenhouse had a Tarzan motif (!) with treehouse, real alligators—really—water lillies, caged peacocks, and many jungle-sized plants.

Outside, a cliff-sized waterfall cascaded into a pool filled with brilliantly colored carp.

Perhaps the most absorbing corner of the vast complex was the Suginoi Museum with an excellent display of intricately decorated armor from the fourteenth to the seventeenth centuries, ceramics, weapons, gorgeous screens, statues, temple guardians. A first-class collection.

Back in the room, the decision was "to bathe or not to bathe" in the public bath.

The Suginoi mineral waters, if you believe the literature, cure lumbago, reduce swollen lymph glands, erase ugly warts and straighten out mental disorders. What would they do for a head cold—a bad, bad, head cold?

The Suginoi has two minor baths and two major baths, each segregated, each beguilingly named. The major bath for men is euphorically called the "Dream Bath." Its counterpart for women is the "Flower Bath." Each is the size of a football field and ornately designed.

Forward! Cold or no cold, it had to be experienced.

I changed into kimono, clutched a change purse, a hotel map and a room key, and headed out in the general direction of the "Dream Bath."

Occasionally I would stop a waitress or a counter sales girl, point to "Dream Bath" on my map, and then follow the pointed finger.

Eventually, I came to a sign in English—one of the few—"For Men."

Inside, behind a counter, was a lady attendant. "Dream Bath?" I asked.

"Yes," she said and signaled me to follow her.

I doffed my hotel slippers in a giant common slipper basket and followed the lady past a set of small lockers and up a ramp. There under an immense, cream plastic roof that filtered the sunlight was the damnedest aquarium for human beings in the world.

It was dazzling. Bigger than a football field, there were a dozen baths of different sizes and decorations. Some were bordered with statues, one had a Japanese red lacquer bridge across it, others had pebbled bottoms. One featured a tiled slide. There was even a replica of part of a Bullet Train. Lush plants, palms, vines were everywhere.

The lady led me back to the locker area, indicating she wanted a coin. I extended a handful out of which she took a Y20 coin for the locker key. She produced a terry towel half the size of a dinner napkin—and waited. She was waiting for me to strip. I looked at her. She looked at me. There was nothing else to do. I stripped with what I hoped was great nonchalance, put my things in the locker and was about to close it when she said, "Watch."

Oh, yes, my wristwatch. Even the most nonchalant forget. I locked the cabinet and then, key in one hand, towel in the other at a strategic position, I paused. What was I supposed to do with the key? Matter-of-factly, the lady took it from me and slipped the rubber string attached to the key around my wrist and went back to work.

Back up the ramp I went to the Dream Bath Washing Wall where a dozen hot and cold spigots were placed at knee height, each furnished with a plastic stool and plastic bucket. Why does everything in Japan have to be so low, I wondered, and why didn't mother give me looser hamstring muscles?

Having read several advisory booklets on bathhouse procedures I made a big show of soaping and washing and rinsing, pouring small buckets of water over my head and body.

Now baby-clean, towel draped casually around my neck, I entered the first pool, twice as large as an ordinary swimming pool and a uniform one meter in depth, as were all the pools.

The place was mine alone, momentarily, until another bather came in and proceeded to the far end, up another ramp, where there were half a dozen smaller pools.

Ultimately I tried almost all of them.

In one corner a large pit was filled with volcanic heated sand. Very hot. If you wanted to try a sand sauna, an attendant would bury you in sand. It was the only thing I passed by.

The upper path led around to the head of the tiled slide. The place was deserted. Who was to know?

A workman below spraying the plants saw my indecision and urged me to try it, illustrating with gestures how to use my towel as a bottom mat to slide on. Wise idea.

Zip! Splash! Great!

The replica of the Bullet Train caught my attention. Besides containing another tub of steaming water, it had a 360-degree shower ring. I tried that too.

That did it. I had spent half an hour in the various pools and then went through the spigot-and-rinse routine again, dried myself as much as possible with the wet-but-wrung-out towel, changed back into my kimono, collected my watch, returned to my room and went to bed.

"Tonight I feel much better," I wrote with forced optimism in my notebook. Secretly I thought I had pneumonia.

The next morning the cold was almost gone.

Conversations in Miyazaki

The train ride to Miyazaki is a hundred and fifty kilometers down the east coast of Kyushu from Beppu.

On the first leg, my seat companion, a blue-suited young businessman, was reading a copy of the morning newspaper—then switched to a thick comic book. Hmmmm.

What was this thing with comic books?

The scenery out of the window became less cluttered of houses and factories. Rice paddies and fields of produce stretched out alongside the tracks. Citrus trees were much in evidence. Japan, in Kyushu, was taking on a new, more spacious, handsome look.

Colorful paper carp were flying from poles in front of village houses like airport windsocks. The largest carp dominated the top of the string of paper fish, sometimes being six meters long, with the remainder of the carp diminishing in size as they came down the pole. A pretty sight of moving color.

Boy's Day, a national holiday on May 5, was still two weeks away. Why were the carp flying so early?

The train ride again extended through the lunch hour. One thing that the Suginoi didn't have was a pastry shop. No sandwiches. None on the station platform. I was sandwich-less and famished.

I stopped one of the passing attendants laden with oranges, and drinks and mysterious boxes and asked, "Sandwich?" (The Japanese word is *sandoichi*. The English word is close enough to be understood.)

There were no sandwiches or sandoichis.

My instructions at Miyazaki were to proceed from the station to the Sun Hotel Phoenix, twenty miles away by taxi. Contact: K. Nishimura.

I was no sooner through the exit gate than a pleasant lady stopped me and asked in colloquial English: "Are you Mr. McDermott? I'm Kazuko Nishimura."

For the next day and a half Kazuko made Miyazaki an enjoyable, rewarding stop. By this time, I had a million questions to ask and she opened many doors of understanding to my fumbling queries about Japan and her people.

"May I call you John?" was her first question after we had shoehorned ourselves into her Honda Civic whose engine cough was worse than mine. To ask to use the first name at first meeting meant that she was well trained in Western ways. We obviously were going to get along. "We will go to the hotel, and you can see your room, wash up and we'll have lunch. Okay?"

Lunch? Oh, yes, please.

"Before the train pulled into the station I could see two tall, white buildings over there," I pointed in the direction of the ocean. "Would that be the Sun Phoenix Hotel?"

"One of them, yes," she replied. "The other building is the Seaside Phoenix Hotel. Downtown, on the river, we have the Hotel Phoenix which gives us about six hundred rooms altogether. In front of your hotel is our Phoenix Golf Course with 27-holes, and back on the plateau behind the city we have a 36-hole course, all part of Phoenix Kokusai Kanko, a company owned by Mr. Toryo Sato."

"Who is he?"

"He is best known for his paper company in Osaka plus other activities in other places. He now has seventeen companies."

En route to the hotel we passed several houses decorated with flying carp.

"Why the carp now?"

"Boy's Day," said Kazuko.

"But that isn't for another two weeks."

"Oh, but many people put them up early. Others, particularly in the country, celebrate Boy's Day according to the lunar calendar which puts the event a month later so you can see flying carp from April through June."

"Why carp?"

"The carp is known as a strong fish able to swim upstream. The fish symbolizes the hope that the sons will be able to emulate the strength and courage of the carp."

The Sun Phoenix Hotel proved to be an accommodation of international class. Most of the counter personnel spoke English as did the petite Japanese hostess, Miss Fujimoto, who showed me to the room.

Twin beds, a stocked refrigerator, one yukata kimono plus one deep blue samurai kimono which I thought was silk but was of thick cotton.

Yes, said Miss Fujimoto, they could do my laundry overnight.

One instant appeal of the room was to look out from the room, across the golf course, across a green park and onto the ocean. Not another building in sight. Fairways, trees and sea. Green, green and blue. How tranquil in crowded Japan.

"How long have you been with the hotel?" I asked Kazuko over lunch in the rooftop restaurant with views in all directions.

She wanted to talk about the properties and I wanted to know more about a woman hotel executive.

"How long have you been with the hotel?" I repeated.

"Eight years." Pause. "There are 600,000 azalea plants on the property and they are all now in full bloom. Tomorrow is the Azalea Festival Day and the television stations will be here to televise the ceremonies."

"Where were you before?"

"We also have on property six tennis courts and a zoo."

"Before the hotel—?"

"I was with a furniture rental company in Tokyo—the first such company in the country—and we did much business with American, English, Australian and New Zealand people. I majored in English in a junior college in Tokyo so I was the principal contact with the clients, speaking English most of the time."

"Why did you come here?"

"I was born here—or near here—at Nichinan where there is a famous Udo Shrine."

"Your card reads 'Sales Manager for Inbound and Convention'. What does that mean?"

"When I first came here I was in the reservation office but dealing with English-speaking guests or potential guests, which is now more and more important to us.

"At one time Miyazaki was a thriving city for honeymooners but the travel agencies started giving business more and more to bigger ticket destinations like Guam, Honolulu, Hong Kong, so conventions, including those from overseas clients like the one we just concluded for the Australians, is part of our marketing plan. The Australians went to sessions in the morning, played golf in the afternoon and then went into Miyazaki and played all night. They had a great time."

"Australians usually do. How many women in the organization hold positions at your level?"

"I am the only one."

"How many employees are there and how many are women?"

"Out of eight hundred employees there would be five hundred women. We just added seventy-five trainees."

"Why so many?"

"Because so many get married and leave."

"Can't they get married and stay?"

"No."

"What!"

"The company rule is that no one on the permanent staff can be a married woman. But eighty-five percent of the men on the staff are married to former staff members and that is good because their wives know from experience how demanding hotel business hours—and days—can be."

The card, on being reread, said Miss Kazuko Nishimura.

"In the tourist industry generally and in the hotel business specifically I see examples of women assuming more and more responsible positions. Is that happening in Japan?"

Miss Nishimura, the only feminine staff member not in a blue uniform, shook her head.

"I went to the Pacific Area Travel Association conventions is Canberra, Australia and Seoul, Korea, and I was the only woman executive from Japan there."

"Back to the carp flying. There is a Boy's Day but not a Girl's Day?"

"No, there is a Girl's Day. It's in March. But unlike the Boy's Day, it is not a national holiday."

"Women in Japan have a way to go."

"Let's go see the country club," said Kazuko, turning the subject back to the property.

Adjacent to the Seaside Phoenix Hotel is the clubhouse of the Phoenix Golf Country Club where you can play golf for about $100 a round—half the price of Hakone—including a uniformed girl caddy who pushes a cart carrying four bags. Strapped to the cart is a can for cigarette butts.

The name and locale of the Phoenix Club is well known to the international golfing elite because it is the site of the annual Phoenix-Dunlop tournament, drawing the biggest field of international golfers playing for the biggest purse in Japan.

Seve Ballesteros has won twice. Other winners include Tom Watson, Bobby Wadkins, Andy Bean, Graham Marsh, Hubert Green, Johnny Miller. Calvin Peete, the poetry-swinging black, won the tournament in 1982 and a check for $66,000.

The clubhouse menu is unique. Opposite each item on the menu is a time it takes the dish to be served. The manager of the club said with pride: "Every golfer is impatient and has a hot temper. We can fix and serve noodles in five minutes."

Miyazaki is a prosperous, modern city of 250,000. It is going again through a period of growth after a slump when its youth took off for the city jobs in Osaka and Tokyo.

You are reminded that it is on the same latitude as Los Angeles when you see its mainfare divided by tall palm trees.

Historically, the area goes back to the very beginning of Japan.

Scattered around Miyazaki are ancient burial grounds thought to have belonged to the first inhabitants of Japan. Where did they come from, the first inhabitants? Evidence indicates that the immigrants could have come from Korea but that is not a popular theory. Korea is not the most popular country in Japan.

Also, the legendary Jimmu, the first emperor of Japan, started his military conquests around Miyazaki, eventually forming the Yamato Court in the Nara Prefecture at the beginning of the fourth century.

You are reminded of both of these historical times when you visit the hilltop Heiwadai Park and find the "Peace Tower" and the Haniwa Gardens.

The "Peace Tower" was built in 1940, at the beginning of the war, and is dedicated to the 2,600 years of Japanese history.

The monument looks like an asparagus tip from the Jolly Green Giant. If you ranked the ugliest monuments in the world, here is a certain candidate for the top ten. It might even take first.

The inscription written in 1940 is not endearing either. "We spread our power all over the world."

In the corners of the asparagus are four figures representing the merchant, the farmer, the fisherman and the warrior. The military figure was taken down by sensitive local authorities after World War II, but then replaced in 1962.

But wait. Don't turn away.

Twenty meters in front of the monument is an octangular stone where, if you stand and clap your hands, you get an echo.

Japanese tour guides tell their followers "Clap your hands twice and pray for happiness."

They all do as they are told. The echo bounces back and the tourists go away smiling.

On the door of the tower are the symbols of the Shinto shrine: the mirror, the sword, the jewelled necklace.

Also embossed on the metal doors is the ship of the legendary Jimmu as he sails from Miyazaki to conquer Japan.

Fifty yards away is the Haniwa Garden. Here, scattered around many trees, are reproductions of clay figures found in excavations dating back to the third century when an obviously artistic and cultured society existed.

The figures take many forms of the day: horses, dogs, houses, soldiers with shields, soldiers with daggers.

The vacant, hollow-eyed reproductions are made in Miyazaki and can be found in souvenir shops throughout Japan—and may remind you of Aztec pottery.

At dinner on top of the Sun Phoenix it was question-and-answer time again.

"I'm under the impression, Kazuko, that since my last trip to Japan twelve years ago everything has been upgraded: better designs, better quality, even better marketing. Clothes, for example."

"Definitely," said Kazuko. "One instance. I'm not a little

woman. But it hurts to go into a store and to a section marked 'LL'—large lady. Today it is called 'Carnation Corner' or somesuch. Much better."

"Something else I don't recall seeing before which really has aroused my curiousity." And I told her about the couple on the train reading the comic book, the men in the noodle restaurant reading comic books, my businessman seat-mate that morning with a comic book. "What's this all about?"

Kazuko shook her head. *"Manga,"* she said. "Manga is the Japanese word for comic books, or illustrated story. It is a national disease, and I can't explain it. It seems as though in the last ten years the young people in universities, the young businessman like you saw, the general population of young people don't seem to have a serious thought in their heads.

"No one reads good literature any more. Classics or good novels are unknown to the young. Perhaps it is because this new generation grew up on animated television programs—adventure stories, science fiction, blood-and-guts stories. Today's way of communication is through picture graphics and manga, the illustrated pulps, are now part of the Japanese way of life."

Later I learned that manga accounts for thirty percent of all publishing sales. As many as three million copies will be sold each week.

"Another subject. I hear so much Western music on the radio, on the street, on television. So much of it is in English."

"Sure. Remember we all have had three to six years of English in school. We can read it. We can even write it. In music we can hear it and mimic it. We just can't speak it. I have lots of English records in my house. LP. Stereo. Tapes. All in English."

(In my notebook I recorded the remark that her favorite record was "France Inatra and his song, *Spring Is Here."* Later, rereading my notes, I understood my error.)

"As a single woman in Japan in an executive position, you are obviously unique. Do you have a difficult time doing your job?"

"Not at all. Remember I am dealing with English-speaking clients almost exclusively. Where I have trouble is making my peers appreciate what a woman wants in a hotel. All hotels are designed by men, right? Yet, most international travel for pleasure is done by women. And also an increasing number of convention attendees are women, not just as wives but as delegates.

"When I look at a hotel I look at it from a woman's needs."

"For example?"

"Okay, for example. First of all, where is the dressing table and is it properly lighted? Nine out of ten times it isn't. The man who designed the room never had to put on make-up in the dark. And is there room for cosmetics?

"There should be space for at least three pairs of ladies shoes—particularly at a convention hotel.

"The wardrobe should have hangar rods high enough to accommodate floor-length dresses.

"Showerheads are another item of horror. They are not designed for a lady who has just had her hair done. A flexible, hand-held showerhead is better for a woman."

"What's the biggest complaint of your international visitor? Do you have any problems with security?"

"You mean robberies? Never. Oh, sometimes a person is missing a billfold but it is inevitably found in the suitcase where it was hidden. And international guests sometimes worry about their door being open too long. The Japanese housekeeping routine is to clean eight rooms at a time. 'Why can't you just clean one room at a time?' they ask. But eight rooms at a time is our system.

"Also guests in less expensive rooms occasionally complain about the lack of storage space. But the Japanese traveller is accustomed to travelling very lightly and doesn't require storage space."

"Or laundry?"

"Or laundry."

"Is that why I couldn't get my laundry done in the last hotel?"

"That's it," said Kazuko.

The next morning Kazuko met me in the hotel lobby.

North of Miyazaki, JNR has a research facility and a test track where an experimental magnetic elevated train has been run at speeds over 500 k.p.h. I had hoped for an interview with one of the engineers but the facility was closed on Saturday.

Sitting in the lobby planning our day, I asked Kazuko if there is a difference in the young people of Japan today as contrasted to yesterday.

She said it is a new generation.

Newly married couples do not move in with the parents as their parents probably did when the houses were big enough for three generations. Sleeping in large family groups on tatami mats is not

attractive to the new generation.
They want their own apartments with Western furniture, plumbing, appliances.
He wears a blue suit to work but he doesn't come home, slip on a kimono and go out into the garden for an hour to contemplate the beauty of a camelia. He puts on his blue jeans, a T-shirt, and plays the latest tapes of the Bee Gees.
She does the same.
These are called the "new family."

In the hotel shopping area just off the lobby Kazuko showed me samples of the local pottery, *takasaki-yaki,* a lovely pottery with patterns developed from oil drops.
A cup and a saucer could be bought for as little as $6, a handsome vase for $150.
Another local product she had me sample was *shochu,* a strong alcoholic drink made from buckwheat or rice or sweet potato or chestnut.
We continued our Japanese shopping excursion by driving to the Daiei Super Market, a small shopping center, in Miyazaki.
First we went to the bookstore where Kazuko pointed out how different magazines were targeted to different age groups. High teens. Early twenties. Late twenties.
Adult books. *Focus,* a picture weekly. Sexy Focus, a pornographic satire on *Focus. Penthouse* and *Playboy* for men. *Eros* for women.
And stacks and stacks of manga.
We visited a kimono shop, a record store, a food store.
In the food store I told Kazuko about a delicious dish I had seen prepared and sampled in a Okayama department store basement.
"*Okonomi-yaki,*" she said. "Come over here." And there in a window was a woman making okonomi-yaki. "Would you like to go to a little okonomi-yaki restaurant for lunch?"
"Yes!"
In the middle of the city, in the Sanyo-Beniya Building where restaurants dominate every floor, we went into the okonomi-yaki restaurant and sat at a counter about five meters long—not quite twenty feet—with a hot plate running its length. Modern, neat establishment.
The base of okonomi-yaki is flour, egg and water into which is

chopped onion, cabbage and green pepper. The diner then has a choice of what other ingredients to add. I selected pork and shrimp. Kazuko took octopus and cuttle fish.

The chef poured the batter into pancake rounds on the counter's hot plate and added the ingredients, turning them over with a spatula from time to time as they became firm. When the dish was almost cooked, it was basted with a sauce.

"What's the sauce, Kazuko?"

"Barbecue sauce. Any sauce. If it comes in a bottle from America, it is *sauce.*"

The chef gave each of us a small spatula, moved the rounded okonomi-yaki to the edge of the hot plate. We served ourselves, cutting off portions as we ate. A tasty lunch.

"I feel so sorry for foreign visitors who come to Japan and never get to enjoy anything like this. They come and leave and never know it is here."

"Ask," suggested Kazuko. "All you have to do is ask. People in Japan will direct you. If your readers come to Miyazaki, tell them to call me. Really. I'll show the way. Now what do you want to do?"

"I would like to play pachinko."

Pachinko is another Japanese craze. Throughout Japan you will pass pachinko parlors filled with hundreds of vertical pinball machines before which hundreds of Japanese sit mesmerized as thousands of steel balls rattle around a series of set pins, hoping that balls will drop into winning holes which then reward the players with more steel balls.

Many years ago the game was started for children. The pins were laboriously pounded in by hand.

Today children are not allowed in pachinko parlors and the machines are designed and the pins set by computers.

Bringing newly designed machines onto the market and into the big city pachinko parlors is as necessary as introducing new dress styles. The older machines go out into the suburbs and then into the country and then into oblivion.

Kazuko clapped her hands. "Good. I love pachinko. Five thousand yen is my limit. Some players will lose thirty to fifty thousand yen. Terrible."

"Why do they do this? Is it a psychological relief? All I've seen anyone win is a pack, or carton, of cigarettes."

"Ah," she winked. "There's a little empty room someplace nearby and a small low window in the back. There you can turn in the chit you have won—or the cigarettes—and you will receive cash in return."

"Ah-so?"

"Ah-so."

From the restaurant she led me to a major pachinko parlor but instead of going in we walked around the corner and there in a little hole-in-the-wall-store was a hole in the wall.

"Ah-so."

We returned to the pachinko parlor, bought a thousand yen worth of steel balls from a machine which dropped them into a plastic basket. We had difficulty finding an empty machine . . . and there were seven hundred of them.

You can't imagine the megacycle din of seven hundred pinball machines.

Finally we found two machines, divided the balls, poured them into inclined trays in front of the machine. By turning a knob, the balls automatically shot in a steady stream to the top and then rattled down through the pins to the bottom, occasionally dropping into a hole, the reward being a fresh bunch of steel balls dropping into the inclined tray.

The only control the player has is by the knob which starts or stops and slows or accelerates the speed of the steel balls.

It took us ten minutes to lose our thousand yen.

"There are people—professional gamblers—who will do this all day long," said Kazuko.

In one corner of the parlor is a wash basin and clean roller towels to wash the grime of gambling off your hands.

That evening I returned to the Sanyo-Beniya Building under Kazuko's direction for a yakitori dinner—serving after serving of various items grilled on a stick and brought one at a time to the diner.

At one point I beckoned the waiter who spoke a few words of English and asked, pointing at the last serving which tasted like grizzled beef, asked, "What is that?"

"Fish."

"No, not fish," I said.

"No. Wrong. Cock," he said and flapped his arms like a fowl.

"No, not chicken," I said.
"Yes, chicken," and he pointed to his stomach. Something from inside the chicken? Heart? No. Liver? No. It was grizzled. Gizzard! I *never* eat chicken gizzards. I did that night. Also barbecued pork, chicken breasts, beef . . . and drank lots of beer.

My dinner was a different, delicious experience—with great gizzards.

Two breakfast buffets were offered in the dining room—one Japanese, the other Western.

I was surprised by the number of the Japanese, predominantly golfers, who preferred the Western breakfast.

With my tray of orange juice and eggs I sat at a long table and was soon joined by another American who gravitated to my table in the natural reaction of two people of common language and race in a room of other nationalities.

He was a quality control engineer from Detroit with the tractor division of Ford Motor Car Company. I envied his full head of hair lightly sprinkled with grey. A solid looking citizen of regular features and deliberate speech.

Had he been in Japan before?

"I've been coming to Japan, it seems, all of my life. I was in the Navy and my ship was the second ship behind the *Missouri,* the battleship on which the Japanese surrender was signed.

"In the last ten years, I've come to Japan four times a year."

"I haven't been here for twelve years," I told him. "I see lots of changes. Do you?"

"Oh, my, yes. For one thing the Japanese are less withdrawn. They are more willing to try the English they learned in school—eager to, in many cases. They smile more and are more friendly on more levels of the society."

"Japan has had so much publicity about its fantastic production, particularly in the car industry. Is this merited or is it just a case of publicity in an isolated industry?"

"Oh, you had better believe it is merited. Let me give you an example. Near Detroit we manufacture tractors of 40-horsepower and above. In Japan, in a cooperative manufacturing venture with a local company, we manufacture tractors of 13-horsepower up to 40-horsepower.

"I have sat down with the local people when we are going to bring out a new tractor and, with all their parties and our parties involved, we will eventually agree upon the specifications and details of the new tractor.

"In ten months they will have the complete product on the line. Tractor. Spare parts. Operations manuals. Parts manuals. In Detroit it would take us four to five years."

"What about quality?"

"As a specialist in quality control I can tell you that we can't teach them anything about quality control."

"What makes the difference between their efficiency and ours?"

"What I see is that the Japanese assemble the people responsible for all areas involved and work out the objectives together, and at one time. We tend to give each department a time-period to work out its own details, often independently of what the other departments are doing. By the time we get our whole act together the Japanese are already on the market with a product. I see this happening in all industries."

I told my engineering friend from Detroit about the Fujiview Hotel constructing a new facility in a one-year period of time.

"Oh, that's not surprising. And the hotel will also have an extra amount of time-consuming, earthquake resistant steel construction in it.

"Listen, I have stayed at the Keio Plaza Hotel in the Shinjuku District since it opened because the companies I deal with are in that area and, also, it is a ten-minute, rain-free walk to their offices or to the train station. The Keio Plaza was the first high-rise in Shinjuku.

"Well, you know what it looks like now. High-rises everywhere. And I've seen it happen. A hole in the ground in January, but by the next January there stands a completed building."

It was a good morning for people.

On the train from Miyazaki to Kagoshima, my reserved Green Car seat companion was a quiet Japanese businessman and across the aisle was a grey-haired Westerner, slightly florid, well-fed and baggy eyed, holding an empty beer can. His first words of greeting, "G'diy, Mate" confirmed what the empty beer can in the morning implied, an Australian.

His lady companion was of his same vintage but nevertheless a beauty, a happy, hearty, and humorous lady. The best kind.

They were into the third week of a six-week tour of Japan, he said, travelling with 21-day rail passes and also a JTB hotel coupon book. Their coupon book had failed them once in Kyoto when a hotel turned down their request for a reservation. He wrote a properly indignant note to JTB in Tokyo.

"Wouldn't happen again. Confirmed now all the way through."

He estimated their travel budget, less the airfare, for the forty-five days at about Y25,000 a day.

I admired his organizational system. Into a "Daily Envelope", a clear, plastic bag, he put that day's railway Green Car seat reservations, that night's hotel coupon and the city map of the destination supplied by JTB.

We exchanged Good Samaritan stories.

One of his several stories was of getting off at the wrong station in a city. They were lost. He showed his hotel-marked map to a Japanese stranger who was personally upset by the mistake, rearranged his car so that he could fit their luggage in it, and drove them across town to their hotel.

"That's wouldn't ever happen to you in Melbourne," snorted the Aussie.

It wouldn't happen to many visiting Japanese in Honolulu either and I made a resolution to look for chances to be more helpful when I returned home.

I said something about how the Australian stockman would faint at the prices asked for beef in a Tokyo supermarket.

"Well, be careful," he said. "It all depends where you are. Two and a half years ago I was in Hokkaido, the northernmost island, and I went snooping around a butcher shop.

"Thinking the same thing you do, I asked the butcher to show me a filet. He disappeared and came back with an uncut filet which would have cost me about fifteen hundred yen a kilo in Melbourne. 'How much?' I asked.

"The butcher said, 'Fifteen hundred yen a kilo.' So there you are."

We exchanged other impressions of Japan and I asked them if they had noticed the predominance of comic books.

"Don't you know?" the Aussie said, "They are pornographic. The cartoons are so explicit in those comic books that we wouldn't even allow them in our country."

East Coast of Kyushu 121

The pastoral countryside between Miyazaki and Kagoshima on a spring day, happy with clean sunshine, is as pretty a picture of Japan as you will see.

Vegetable farms with meticulously laid out rows of green plants, row after row, occasionally covered with plastic. Neat hothouses growing things red and green—tomatoes, beans, asparagus.

Volcanic hills slope up from the farmland in patterns of varigated greens according to the types of trees. A swash of deep green here, a splash of light green there, a soothing, pastoral painting.

At Kirishima-Jingu many people left the train to transfer to the line taking them into Kirishima-Yaku National Park where there is excellent vacation hiking trails, golf courses, hot springs.

As the train approached Kagoshima, the conductor said something in Japanese in an excited tone of voice and pointed out the window. "Sock-ur-ah-jeema" he said.

We could see profiled against the now hazy sky, Mt. Sakurajima, an active, smoking volcano, sending up bellowing puffs of fresh white steam clouds. It was putting on a show.

Mt. Sakurajima is across the bay from the city of Kagoshima and is a tame if untidy volcano. Its last major eruption was in 1914 but it still blows ashes into the sky. When the wind turns north toward the city, the cinder dust is so dense that pedestrians carry umbrellas for protection. In every corner of Kagoshima are piles of fine, black cinders.

> Note: Kagoshima is a good example of how you can get lost at a railroad station, as the Australians did. When the train stopped at Kagoshima Station, it was my inclination to say, "This is where I get off." Wrong. My directions and ticket said "Nishi-Kagoshima Station" or "West" Kagoshima. Often there is more than one station around the city and it will stop at a directional name like *nishi*. Believe your ticket.

Kagoshima is a prosperous city of half a million with a sea port and an international airport.

The subtropical weather makes it an attractive year-round district except for the rainy months of June and July but the subjects of interests to overseas visitors are limited to two: pottery and Christianity.

Kagoshima is in Satsuma Prefecture and abounds with the famous Satsumaware pottery. The nobles preferred the delicate white pottery. The peasants used the everyday black—which I personally find more handsome. The local museum—closed on Mondays—has an excellent collection of Satsuma pottery and other local crafts.

Christianity was introduced to Japan in the year 1549 when St. Francisco Xavier—not the St. Francis of Assisi—was brought to the city by a Kagoshima patron as the first missionary to preach the fundamentals of Christianity in the country. His mission lasted ten months during which time he built a church, made converts, and then Buddhist pressure forced him to move on to Nagasaki.

Xavier's rock church was destroyed by bombs during the war but in 1949, commemorating the 400th anniversary of his appearance in Japan, a new church was built. Across the street is a re-created portal of the old church and also a bust of the saint.

South of Kagoshima, an hour by train, is the famous hot springs resort of Ibusuki, a favorite spot for tour groups and honeymooners, and the wondrous world of Mr. Iwasaki.

The little city, the most southern in Japan, has sixty hotels but the dominating inn is the 600-room Ibusuki Kanko which also includes the new western wing known as the Ibusuki Iwasaki Hotel.

The hotel complex has a bowling alley, several restaurants, a museum, a major souvenir shopping area, a 1500-person restaurant-theater known as the Jungle Park and hot baths similiar to those at the Suginoi Hotel. Known as the Jungle Baths, the covered pool area is big enough to hangar a Boeing 747. The dozen or more pools are suitably garnished with trees, ferns, statues, waterfalls—everything but Tarzan and Jane.

Owner of the resort is Yohachiro Iwasaki, 82, whose empire involves eighty companies. Not bad for a man who started with a lumberyard.

Our first encounter with Mr. Iwasaki's name was in the little cattletown of Rockhampton on the Queensland Coast of Australia where Iwasaki had bought for development a major piece of beachfront land known as Yeppoon.

The state of Queensland is Caucasian-biased, to put it gently.

The fact that Mr. Iwasaki was able to buy land not only as a foreigner but a Japanese foreigner was a remarkable accomplishment further broadened by making Rockhampton a sister city of Ibusuki and building a Japanese garden in Rockhampton and, in turn, having Rockhampton complete the exchange by building an "Australian Garden" in the middle of Ibusuki! A magical performance.

When I arrived at the modern, ten-story hotel, I wandered through an empty entranceway and into an empty lobby. No one in sight except for two people at the front desk. Was it open? Off-season or off-off-season?

I was expected but my room wasn't ready. The assistant general manager wanted to see me. Osamu Shimpuku—black hair, neat blue suit—made his appearance and we bowed and shook hands and exchanged cards and shook hands and bowed. His English was spotty but his heart was pure and for the next four hours he showed me Ibusuki.

First we had a tour of the hotel starting with coffee in the Skyroom and then lunch in one of the hotel's restaurants—buckwheat noodles, cold, dipped in a piquant sauce, and cucumber sushi.

We left the hotel in Mr. Shimpuku's aged Toyota, stopping first at the "Australian Garden", then cut inland through lush farms of tobacco, rice, wheat, vegetables—to Lake Ikeda, the largest lake in Kyushu. It is known for its giant eels, two meters and more in length and over fifteen kilos in weight. If you want to see such eels live, close up, stop at the souvenir shop in Obama where they have several in a glass tank. It will do nothing for your lunch.

Our next stop was Mt. Kaimon where Iwasaki operates two concessions: a restaurant-resthouse, filled that day with twittering uniformed schoolgirls, and nearby, a very attractive hillside golf course where, on a weekday, you can play a round of golf for $20 —including caddy. That is practically free in Japan.

This is the best part. As a part of the obligations that went along with these concessions, the company had to landscape the area. Mr. Iwasaki's idea, which he instituted fifteen years ago, was to let the honeymooners landscape the mountain. For a price.

For $25 a honeymooning couple can buy a seedling and plant it on the mountainside along with a plaque bearing their names and date. A living monument to their glorious future. Who could resist.

No one. Today there are 100,000 plants flourishing on the green mountainside. Talk about Huck Finn and his white-washed fence!

And, of course, the honeymooners have to come back every two or three years to see how their memorial is doing, eventually bringing their children to share in their heritage—a sure source of repeat business.

That's why Mr. Iwasaki has eighty companies.

At Nagasakibana Point we stopped so I could take a picture looking out over the ocean, one of the few places in the world where three bodies of water come together . . . in this case Kagoshima Bay, the Pacific Ocean and the East China Sea.

Nearby a professional photographer was taking a picture of a newly-married couple whom he had draped with plastic leis and posed against the Fuji-like cone of Mt. Kaimon. The color photograph would then be transposed to a dinner plate which the newly-married couple, a "new family", could then display in their new apartment with Western furniture as a testimonial to these wonderful days.

Removing money from honeymooners is a major business in Japan.

"This is one of the few easily found mixed baths in Japan," said the *Survival Kit* guide book about Ibusuki. I had visions—and copy already mentally written—about the pains and pleasures of bathing with two hundred naked strangers.

Wrong, wrong, wrong.

Men upstairs. Women downstairs.

However, Ibusuki is correctly known for sandbathing in the lava-heated sand where you are covered from neck to toe and left to cook underground like a pig at an Hawaiian *luau*.

At another hotel I took a picture of people at oceanside being steam-cleaned in such a manner. This I had to try. The Ibusuki Kanko advertised sandbaths, so we hurried back to the hotel and parted, Mr. Shimpuku for work and me for the baths, promising to rendezvous at 6:15 for dinner and the "Polynesian Review."

The formerly empty lobby was beginning to fill with touring Oriental vacationers getting off their busses.

Hurrying to get to the baths before the hordes of people, I changed into a yukata robe, took my change purse and went down to the sub-level Jungle Bath.

"Sandbath," I said to the woman attendant. She gave me a slip of paper to sign (Y800), another robe and the usual postage-stamp towel.

She followed me upstairs and waited while I doffed my slippers, went to a locker (Y100) and changed into the second kimono. She beckoned me to take off my shorts. (Old nonchalant had already put his watch in the locker.) She turned the key in the locker and put the rubberized band with key around my other wrist.

She motioned me to the ramp of the Jungle Bath indicating that I was to follow the signs in English saying: "Sand Bath." I threaded my way past pools varying in size from backyard jacuzzi tubs to full-size swimming pools, past plants and statues, in this huge room where natural light filtered through. I found a staircase leading down, down to the sand baths.

In another plastic-roofed room about fifteen meters long and five meters wide was a level sandpit. It was empty except for two men in white pants and undershirts with shovels standing at the far end. They were standing over a shallow grave. Mine.

They beckoned me to come forward. A strong urge to return to my room and take a siesta was rejected.

In pantomime I queried if I were to remove my number two kimono.

No, you dummy, was the pantomimed response, keep it on and come here.

Dutifully, I went to the burial ground where one man took my towel and put it down for my head, motioned me to lie down—no, lower—and then the two men shovelled sand over my kimono-clad, frightened body.

Being buried alive was never my idea of a way to go and copious perspiration from heat and nervousness appeared in the first sixty seconds. A clock on the wall was just out of visibility but by minute three the sweat was dripping in my ears. A sense of claustrophobia began to rise.

"Don't think of it." I told myself. "You'll flunk the sandbath test and be a disgrace."

A temporary distraction appeared as two new candidates for parboiling came into the torture chamber and were properly encased alongside.

Oh, that one would start a diverting, amusing, time-absorbing conversation in English.

Nothing. In the ceiling I counted brackets holding the plastic corrugated roof to the beams. Thirty to the left. Thirty to the right. One minute. Again and again.

More men came into the room. I looked pleadingly in the direction of the attendants. They never glanced back.

Now, bathed in sweat, it was a matter of endurance—and stupidity. What was I trying to prove?

Enough. I sat up. Then stood up. The attendants didn't seem surprised. I looked at the clock. Ten minutes. The recommended time.

I retreated to the end of the room where a third attendant indicated that I should doff the sand-encrusted robe and get into a luxurious, warm pool where I removed all the sand, and then, with my serviette in the proper place, I moved back to the stairs.

On either side of the mounting stairs were small grottos with various temperature pools in each grotto—cold, cool, warm and hot. I tried them all.

Once back in the flora and fauna of the Jungle Bath, I made a serious mistake. At a particularly pretty pool from which vapors of steam heat rose, I put one foot into the pool before testing the water. It was near boiling. I scalded my heel. *Always test.*

After trying several other safer pools I did the soap-and-water routine at the ankle-high spigots and damp-dried with the towel, and returned to the room. It was almost rendezvous time. I changed into a fresh yukata, donned the heavy blue cotton jacket and, feeling relaxed and well, went to join my host in the lobby.

It was filling with tour groups who had also changed into yukatas and short coats for dinner. A huge group from Taiwan. Another from Hong Kong. Many tour groups from throughout Japan. Large numbers of Japanese come at the end of March when cherry blossoms first begin to appear.

Tomorrow morning, immediately after breakfast, the tour groups would all be gone, the hotel's lobby serenely empty again.

Downstairs at a ringside table, Shimpuku was the chef at our private table where we sat on floor mats. On a grill in the middle of the table he cooked thin slices of beef, fish, mushrooms, onions. We were served sashimi, rice, cold crab, miso soup and cold beer.

The restaurant-theater was two-thirds full which equalled nine-hundred people—about a year-round average said Shimpuku.

Individual groups were introduced and they loudly cheered and applauded their own attendance.

The first act of the show consisted of local folk dances performed by local housewives, nicely costumed.

The "Polynesian Review" followed. Eight girls dressed in Tahitian costumes with grass skirts hanging precariously low on the hips shook, wiggled and bumped to the enthusiastic applause of the crowd. The Samoan fire dancer was a tremendous hit.

The girls came down into the audience to get men to come up on the stage and perform.

In Hawaii, part of the usual act is to get three or four men on stage, roll up their pant legs and teach them to hula.

Not here.

Every man who could walk was urged to get on stage where they were lined up, did a few Tahitian shakes, and then pushed into small groups to the front of the stage where they had their pictures taken with the "Polynesian" girls with coconut shell halves for brassiers.

Quickly they were hustled off-stage, given another short shimmy shake, and the way was cleared for the next group.

When the mob of men had been photographed, they started on the women. That's when I left.

"How many buy pictures?" I asked Shimpuku on the way out.

"About seventy percent," he said. "At eight hundred yen each," he added without waiting for me to ask.

"How many nights do you do a show?"

"Every night. Three hundred and sixty-five days a year."

I quickly did the arithmetic.

"If I take your average attendance and multiply it by three hundred and sixty-five, multiply that by seventy percent and multiply that by eight hundred yen, that means you take in something over one million dollars a year just for a photo gimmick!"

"That's right," Shimpuku-san beamed proudly. "It was Mr. Iwasaki's idea."

7. The West Coast of Kyushu Castles and Gardens and Nuclear Bombs

The west coast of Kyushu is rich in pleasure for the adventuring traveller. Here it is not so much the "new" Japan and its thriving, vibrant, post-war modern cities which intrigue the wanderer but the history, ancient and modern.

From the sybarite pleasure of Ibusuki, I was heading for the castle town of Kumamoto necessitating a change of trains at Kagoshima and an hour's wait on an almost empty platform.

I went in search of a newspaper. There are four English language newspapers printed in Japan: *Japan Times, Mainichi Daily News, Daily Yomiuri* and *Asahi Evening News. The Herald Tribune,* printed in Hong Kong, is flown in daily. My preference is the *Japan Times* which I like for very serious journalistic reasons. They run the crossword puzzle—and the solution—in the same issue. No English newspaper of any sort was available. I turned away.

Wait. Comic books. Manga.

I turned back and picked out a thick comic book with an illustration of a girl in tight shorts on the cover and opened the magazine in the middle.

OH!

I closed it as fast as a photographer does when he opens the back of his camera to find there is still film on the reel.

Popped the magazine into rack, walked away, casually.

That night in the *Mainichi Daily News,* I read about Japanese Customs confiscating pornographic video tapes and magazines that Japanese tourists, mainly honeymooners, were trying to smuggle back into the country.

Ho, ho, ho. They should confiscate the manga instead.

Kumamoto, a prefectural capital of half a million people, is famous for several things.

It has one of the three most famous castles in Japan; the other two being in Osaka and Nagoya.

The Suizenji Garden is an outstanding example of classic landscape architecture.

Also the city is the entrance to Mt. Aso National Park, a spectacularly sized volcanic crater, and one of the scenic wonders of Japan.

Lastly, the nightlife in Kumamoto, according to tourist literature, is among the raunchiest in the nation.

I didn't see any nightlife, and I also missed going to Mt. Aso, the most serious omission of my Honshu-Kyushu swing. The crater basin of Mt. Aso is the largest of its kind in the world, 24 x 19 kilometers. Five volcanic cones are within the crater, including a live active volcano. In case of a serious eruption when the volcano can throw huge rocks in the air, the park service has provided concrete shelters where tourists can find protection.

The park includes vast areas of grassland, lakes and forests, and I missed it thinking there was not enough time but I was wrong, especially when I found out that getting from Kumamoto to the center of the park takes only two hours or less by train and bus. Next time.

Staying across the street in the Kumamoto Castle Hotel made the visit to the castle quite simple.

Dating back to 1607, a large part of the castle was burned in the rebellion of 1877—a common occurrence, you find as you go castle collecting in Japan—but the donjon or main tower was rebuilt in 1960 and now houses a museum, also a trademark of Japanese castles.

What always impresses you about Japanese castles, and this is true of Kumamoto, is the immense size of the stones that went into the construction of the castle walls, and the harmony, almost delicate symmetry, of their position to each other.

It is known as "The Ginko Castle" because of a giant ginko tree said to have been planted by the builder around 1600.

Suizengi Park is not difficult to find by taxi if you have the name written by the hotel porter—and is a short taxi ride from the castle.

As would be expected the Japanese become very esoteric when creating anything. For every creative process there are a dozen different schools. Example: the *Ikebana* art of flower arranging involves more than twenty well-known schools plus innumerable offshoots and branches of these schools.

The same variations apply to the tea ceremony and, of course, to garden landscaping in which the spiritual is historically involved.

Two principal types are *tsukiyama* or hill garden and the *hironiwa* or flat garden, styles which go back almost to the beginning of Japanese history and were developed by Zen priests, tea masters and, later, professional landscapers.

Pride in the beauty of his garden was part of the motivation in building a nobleman's villa and so it was in Kumamoto when the villa for the Hosokawa clan was laid out in 1632. It was customary that the front of the villa, where there was space, would be devoted to a hilly type tsukiyama garden and the back areas, where the space was more restricted, would be given to a flat or hironiwa garden.

The reputation of the Suizenji Park is its unusually expansive size in the tsukiyama tradition.

I thought when I entered the garden that it was not so much planted as molded. Across a pond, shaped in the form of Lake Biwa outside of Kyoto, is a replica of Mt. Fuji.

Along its gravel paths are signs recalling scenes from the "Fifty-Three Stages of Tokaido", the famous road in the Shogunate Period from Kyoto to Edo (Tokyo), a part of which is seen in Hakone.

It is a graceful garden, the landscaping rising and falling in soft mounds with water, bridges, stone walks, clipped bushes and trees pleasing to the eye.

In one corner of the garden a small Shinto shrine with multiple, red-lacquered poles lead to the altar. I put a Y100 in the altar box and pulled the giant rope and clanged the attached bell, thereby getting the attention of the spirits.

Charming spot. I sat on a shady bench and read my first *Japan Times* in a week and watched the tourists walk by. On the way out I stopped at a Baskin-Robbins for a rocky road ice cream cone. A little Japanese Shintoism and American ice cream—it's all part of the experience.

Later I walked the downtown district—it has a covered arcade with a sliding roof—past a cling-clanging pachinko parlor filled with intent customers. Sure enough, in an alley adjacent to the parlor was a hole-in-the-wall store with a hole in the wall.

West Coast of Kyushu 131

During my stroll at the castle and in the park, even walking downtown, I didn't see another European. Not one.

At midday, at the station waiting to catch a train to Misumi and then a ferry to Shimabara and finally a taxi to Unzen National Park, I saw a bearded, bespectacled character who looked as if he were a professor at a New Zealand university and I said facetiously to him, "I didn't think there was another one in town."

He spoke no English.

The slow, open-windowed train to Misumi was a ride into yesteryear because the wooden cottages were built up to the edge of the tracks and one could look into the back windows and through shoji doors and witness the life as it had been lived for generations.

Another unusual sight, as the train went along the Ariake Sea, were the mudflats at low tide filled to the water's edge with pickup trucks and literally hundreds of people searching the sand. For what? Mussels, clams, oysters?

At Misumi a taxi driver refused to drive me the two blocks to the ferry terminal so I hauled my two bags, loose umbrella, shoulder strap camera and my clutch bag down the street to the ferry office, bought a first class ticket to Shimabara for an hour's ride. It was not a JR ferry or I could have used my rail pass. A second class ticket would have cost half as much but the ferry was already filled with school children. For privacy and deep-cushioned comfort, go first class.

From Shimabara, a port town of about 50,000, to Unzen National Park is a half-an-hour taxi ride and about $16, my most expensive taxi bill in Japan, which left me at the doors of the timbered Unzen Kanko Hotel, set back from the road behind a long, tree-lined driveway.

While checking in, I realized I was missing something. Not my umbrella. I was missing my camera. I had left it on the ferry.

The desk clerk was immediately on the telephone and in ten minutes reported that the camera had been found, turned in and it would be delivered to the hotel before dinner that night.

Unzen National Park in the middle of the Shimbara Peninsula was the first national park in Japan (1934) and boasts of the first golf course in Japan, (nine holes, 1913).

How to Get Lost and Found in New Japan

Generations ago when the summer weather in Hong Kong became too intolerable, here is where the nabobs from the Crown Colony came to cool off and play.

The Unzen Kanko Hotel was a favorite among foreigners being one of the few of the twenty-eight hotels in Unzen with Western rooms. It is still a gracious hostlery with a sulphur bath and a timbered dining room, with neatly uniformed young boys and girls, carefully trained. All very 'upstairs, downstairs' in domestic feeling.

The toilet in my bathroom was banded with a piece of paper which read: "Perfectly Disinfected."

The Unzen Visitors Information Center dispenses a pamphlet-map in English with suggested village walks.

Behind the Visitors Center is the "Hell Zone," sulphur-bleached acres of hillside filled with hot springs with bubbling, boiling water burping out of the ground. You can hear it, smell it and see it.

Extensive walks lace the area which is also gridded with pipes taking the mineral waters down to the hotels for quick-cure soaking baths.

At a spot above the Hell Zone is a memorial cross.

In 1637 the Amakusa War broke out as Japan's Tokugawa Shogunate moved to suppress the growing Christian movement. Christian captives were brought here to denounce the faith and, refusing, were boiled alive in the hot springs. A plaque in Japanese near the cross reads "Red flowers remind us of the blood of Christian martyrs."

I arrived in sunny weather and the young man at the desk said it was not too late to catch the bus to Nita Pass and take the "rope car" to the top of Mt. Myoken where, on a clear day, you can see forever.

Instead I elected to visit the Center, walk the Hell Zone and the village, write letters and go to the top of the mountain the next day.

That night it rained and the next morning the fog was down to the bottom branches of the trees.

The lesson in Japan—or anywhere else—is to take advantage of good weather when you find it.

It was a dull day in Unzen. I went back to the Visitors Center and saw an outstanding 15-minute, fully automated, multi-projection slide show. I had noodles in a small restaurant. Took a sulphur bath. Was the only diner in a tempura restaurant where I had a lovely but lonely dinner of batter-dipped, deep-fried pieces of fish, cheese, sweet potato, turnip, mushroom, cauliflower, parsley— each morsel put on my plate as it came out of the pan.

On the side was tea, rice, miso soup, and, for dessert, an orange. I remembered from a past experience and drank all of the tea because the tannic acid of the tea dissolves the fat of the deep-fry cooking and cleans out the plumbing.

The next morning was foggy again and a taxi driver took me to the Unzen bus station, carried my bags inside, assisted me in buying a ticket from a vending machine, took my bags to the proper gate for the bus before leaving me.

I had to make a train connection to get to Nagasaki and I wondered how the bus driver could make it in such weather.

Despite the foggy morning, despite the picking up and letting out of random passengers, the bus service was as prompt as the train service. Right on time. Instead of worrying about missing the train I could have enjoyed the vistas of the seashore and fields of tea bushes.

I arrived in Nagasaki before noon, one of the rare times I wasn't travelling during the lunch hour. Not surprisingly my room at the Nagasaki Tokyu Hotel, part of a major chain, was not ready.

However, the girl at the desk was most helpful. She spread out two city maps with English titles and advised me where to go.

1. The Glover House, one of the first English residences, right behind the hotel.
2. Dejima, the former man-made island, where the Portugese and then the Dutch traders were isolated.
3. Sofukuji, one of the few Chinese temples in Japan.
4. The Site of the Martyrdom of the Twenty-Six Saints of Japan.
5. Peace Park, site of the second atom bomb.

Glover House was a good place to start a visit to Nagasaki because it was a reminder of the city's rich, historical heritage.

The world-wide publicity of the atom bomb obscures the historical importance of Nagasaki which, for literally hundreds of years, was the Japanese peephole to the outer world, and the rest of the world's peephole into Japan.

Ships came from Spain, Portugal and Holland as early as the sixteenth century to trade for silk and pearls. Japanese ships sailed from here to trade with China and the Philippines.

When the Tokugawa Shogunate closed the doors to Japan in the seventeenth century only the Portugese traders were permitted to remain in Nagasaki but they had to live in isolation on the manmade Dejima Island. The Portugese were displaced by the Dutch who were also confined to Dejima Island at the edge of Nagasaki Bay for over two hundred years, from 1641 to 1854.

As the power of the Shogunate government started to crumble and the Western powers forced amity treaties on Japan, Nagasaki was made a freeport in 1858. Among the first English traders to arrive was Thomas Blake Glover who quickly took advantage of the needs of the warring classes fighting for the reins of power by profitably supplying them with imported firearms, ammunition and even warships.

Glover expanded his enterprises by starting the first railroad, opening coal mines, operating a shipyard—now Mitsubishi—and importing the first Western printing press.

Culturally, he made the first in-depth study of local fishing, hiring a painter to render in color the specimens found in surrounding waters.

More importantly, he arranged for the sons of prominent clans to go to England to school. The understanding of language and customs proved beneficial to future East-West relations and aided in the advancement of the Meiji monarchy following the downfall of the Shogunate.

In 1863 Thomas Glover built a wooden Western-styled house with a wide verandah surrounded by a large garden on a hill overlooking Nagasaki Bay, a modest house by today's standards but a mansion in early Nagasaki.

Other foreign residences were built in the same neighborhood reflecting the western-style of building in the early Meiji Period. The neighborhood became known as the Meiji Village of Nagasaki.

Today, the Glover Garden is a public park where other buildings of the same era have been assembled.

The admission is Y600—high by Japanese standards. Two moving sidewalks carry visitors to the top of the garden and, from there, they have an easy downhill walk through the different attractions.

On top of the hill the Mitsubishi Dock House, a two-story wooden structure, contains a pictorial history of Japanese warships and merchant ships.

Below it is the former residence of Frederic Ringer, a successful tea merchant, who built the unprecedented stone structure in the early Meiji Period.

Other buildings are the Old Alt House, a columned, elegant structure, and the Old Steele Memorial Academy.

The Glover House is most interesting for its contents. Some of the original fish paintings. Photographs of Thomas Blake Glover, by then a white-moustached patriarch, show the entrepreneur at work and at play and with his family. (He married a Japanese lady and they had one son and one daughter.) The colonial arms merchant died in 1911 at age seventy-three.

Throughout the gardens are pleasing, modern waterfalls.

The Glover House keeps getting associated, erroneously, with the legend of Madame Butterfly. What does exist is a memorial statue to Tomari Miura who, for thirty years, played the part of Cho Cho San in the Puccini classic opera. Near the statue is a wall plaque bearing the profile of the Italian composer.

You leave the Glover Gardens through the Nagasaki Traditional Performing Art Museum and it's wonderful!

In floor-to-ceiling display cases are reproductions of early Japanese ships, some up to six meters long, which become floats in the Kunchi Festival in March, accompanying the sacred Suwa Shrine.

The floats are part of each district's contribution to the shrine and a corp of finely trained men, *odori-cho,* show tremendous coordination as they carry or push the floats through the streets, all the while going through twirling, lifting drills with the float.

A rousing color film reflecting the vibrancy and the noise and the physical effort of the men makes you want to get to Nagasaki in March and see the festival in action.

> Note: one economic writer's advice to the Western world trying to understand Japanese production was to watch the odori'cho in action. The dedication, the training, the sacrifice that goes into the odori'cho performance is a reflection of all the qualities that make Japanese production what it is.

The man-made island of Dejima no longer exists. Landfill has attached the historic island to the mainland but its boundaries are marked with metal studs in the pavement. Facing the river inside a walled garden is a model of the island, perhaps twenty meters in length, with miniature buildings in place at the time of the Dutch occupation.

The buildings are labelled in Japanese but an interpreter pointed out barracks, cattle barns, warehouses, the captain's villa, living quarters for the local governor, secretaries, interpreters, sentinels, black men, and women of pleasure.

A curiosity in the garden is a cast-iron diving bell imported from England by the last shogun. The bell was open at the bottom except for a platform on which the observers stood. On top were half a dozen glass portholes. The occupants were evidently limited in their dive to the amount of oxygen trapped in the bell.

Another mile away is a grimmer reminder of Japanese history —the hillsite where, on February 5, 1597, six foreign missionaries and twenty Japanese Christians, arrested in Kyoto and Osaka, were crucified.

On the plateau of the hill is a large wall where each of the canonized martyrs is depicted and named.

Still another mile along is the hypocenter of the second atomic bomb.

On August 6th, the *Enola Gay* dropped the first atomic bomb on Hiroshima. "Little Boy", as the bomb was named, was made of uranium material with an explosive equality of twelve kilotons of TNT.

On August 8th, the B-29 *Bockscar* left Tinian Island in the Marianas for the second atomic bomb target, Kokura. It's load was "Fat Man", distinctly different from the Hiroshima bomb. Fat Man was composed of plutonium 239 with an explosive equality of twenty-two kilotons of TNT.

Kokura, the primary target, a railhead connecting Kyushu Island with Honshu, was covered with clouds. Three times *Bockscar* attempted to find the city and, failing, left for the secondary target of Nagasaki where parting clouds revealed the Nagasaki Steel Works.

The second atomic bomb was dropped and exploded at six hundred meters above the ground at 11:02 A.M.

Everything within a radius of four kilometers was completely destroyed through immediate incineration or subsequent burning. People and buildings simply disappeared.

The people who died instantly were the lucky ones. Others, horribly burned, lingered an hour, a day, a week in the most excruciating pain.

More than 70,000 people died. More than 18,000 houses were destroyed or damaged.

Ironically, Nagasaki had the largest per capita population of Christians in Japan.

The Urakami Cathedral, the largest Roman Catholic cathedral in the country, was six hundred meters from the hypocenter, and most of the 13,000 members of its congregation who domiciled around the church were the first to die.

(Hiroshima was the center of the strongest Protestant movement in Japan.)

A black stone monument marks the site of the hypocenter. Nearby, in Peace Park, people come from all over the world to pray for peace on August 9.

Adjacent to the hypocenter is the A-bomb Museum and the new (1981) Peace Hall. I had an appointment with Yoichiro Yamaguchi of the museum staff and Terumasa Matsunaga, the deputy chief for peace education employed by the Nagasaki Municipal Board of Education.

They had given up their holiday on the Emperor's Birthday to come to the office and talk with me.

Mr. Yamaguchi, a delightful cherub of five feet, had a memorized speech in English which he asked if he could deliver.

He traced the history of Nagasaki saying that it was always an important port city, the oldest, most famous in Japan from the time the Portugese landed in 1570 and even with the shutdown of Japan by the Shogunate, Nagasaki remained the one open eye to the world.

(By habit, I would interrupt with questions and, after being answered, Mr. Yamaguchi would ask somewhat plaintively, "Please, may I now continue?")

He continued: Nagasaki had always been a center for fishing and shipbuilding and for centuries has been attractive to visitors, now numbering five million a year.

Nagasaki has played an important historical cultural role in Japan as exemplified by the Glover Garden now a "national treasure." Next to Glover Garden is the Ohura Church, built in 1865, and is the oldest Gothic church in the country.

Economically, the reborn Nagasaki with more than half a million in population is also important. The city prospers as a fishing center—200,000 tons of fish are brought through the port annually, most of which goes to Osaka and Tokyo markets.

The Mitsubishi Shipbuilding Works, while suffering from the drop in oil-tanker production because of world oil problems, is still producing roll-on-roll-off freighters and tankers for carrying liquified petroleum, LNG. LNG tankers are distinguished in the harbor because they look like hump-backed monsters with the top part of their spherical containers appearing above decks.

The shipbuilding company is diversifying its production by manufacturing electric motors and desalination plants which are shipped to Saudi Arabia.

Mr. Matsunaga then described the newest effort of their peace movement which had been organized the previous February.

One had to be sympathetic to the movement, and I gladly gave him Y10,000 for a membership and I also told him that Matsunaga was a very familiar name in Hawaii because that was the name of one of our U.S. senators, and, in addition, I told Mr. Yamaguchi, that there were hundreds of Yamaguchis in Honolulu and that they all were rich.

We became friends.

They gave me stacks of materials and then took me through the four levels of the museum.

It was more of Hiroshima.

Ghastly pictures. Physical mementos of horror: a clock bent out of shape, its hands still pointing to 11:02. A piece of melted glass and the skeleton of a hand inside.

Video machines with Japanese and English narration recaptured the day of August 9 and the obliteration of a city.

Everywhere in the museum the walls were lined with long garlands of multi-colored paper leis assembled by students who came to the museum by class with their offerings—offerings for peace.

"The 'Fat Man' was a snap of the fingers compared to the destructive power of today's hydrogen bomb," said Mr. Matsunaga. "The average H-bomb can destroy ten million people. Four hundred could eliminate mankind. There are now what—fifty thousand H-bombs in the world? It's madness.

"People tend to think that the Nagasaki bomb was just another large bomb. It wasn't. It was the prototype that could destroy the world.

"Next time there will be no reconstruction.

"Albert Einstein said when he learned about the possible success of the A-bomb and its ultimate potential, 'We are going to have to alter our way of thinking.'

"Have we done that?" asked Mr. Matsunaga.

"You've altered mine," I told him.

Nagasaki, like Hiroshima, is a very sobering experience.

We went to happier subjects.

Mr. Matsunaga had not had lunch—neither had I—and the three of us repaired to a nearby noodle shop for bowls of hot udon noodles in broth and cups of green tea.

"It's Emperor's Day but there aren't any parades or flags or special celebrations?" I asked my luncheon companions.

"No parades," said Mr. Yamaguchi, "but today the Emperor makes his only public appearance of the year at the Palace." (Later we learned that a psycho had thrown an axe or hammer in the direction of the Emperor that day which caused no harm. Like the terrorist who took a shot at the Pope, he'll be a long time gone.)

"Also today is the biggest horserace of the year, and a major summo wrestling championship starts this afternoon at four o'clock on television."

"Another question," I said, between noodles. "In Kagoshima there is a St. Francisco Xavier monument in the church park and a plaque saying that after St. Francis was expelled from Kagoshima, he went to Nagasaki. Where did he live here?"

"Not here, no," disclaimed Mr. Yamaguchi. "He stayed near here for a short time but never in Nagasaki. He was invited by the lord of Yamaguchi Province—same name as mine—which includes Hiroshima—to go there and preach. Now, you have to remember that in those days the traders and the missionaries always went together. Same as in Nagasaki. The Portugese and the Spanish brought the Bible but they also brought rich trading."

"Are you suggesting that the lord of Yamaguchi wasn't seeking Christianity as much as he wanted to attract trading?"

Mr. Yamaguchi smiled his cherubic smile and nodded.

My friends would have stayed with me all afternoon and showed me every part of the city but it was almost four o'clock—summo wrestling time—and I insisted I could carry on by myself to the Sofukuji Temple.

We parted on a street corner. As I caught a taxi to the Sofukuji Temple, they said "aloha" several times, each time louder and with mounting enthusiasm. I almost cried. Such nice people.

The Sofukuji Temple is known as the "Red Temple" because of its vermilion-colored main gate and main hall.

Dating back to the Ming Period, this exceptional Chinese temple had Chinese abbots who had to come from the same province in China.

(I'll never forget the temple because of a memory I have of a stunning black-haired beauty dressed in a bright red motorcycle jump suit and carrying a white helmet stepping through the vermilion gates looking like an exotic model in a *Vogue Magazine* photograph. I couldn't get my mouth closed fast enough to get my Rollei out of my pocket to get a photo, but the mental picture still remains.)

The burn from the boiling bath in Ibusuki had now turned into a painful blister and I sought out a pharmacy near the hotel.

My problem was not understood by the pharmacist until I took off my shoe and sock and showed him the wound.

"Ah." A package of tape and a tube of salve were produced, money was exchanged and I was on the road to recovery.

You can get by.

The next morning at the Nagasaki Station a Japanese woman with three children introduced herself in English. She had spent three years in Madison, Wisconsin where her husband had worked at the university. He was now back in Japan developing better tasting feed for cattle. Still another example of my quality control engineer's opinion that people in Japan are friendlier than ever and more willing to try their English.

West Coast of Kyushu 141

At the station platform I had my morning can of "High C", an apple juice drink which I purchased daily from vending machines. Vending machines smother Japan. They sell soft drinks, beer, candy, food—and they always work. Always.

Also it should be noted on station platforms one often finds quick noodle stands where you can get a stand-up meal of hot noodles before catching a train.

I was on the way north to Fukuoka, often referred to as Hakata. At one time, separated by a river, there was a commercial town of Hakata, and a castle town of Fukuoka. Today they are offically joined under the name of Fukuoka and boast a population over a million, the largest city on Kyushu.

On board the Green Car and getting comfortable in my reserved seat, I looked across the way—and "hello, mates"—there was my Australian couple.

It was old home week. We played catch-up.

In Nagasaki they had had a disastrous day trying to find a non-existing kite flying contest. They had gone to the Glover House, but discouraged by the hill climbing, they had turned away, and were chagrined when I told them about the moving staircase to the top of the hill and how satisfactory the whole Glover complex was.

In the subtle game of travel-story oneupmanship, however, they story-dropped their own victory prior to coming to Nagasaki.

"We went to Mt. Aso by train and joined a bus tour through Aso National Park—it was magnificent—perfect weather—and then we continued on the bus back down through the five islands of Amakusa, all of which were first rate. You shouldn't have missed it," he said.

Damn!

My Australian friend turned out to be a doctor. I immediately showed him my damaged foot and he pulled down a bag from overhead saying he always carried a complete medical kit—and supplied me a jar of another salve.

I bought a round of morning beer in return and offered wedges of cheese and crackers from my bag, part of my own survival kit. While digging around in my hand bag for the cheese and crackers, I also showed them my faithful pottery cup and an American immersion rod for heating water for coffee.

"You do that, too?" she exclaimed. "We carry a small menthol camping stove for hot snacks. Yesterday morning he made me a Spanish omelette for breakfast! We carry fruit and juices with us all of the time. But eggs are tricky."

Another incident they related reminded me that cities are rated "great" or "poor" by the experiences you have and by the people you meet.

Example. In a previous trip we had taken a boat across Japan's Inland Sea to the island of Shikoku and the city of Takamatsu. Takamatsu, we always referred to after the trip, as "Sewer Pipe City" because our hotel overlooked a concrete pipe plant. Not very thrilling.

We had decided to leave Shikoku out of the New Japan book because it is not ready for tourists.

"What!" said the Australia couple indignantly. "Takamatsu is one of the finest cities in Japan."

Takamatsu? Why?

"One night at dinner we got into a conversation with an English-speaking chef who subsequently said that the next day was his day off and offered to give us a tour in exchange for the chance to practice English."

"He showed up the next morning in a sparkling, new Prince automobile with white linen seat covers and proceeded to give us a nine-hour tour including a delicious Japanese lunch."

The Australians couldn't say enough kind words about Takamatsu. People make the difference and the Japanese people in the new Japan are eager to meet visitors more than half way . . . even in Takamatsu.

Weather, too, makes a difference in ranking cities, of course.

Fukuoka-Hakata was superlative when I arrived. Bright, clean air, a spring day, not too warm, not too cool. It was San Francisco, Auckland and Sydney at their finest.

At the hotel, remembering the help I'd received from the girl at the desk in Nagasaki, I solicited advice from the desk clerk.

"Where should I go?"

When I came back down from depositing my bags in the room, he had marked a map for popular destinations with written instructions in both English and kanji telling me how to get to the different places by train or subway or taxi. Also on the note, written in kanji, were instructions to the taxi driver, or whomever, saying that I wanted to go to Usenti Park, to Fukuoka Castle, to Nishi

(West) Park, to Oobori Park and back to the Hakata Tokyu Hotel.

"Your timing is right. The flowers are in the peak of blooming," the clerk said.

Perhaps it was the sun or the spring air but the Usenti Park was the most pleasant, restful Japanese garden I visited in Japan. Small, less than two acres, hidden from traffic and the traffic noise behind a tall wall, it was a garden with gravel paths alongside a crooked, stone-filled running stream with water gurgling among the ferns and bushes.

The stream fed into a large pond overlooked by a tea pavilion stretching out over the water and was romantically framed against a background of trees of different greens.

Colored carp were numerous in the small lake, and a pretty Japanese lady, with a parasol to protect her silken skin against the spring sun, knelt by the lake and fluttered her fingers in the water and the carp came to her and she scratched their backs. Amazing.

Later I saw a man calling the carp to the shore by clapping his hands and he flicked water at them with his fingers as though he were playing with children.

A fern-lined shaded walk encircled the lake. At one open spot a foursome of ladies had spread a cloth and were sharing a picnic lunch.

The perfect place at the perfect time.

Go to the top of the remains of the Fukuoka Castle and view the city. It is a favorite place for lovers. If you go alone, you'll feel very much alone.

The once massive structure took ten years to complete.

Now all that remains are the huge stone walls.

A different view of the city is from the top of Nishi Park where you get a good perspective of this port town with its oil tanks and dock facilities bordering Hakata Bay.

Historically, these waters were the scenes of fierce fighting in the thirteenth century when Kublai Khan made two attempts to invade Japan. The first attempt was turned back by the Japanese troops. The second thrust was a major effort with 100,000 Chinese and Korean troops attempting to land at Hakata Bay but a Divine Wind *(kamikaze)* destroyed the Chinese fleet resulting in

an almost total loss of the invading army.
Take a taxi to the top of the hill but walk down, enjoying the flowers in bloom. The 4,000 cherry trees had finished their spring show before my walk but the azaleas were magnificent.
The main street extends from Nishi Park to Oobori Park.
Oobori Park is a lake divided by a foot path. Originally part of the moat for the nearby castle, it was swarming the day of my visit with foot-powered paddle boats and rowboats full of schoolgirls and couples.
The shady path between the two bodies of waters was lined with families taking the sun and picnicking on the grass. No litter anywhere. The people were happy, enjoying themselves but reserved. I even passed two teen-age boys listening to a portable hi-fi stereo machine which they were playing *softly!*

When I returned to the hotel, I went directly to my counter-clerk counselor.
"Tonight," I said. "Dinner."
"You want Japanese dinner? Tempura dinner? Best tempura dinner in Hakata is in hotel."
"No."
"You want night clubs? Girls? Bars? Biggest nightlife district in north Kyushu is right across river."
"No. I'd like okonomi-yaki for dinner."
A whole counter of people snapped their heads in our direction. What was the *gaijin* doing asking for okonomi-yaki?
My clerk wasn't fazed a bit. "You like *conga?* In Hakata we are very fond of okonomi-yaki with conga."
"Conga? You mean eel. Do I have to have eel?"
"No, no. You have your choice."
He directed me to an eighth floor department store restaurant a few blocks from the hotel. En route at an intersection's traffic light, I stopped and listened. What was that?
In several cities of the world a traffic light signalling "walk" is accompanied by a musical tune for the benefit of the blind or near blind. In Nagasaki and in Salt Lake City, Utah it is a cuckoo bird theme.
In Hakata the melody is *Coming Through the Rye.* (Later in Hokkaido we were to hear that Scottish song all of the time.)
The restaurant was packed. I took the last seat at the counter,

the only Westerner in the establishment.

I knew they had had experience in taking care of foreign visitors when the counterman came over to me and communicated by holding out two hands. One was filled with a white mass—eel. The other was filled with shrimp. I pointed to the shrimp.

He came back and held out one hand. In it was an egg. "Hai," I said. Yes, I'll have the egg.

Soon he delivered a huge plate of okonomi-yaki cut into squares. A jar of mayonaise was shoved in my direction.

With a large beer it was exactly what I wanted. And so was the bill: Y800.

When I left, as they do with all customers, every employee joined in a chorused farewell, another unique Japanese custom.

The next morning the sky was down to the ground, a misty, steady rain falling, destroying my plans to take a quick train trip to Hakozakigu Shrine established in 923.

My fair Fukuoka-Hakata of yesterday had turned into Grim City.

Weather does that.

8. Western Villages on the Sea of Japan

Japan has a strong, individualistic visual quality.

You don't wake up in a train or a hotel, look out the window and think: "It's Tuesday, it must be—."

You always know you are in Japan. Especially in the country, the sight of the fields, the farmhouses, even the arrangement of the trees is distinctly Japanese.

Seeing it from the train from Fukuoka to Hagi, the coastal landscape was a painting broken occasionally by small villages. The flat sea was bordered with beaches of sand and pebbles. Offshore were tiny islands topped with one or two twisted pine trees, softened by light rain. The muted vistas were ideal for Japanese wash drawings.

I was on the way to a string of small coastal towns facing the Sea of Japan. The idea of seeing and feeling this remote part of this exotic land was to satisfy a long ambition. At the same time it was accompanied by some trepidations.

Would it be too remote, too raw? Low wooden houses with mud-thatched roofs, shoji doors and smoke curling from underneath their eaves, dirt streets muddied by rain. Villagers still in traditional costume and speaking no English at all.

It was a scene found in samurai movies featuring Toshiro Mifune or Richard Chamberlain in *Shogun*.

The misty weather out of the train window stimulated the stage-set expectations. (The villagers were terrified by bandits who were blackmailing the inhabitants. Mifune, the ex-samurai warrior, the John Wayne of Japan, came to town with his broad sword and saved the day by slaughtering several dozen bandits in one splendid sword fight—and saved the beautiful daughter at the same time.)

Dream on, oh, traveller.

Hagi, my destination, did not turn out to be the simple, country, motion picture village but a popular beach resort—high-rise hotels, modern shops—a port, a fishing center, and famous for Hagi-yaki pottery.

My accommodation was a Japanese-style hotel facing the

Village on the Sea of Japan 147

beach, a prime location. Because of the Emperor's Birthday and the resulting "Golden Week" holiday when the entire Japanese nation takes to the road, I had to pay a double rate at the hotel, Y15,000 a day, but that included two Japanese meals.

> Note: A foreign visitor would do well during Golden Week to stay and play in Tokyo which has been abandoned by the hordes. A perfect time for exploring the city.

Once the time for meals was established with the proprietor who spoke a bit of English I was escorted to a room on the top floor facing the ocean. It was a western-style room with twin beds.
"Where do I take dinner? Downstairs?" I asked the young maid who had bought me upstairs.
"No. Here."
Here? How strange. Did I eat it on my lap sitting on one of the twin beds? And there was no television set. No thermos jug with tea-making service. No yukata robe set out.
This was Y15,000 a day?
As if reading my mind, the young lady slid open shoji doors behind me, and, when I turned around, there was a large, elegant tatami-matted Japanese room with a customary low table, cushioned-back floor seats, a television set (Y100), a lockable safe (Y100), and a refrigerator stocked with beer (Y500 each).
In the closet were yukata and a handkerchief-sized towel. No bath towels in the bathroom. Thinking this an oversight I asked for one.
"Japanese style," she said, indicating that was it.
That was it? For Y15,000 a day?
That evening, in lonely splendor, I dined on all sorts of odds and ends including a large plate of sashimi (raw fish).
The next morning was brilliant with sunshine. From my large terrace I could see across the beach in front to the expanse of the Sea of Japan, dotted with white fishing boats, a soothing, scenic sight.
Breakfast was served downstairs.
Confession: I found that I enjoyed Japanese dinners but the Japanese breakfast which usually includes miso soup and rice and a salted cold fish staring at me with one salted cold eye is more than

I could handle. That morning I couldn't and didn't.

Within easy walking distance of the hotel, if you don't have a blistered heel, is the castle built by the Mori family but destroyed in 1871, and other sight-seeing attractions. I limped off to get ahead of the crowds.

At the admittance booth to the castle grounds, the dear attendant lady told me in a happy stream of Japanese what I should do as she sold me a ticket and I nodded back as happily and took off to walk the remaining ramparts of the castle walls.

At one time I followed a series of directional signs I thought were important. The signs led to the restrooms.

Zipping along the paths were teen-aged boys and girls on bicycles—obviously rented bicycles. What a good idea.

Another group I saw on wheels were members of a motorcycle gang only these were not Hell's Angels in German helmets and raunchy clothes but sleekly outfitted riders with gleaming, high-powered bikes.

After walking the castle walls and admiring the giant gnarled pines, the arched stone bridges, the black butterflies and the blue azaleas reflected in castle ponds, I went to a nearby tourist center abounding with restaurants, a museum, a former samurai barracks, and found a souvenir shop which also rented bikes.

The price quoted I understood to be $6 an hour, pricey but anything was better than walking on a blistered heel. Misplaced zero. The correct price was 60¢ an hour.

What a lot of a small town you can see quickly and effortlessly on a bicycle.

When I first encountered bicycles in Japan coming up behind me on sidewalks and even in covered arcades tinkling their bells for the right-of-way, I remembered rightously resenting them. No longer.

I wobbled and tinkle-belled all over Hagi.

I pedaled down quiet lanes, back alleys, down the covered arcade, into residential areas, past backyards and frontyards of the rich and not so rich, many with exquisite gardens.

I bicycled across town and up to the Shoin Shrine, dedicated to Shoin Yoshida, a famous rebel-loyalist who taught school here and was executed by the Tokugawa government. Yoshida was highly lauded in Robert Louis Stevenson's book, *Familiar Studies of Men and Books*.

Village on the Sea of Japan 149

Past many pottery shops, a cattle yard, and orange groves I pedaled, past a fight between two alley cats, even a tucked-away cemetery with Christian crosses.

Never did I feel so close to a Japanese town.

Four hours I bicycled around Hagi under a brilliant sun which produced a beet-red forehead. The sunburn and a very sore *derriere* forced me to turn in my wheels and pay the proprietor Y500.

(The brand of my bike was "Lemon". That was the trade name. When you remember that there is a soft drink in Japan called "Sweat", you realize that there are marketing people in Japan with instincts for the distinctive.)

That night when dinner was served in my tatami-matted room the *piece de resistance* was presented in a diminutive bamboo ship. Out of the middle of the ship arched a raw fish—whole—which looked as if it had just broken water and was still alive.

Artistically, it was magnificent. Gastronomically, I couldn't face it. Even knowing how ungracious it was, I asked the bewildered mama-san to take the masterpiece back to its master.

The next morning, after a Western breakfast of cold scrambled eggs, delicious toast and black coffee, I had three hours before catching a noon train. Now infatuated with Hagi, I rented another bike and spent the morning exploring more back streets and several pottery shops.

Three well-known kilns are in the area and the streets are lined with tempting pottery collections. Every souvenir shop is wall-to-wall with the delicate sand-colored pottery. Having dragged my bags three weeks through train stations, I wasn't about to buy so much as an ash tray but many of the large vases were tempting. Yes, they would mail in protective wooden boxes but prudence said the decision for a Japanese souvenir would be best left to the Lady Navigator when she joined me for the second half of the tour in early autumn.

Each time I went down a different street I was greeted by a different sight. At one spot I saw an elaborately gold-cloth gowned priest in a sideyard ceremony obviously blessing a new house with the family lined up in attendance. Was he a Buddhist priest or a Shinto priest? I should have known that Buddhist priests are simply gowned in black and white and, secondly, all such blessings are done by Shinto priests who are beautifully, colorfully robed.

The bike hastened my needed errands.

Went to supermarket and bought snacks. Went to pastry shop and bought sandwiches and a dessert for lunch on the train. Went to pharmacy and had a hilarious conversation in pidgin-English with proprietor, aided by curious customers in a desperate, finally successful attempt to buy tape for my battered heel. We all thought it very funny.

"Tape."
"Type?"
"Tape."
"Top?"
"Tape."
"Take?"
"T-a-p-e."
"Ahhhhh. Tape!"

The only Westerners I saw in Hagi were at the railroad station as I was leaving. An American couple from a town near Seattle, Washington were visiting his former pupils of a two-year "practical" agricultural course conducted in the U.S.

"The hospitality is unbelievable," he said. "We have been entertained, housed, fed and toured all over the country for six weeks. We don't have any budget because we can't spend any money. The people are so nice."

People are so nice. It is a phrase you hear everywhere.

Listening to the tales of hospitality made me feel very appreciative of the graciousness of the Japanese.

I never should have sent the fish back.

The scenery between Hagi and Izumi is broken by semi-industrial cities, Japanese names in a litany of rail towns: Masuda, Hamada, Odashi.

Between the towns and their smokestacks are miles of rich rice paddies, formed in sunken green squares, most of them an acre or two, separated by boundaries of mounded dirt.

A stack of covered long poles lying to the side was always part of the farmer's plot. The function of the poles was never made clear to me despite my frequent questions.

The farmers, even with the smallest acreage, were using mechanized tools. Their houses were not mud-thatched but tiled roofed and the doors not paper shoji but were sliding aluminum.

The cars they drove were new.

The fifteen-minute taxi ride from Izumoshi Station to Izumo-taisha left me off in the main street in front of the Ryokan Hinodekan, a Japanese inn with a lovely entry courtyard. A wedding ceremony had just taken place and the banquet had begun and the inn was swirling with activity. The men in attendance wore the traditional black suits with white or grey silk ties. The ladies were mostly in kimono.

After putting on slippers, I was led by the manager, Mr. Ogawa, who spoke a few words of English, to my room, a simple six-tatami-mat room with a small sun room, a refrigerator, a television set. Adjacent was a private Japanese bath and toilet.

Mr. Ogawa and I sat and exchanged pleasantries in the ritual of the ryokan. A mama-san appeared to pour tea and offer tea cookies. The registration card was presented and filled out. How civilized a custom.

"Ah, Hawaii," said Mr. Ogawa when he saw the registration form. He had spent his honeymoon in Hawaii ten years before.

He advised me to visit the Izumo-taisha Shrine, the oldest Shinto shrine in Japan, that afternoon and the next morning hire a car and driver and go to Cape Hinomisaki, famous for its lighthouse and scenery. The car then could take me to my noon train.

The little village of Izumo-taisha exists because of the shrine. I walked five minutes up the hill past souvenir and camera shops and restaurants until I reached the torii, the two giant cross-beamed pillars that mark the entrance to the shrine grounds.

Shintoism which pre-dates Buddhism was, until the end of World War II, the state religion of Japan and the shrines were supported by the national government.

The original concept of Shintoism related to the spirit of the surroundings—the mountains, the trees, the animals. It is, therefore, not surprising to find the setting of the shrines reflecting this concept in the landscaping: the giant pines, the gravel walks, the bridges, the fruit trees in blossom. All combine to establish through nature a sense of tranquility, of peace, of natural spirituality.

The mind shucks off the tight coil of twentieth century restrictions and is ready to accept another kind of inner communication.

Worshippers washed their hands and rinsed their mouths, acts of purification performed by all, including the jumpsuited motorcycle riders, before passing through a wooden fence to the complex of shrines.

At the first shrine a ceremony was in progress. A Shinto priest thumped a big drum, the slow, booming cadence filling the air. A shrill woodwind counterpointed the rhythmic drumbeats. The smell of incense hung heavily in the air.

It was the perfect sound and scent for visiting the main shrine, considered a classic example of architecture before the influence of Buddhism. What impresses a visitor is the immensity of the square structure. Massive beams. Massive pillars. Massive twisted ropes, a meter thick, over the entrance. In the background is a surrounding hillside covered with trees of equal majesty.

The grounds were filled with Japanese tourists vacationing during Golden Week, happily following their leader with the flag, taking thousands of pictures, buying souvenirs by the ton.

In one corner of the grounds on an elevated stage a stylized kabuki drama was taking place. Naughty little boys on the edge of the stage tried to pull the hems of the elaborately gowned actors, and once, during the drama, when one actor left the stage to be chased around the grounds by a sword-wielding fellow actor in a mock fight, they barely survived the pack of kids in pursuit.

Another light note: a square in the compound is reserved for pigeons where parents buy small sacks of feed for the children to give to the fat, bobbing, waddling birds.

The nearby Treasure House is a museum of valuable samurai swords, statues, ancient cannon and antique screens.

Mr. Ogawa was correct. The simplest, fastest way to see Cape Hinomisaki is by car. I reserved a large black air-conditioned Toyota with driver for a two-hour, not too pricey, tour.

Upon departure the following morning, I was royally bowed out of sight by Mr. Ogawa, my mama-san and Mr. Ogawa's brother. (The idea of being bowed out of sight by an American hotel staff, much less the manager himself, is so implausible it borders on the ridiculous.) The driver swung over to the coast, hugging it all the way to Cape Hinomisaki.

The most important customer group for professional drivers in Japan must be honeymooners which means taking their pictures

Village on the Sea of Japan 153

at every photogenic stop.

Thus it was when we reached the Cape, the driver turned into a local hotel high on a promotory, commanded me into the proper position in relationship to the white lighthouse in the background and took my picture. There was no need to tell him how to operate my camera. He had used them all.

Done, he drove down into the middle of the tourist shops, pointed to where I would find the car, and pointed to the path leading to the lighthouse.

Most of the shops around the lighthouse had small grills in front where women were barbecueing Japanese delicacies: tiny squid, spread-eagled on a stick, cuttlefish and a snail-shaped mollusk. I resisted.

Also I ignored the idea of climbing to the top of the tower, electing to stroll the path on the cliff overlooking the clear-water ocean.

The jagged rocks and the sprinkling of wind-twisted pine trees, overhead seagulls wheeling in the sky bare of clouds, squawking at each other, honeymooners holding hands, cooing at each other, it was all quite pleasant and scenic.

From the lighthouse we drove to another shrine just in time to witness a scene straight from the "Mikado." Down from an elevated shrine came a Shinto priest in elegant, multi-gray robes, black-lacquered, slip-on wooden clogs, a black peaked hat. He walked in deliberate, measured steps down to the level of the compound, in the same measured strides across the gravelled compound to another building. He was followed in mincing steps by a simply dressed acolyte who held a parasol over the priest. A precious picture.

Nearby, at water's edge, a glass-bottomed boat disgorged a tour of flag-led Japanese tourists. I declined the pantomimed suggestion of the driver to take a tour on the boat—I get seasick on glass-bottom boats—and that saved half an hour of the schedule. Now the driver didn't know what to do with me until train time.

We had no method of communication, other than pointing.

He took an extra, most colorful detour driving to a small, nearby fishing village where I took pictures of fishermen repairing their nets in front of a fleet of fishing boats equipped with mast-high strings of high powered lamps to turn night into day, a technique used to attract the fish.

154 *How to Get Lost and Found in New Japan*

Not far away in front of an open building, a couple was packing flat seaweed—*wakame*—in neat layers on bamboo trays. Lining the back wall were clothes washing machines employed in the extra duty of washing seaweed.

My last visual memory of the Cape was of a child standing in the doorway of a shrine at the top of a long series of wooden steps and wearing the inevitable T-shirt decorated with a slogan in English. Across the tiny red breast of the shirt, emblazoned in giant, white letters was the word: GIRL.

Matsue is only a half an hours train ride northwest along the coast from Izumoshi, population well over 100,000, bordering Lake Shinji on the west and Nakaumi Lagoon on the east which leads into the sea.

One experience I looked forward to in Matsue was overnighting in a "businessman's hotel", a new idea of offering relatively inexpensive accommodations with only fundamental facilities for Japanese commercial travellers. Businessmen's hotels do not exclude tourists, or ladies, and are splendid for budget-travel in Japan. They are blossoming throughout the country.

My hotel was the Matsue Station Hotel located, according to my instruction sheet, "in front of Matsue Station." No building carried such a name.

I stopped a passerby and pointed to my instruction sheet with the hotel name written in kanji. He pointed to a building directly in front of me and said in perfect English, "It's right there."

The lobby was on the third floor. The front desk was a simple counter with a single sofa before it. Comic books in stacks. Vending machines. The bill, the lady said, was payable in advance: in cash. No credit cards. No travellers checks, not even yen travellers checks. Check-in time was four o'clock but the hotel was accustomed to holding guest luggage. She gave me a chit for my stowed bags and leather jacket and I went off to see the city.

Matsue has several unusual attractions. One is a castle which was not destroyed either in the revolt of the nineteenth century or the war of the twentieth century. But the attraction of special interest to me was the former residence and a museum dedicated to Lafcadio Hearn.

When I first became aware of the magic of words, a gentle, wave-bobbed English teacher urged me to read Lafcadio Hearn

(1850-1904) whose writings were "model examples of simple, clear, precise English."

A short taxi ride took me to the former Hearn residence next to the moat of the castle. Unfortunately the house where Hearn lived was blocked by construction but the museum next door was open, a small, white, attractive Western building with a garden in front. It housed the library and much memorabilia of the author.

Hearn's life was one of struggle and travel.

Born in Greece of an Irish military surgeon in the British Army and a Greek mother, Patrick Lafcadio Hearn was shuttled from Greece to Ireland, to France, to England in his first years. His parents divorced, he was sheltered by a great aunt in Ireland.

At sixteen he suffered a combination of tragedies. He lost his left eye in an accident. His father died. His great aunt benefactor went bankrupt and the boy had to leave college the following year.

When he was nineteen, he migrated to the United States and eventually became a reporter for the *Cincinatti Enquirer*.

In 1881, now thirty-one, he became the literary editor of the *Times Democrat* in New Orleans where he gained his first reputation as an author of novels and essays, and translator of foreign novels.

In 1890, on the idea of selling free-lance material to *Harper's*, a prominent magazine at the time in which he had been published, Hearn sailed to Japan to continue his successful formula started in the West Indies: write articles about the country while gathering material for a novel. For some reason the author broke with *Harper's* and, uncertain about his economic future as a free-lancer, he signed a contract to teach English in the Matsue Middle School. Here he wrote an essay about life in Matsue, "In a Japanese Garden", which was included in a book, *Glimpses of Unfamiliar Japan*.

He married the daughter of a high ranked samurai, became a citizen of Japan and adopted the name of Koizumi Yakumo. He became famous in his adopted country and his name today is still familiar to every schoolchild in Japan.

For a time he was a professor in Kumamoto in Kyushu, then the editor of a Kobe newspaper but returned to Tokyo in 1895 as an English professor and moved in 1904 to the prestigious Waseda University when he suddenly died.

The museum carries many captivating bits and pieces of the

writer's life. His passport. The contract for teaching in the Shimane Prefecture written in kanji on a wooden tablet.

He instructed his son by overprinting his English lessons in large letters on old newspapers, lessons which started at the age of five and never ceased.

There is a notebook of his jottings in almost illegible writing—I felt a kinship here—a common failing of many journalists.

On display is a long letter to Captain Fujisaki, a soldier at the front in the 1904 war against Russia, a letter clearly written and lucid in tone—and, yet, written only a few hours before his death.

There is a bookcase of his original works and translations, pictures of his study, library, house.

Portraits and photographs of the English writer-teacher-editor were always taken from his right side, the side of the good eye.

In one corner is a four-foot high desk, sturdy, as simple as his writing, which he designed and had built, the unusual height to accommodate his short sightedness.

Next to the desk is a glass case captioned, "One of the tasks of the maid-servant or Mrs. Hearn was to keep Mr. Hearn's many tobacco pipes clean."

In the case on racks are eleven pipes. They appear to be opium pipes but they are tobacco pipes.

Nearby is a charcoal brazier "kept with glowing charcoal for his warmth and the convenience of his smoking."

His biography says that Hearn died of a heart attack.

Down the street from the Hearn house and museum, along the moat of the castle, is a samurai's house of "high rank." Expansive, simple, well-kept, it exhibits swords and armor and handsome, noble kimono such as worn by the hero in *Shogun.*

> Note: don't ask the Japanese if they saw or liked *Shogun.* The idea of a samurai's wife making eyes, much less love, to another man is beyond the inherent Japanese tradition of obedience. Unacceptable. The movie is written off as "bad Hollywood."

The Matsue castle was built in 1611 by one of Hideyoshi's generals, the builder of the castle at Osaka. The three-story donjon still stands and from the top, if you can get in front of the schoolgirls, you can get a view of Lake Shinji.

Back at the businessman's hotel the room was ready. Corner room. Very small. No toothbrush. No *Bible.* No *Teachings of Buddha.* Small television set but no refrigerator. Small double bed. Clean.
At first it appeared there was no bathroom. Mistake. In the corner, behind the door, were quite adequate facilities including a deep tiled furo. Fundamental but satisfactory for the price.
Went to the basement "Club" for dinner. Only person there except for a table of "hostesses." *Oh, dear.*
Ordered small steak and beer and was joined by two of the girls. "Do you mind if we sit down?" Just what I warn people to avoid. They sat down.
How old was I? Was I married? Children? What did I do? Did I make much money?
My new "friends" were both named Miyuki. Miyuki Notsu, the vivacious one, was eighteen. Miyuki Nonomura, who appeared to be slightly zonked, was sixteen.
How long was I going to be in town? That did it. I fled for my life without finishing dinner.

When I arrived in Tottori, a short distance from Matsue, I again went into conference with the clerk at the desk of the Hotel New Otani.
In order to see the city, slightly smaller than Matsue, and to view the sand dunes—the city's claim to fame—it would be best to hire a car and driver.
Done. Shortly thereafter Mr. Nakasuma—no-English-whatsoever—and I departed on a non-communicative two-and-a-half hour tour. Occasionally he would point to a building, say something in Japanese and I would nod as if I understood. Most often he would tap his watch. That I understood.
Our first destination was the famous sand dune area, several kilometers away from the city, Tottori not being on the ocean.
It was Boy's Day, a national holiday, and the location where we stopped near the sea was alive with cars, tour busses, restaurants, souvenir shops and swarming people.

Mr. Nakasuma parked the car, led me up an embankment overlooking the dunes, tapped his watch indicating fifteen minutes and returned to the car.

Stretched out in front of me were endless undulating hills of rose-colored sand. The expanse of sand runs sixteen kilometers along the ocean and two kilometers inland. As far as the eye could see, the dunes were covered with wandering people looking like roving ants.

Immediately at hand the scene bordered on chaos. Hawkers with portable microphones were urging visitors to get into covered wagons and take a tour pulled by a miserable pony.

A string of saddle horses were also being hustled.

Added to the confusion was a tethered, saddled camel which, with the Sahara-like background, looked perfectly in place.

Lines of people were walking the two kilometers down to the ocean. I joined them, the lovers, the families, the struggling tots and elderly people, receiving sidelong glances on the way. This is not common touring country for Europeans.

At the top of the bluff overlooking the ocean, novice hang gliders were using the height to practice take-offs and landings.

I trudged back to the car. Mr. Nakasuma presented postcards he had bought me.

We drove into the country, passing scenic green hills, past rice paddies—much like the scenery I had viewed from the train.

We visited two shrines, one with a hundred stone lanterns and many stone turtles.

The other shrine featured an exquisite Japanese garden where we sat on a open, tatami-matted porch and drank tea and ate biscuits, in silence naturally, and contemplated the lily ponds, the pale blue and white azaleas in bloom against a hill covered with trimmed trees rising to the sky. Tranquility and beauty.

No questions. No answers.

Nakasuma-san tapped his watch.

Back to the hotel.

Excitement in Tottori.

After walking the shopping area and scouting the usual covered shopping arcade, I witnessed a fire in a two-story shop.

The Japanese reputation for efficiency and precision suffered in the ensuing scene of firehose, smoke, shouted directions, countermanded directions, firemen starting one way, then going another, all further compounded with confusion because the street had not been closed off to traffic and cars were carefully guided over the firehoses protected by little wooden bridges. Too much. I strolled on, slightly disillusioned.

A few minutes later I came across a fight in front of a pachinko parlor where four bouncer-type employees were dealing with a fist-swinging customer in the street. Shop owners popped out of doors to watch wide-eyed.

My!

Every now and then, you run across un-Japanese behavior.

The last few miles of the train ride from Tottori to Kyoto pass along the banks of the Hozu River.

One of the attractions in Kyoto is to shoot the rapids on the Hozu River in a flat bottom boat, a sixteen kilometer trip which can take two hours and is perfectly safe but high in thrills.

I had tried to do the rapids during a previous trip to Kyoto but had been rained out by the high waters.

Now from the train, I looked down on several boats, each carrying a dozen passengers and two or three boatmen plus the helmsman. The boats wound their way through the canyon walls, past giant rocks, and in and out of white water.

The boat passengers all waved at the train and the train passengers, all wanting to trade places, waved back.

9. A City of Rice Riches and A Village in the Alps

Shortly after you leave Kyoto on the train to Kanazawa, you reach the west bank of Lake Biwa, the largest lake in Japan, 235.4 kilometers in circumference, larger than the biggest lake in New Zealand.

The publicity says that the lake is named after its shape, the *biwa,* a Japanese musical instrument. What is looks like on a map to a foreign eye is an outline of the African continent.

From the train the popularity of Lake Biwa is evidenced by the many hotels and inns along the way, the beautiful views, the sight of excursion boats and fishing boats.

Two and a half hours after leaving inland Kyoto, you are on the west coast facing the Sea of Japan and the historic town of Kanazawa.

Since the mid-centuries, Kanazawa has been famous as "The Castle Town of a Million Goku"—a million *goku* translates into five million bushels of grain—the richest fiefdom in Japan.

Given three centuries of peace starting in the sixteenth century under the Maeda family, and with handsome income from the crops, master craftsmen from throughout the country were invited to Kanazawa to produce the best in lacquerware, silks and pottery.

It continues to be an art center today with its own master craftsmen rivalling Kyoto and Tokyo.

The internationally famous work of art in Kanazawa, however, is a garden, Kenrokuen Park, one of the three most beautiful gardens in Japan. (The other two are the Korakuen in Okayama, between Kyoto and Hiroshima, and the Kairakuen in Mito, northeast of Tokyo. *en* means garden.)

The time was after one o'clock when I carried my luggage from the station, through an underground passage filled with restaurants, shops, and cinemas and exited into the lobby of the Kanazawa Miyako Hotel.

The Miyako belongs to the same chain that owns the famous Miyako in Kyoto, and is a modern, first-class hotel.

Employing my now-standard strategy of consulting with the room clerk about the points of interest in a new city, the Miyako room clerk produced an excellent city map. More importantly, he loaned me a book, *Kanazawa, the Other Side of Japan* by Ruth Stevens, an American-born teacher who had lived in Kanazawa since 1974.

Before venturing into the city I sat down and skimmed its pages.

Besides the generalities, Ruth Stevens has divided the city into seven areas and microscoped into each area her suggested places to shop, eat and drink. An excellent guide book but hard to find. I couldn't find a copy to buy in any of the bookstores.

Among her suggested Japanese phrases to learn is this gem, *"Watashi wa sashimi wa dame desu"* which translates to "I don't care for the raw fish, thank you just the same."

If you are thinking of spending enough time in a single corner of Japan to learn about the country in depth, her book suggests that you would do well by choosing Kanazawa.

The first stop I picked from among the author's suggestions was the Kanko Bussankan or its second name Ishikawa Prefecture Tourists Products Hall—terrible names—which is a center where the visitor can watch craftsmen at work and also buy products of the district.

Starting in the basement—I always start in basements—I found local specialties like candy and biscuits, and a noodle counter where a bowl of soba noodles cost Y200. The second floor holds a more formal Japanese restaurant.

On the ground floor are the crafts, mostly made by the artisans in the third floor workshops. Admission to the third-floor gallery is Y100 to watch the craftsmen at work in glassed-in ateliers, designing patterns on silk cloth, incredibly intricate and time consuming, painting tiny flowers, smaller than shirt buttons, on Kutani porcelain vases, creating wooden containers out of Paulownia wood, sculpting lion heads out of small blocks of wood, making minute leaves, fish, flowers, birds out of sugar candy.

All were so intense with the project in front of them, and yet so calmly, serenely patient.

The time seemed past the hour when the school children tours would have left the Kenrokuen Garden, which is just around the corner from the craftsmen center, so I proceeded to the entry gate opposite the former Kanazawa Castle, now the site of the local university.

Formerly the castle's private domain, the outer garden was laid out in 1676, enlarged in 1774 and completed in 1822. After the Meiji Restoration, it was opened to the public. Kenroku means "the combination of six", the six elements being vastness, careful arrangement, antiquity, a peaceful, quiet atmosphere, coolness emphasized by running water and scenic charm.

Stevens' book lays the garden out by the numbers which gives a reader the pertinent details of each particular area of interest, i.e. the name of the tree, the reason for the statue, etc. That is one way to enjoy it.

But for me it was a garden to walk through slowly, savoring each pond, each hill, each waterfall and talk to the stones, whisper to the flowers. Kenrokuen is an absorbing garden.

Return for a second visit and do it by the numbers.

Note that the garden is designed so that every season of the year is accentuated in some manner or other.

By a pond is a famed stone lantern which serves as a design motif for the garden.

Adjacent to the garden is a lovely two-story villa, Seison-kaku, built in 1863 by a local lord for his mother. You can visit it for Y300.

The villa is known for its gardens, carved transoms, gold-leafed rooms and the *uguisubari*—"singing nightingale" floors—floors that squeak when trod upon as a security precaution against tiptoeing assassins, bringing back the visions of a samurai movie and Mifune at his best: "Hah!" Slash. "Hah! Hah!" Slash. Slash.

Point #4 in an English brochure cautions: "When visiting the Seison-kaku please observe good, quiet manners of enjoying cultural heritage."

From the second floor I observed the approach of a large group of Europeans. Good, I'd ask questions about their tour. Where had they been? What was of most interest? What had they bought?

No questions. They were Soviets.

I strolled over to the remaining gate of the castle. The Ishikawa

Gate, formerly the rear entrance, is still majestic with massive stone walls, striking white lead shingles, an occasional turret, a contrast to the jean-clad university students walking through its portals.

From the castle site I walked back into the middle of the city and the open-air Ohmicho Market, a market dating back to feudal days, where, then and now, all Kanazawans came to shop among some two hundred open shops selling fruit, fish, vegetables, meat, chickens, live or dead. Here you mingle with local people doing their local things. You'll be the only foreigner there. No souvenir shops but there are restaurants like the *kaki-taki* restaurant which my Australian friends had experienced. Basically a sushi restaurant, the rolls of rice filled with different goodies pass before you on a conveyor belt built into the counter. You take whatever catches your eye and pay according to the empty dishes you stack up.

Kanazawa has much more to offer.

Excellent *noh* theater, a Kaga Yuzen silk kimono shop where you can watch the artisans work their colorful patterns into the rich beauty of the yuzen silk, a gold leaf museum (95% of Japan's gold leaf is made here), a former samurai district of old buildings and houses surrounded by mud walls in narrow streets, giving the contemporary visitor a feeling of the past.

Nearby is Yuwaku Hot Springs where an Edo-era village has been recreated. A better village awaited me, I was told, at Takayama, my next destination.

Should you want to relax and dwaddle in the area, you can explore the Noto Peninsula National Park to the north where the waters of Tsukumo Bay "are protected and calm, feminine in appearance."

Southeast of Kanazawa are two national parks in the Japan Alps and also the delightful alpine village of Takayama, known as the Little Kyoto. It is a bicycle town.

Takayama is clean, calm, a city of craftsmen, a place which inspires creativeness. Several streets have retained the old wooden buildings of another era.

Also it is the location of an unusally pleasant family-owned inn, Minshuku Sohsuke whose owner-manager-chef is Kinachiro Nakajima, a trim, forty-plus innkeeper. He is a never-stop, whirling dervish who professes not to speak any English (he does), who bought a 150-year-old farmhouse in a mountain village twelve years ago, cut it into sections, transported the sections to Takayama where the village carpenters, famous in Japan, created a colorful, quaint, thirteen-room country hostelry in thirty days.

Nakajima-san met me at the station, grabbed my bags, put them in the car and we were off in the fastest station departure I experienced.

The inn was only five minutes from the station and made an immediate favorable impression because it had that Japanese quaintness that foreign visitors expect to find: old wood and polished wood at the entry where I exchanged my street-weary walking shoes for shuffle-along slippers.

Off the entry room, the "main" room encircled a sunken firepit. An iron bar, sometimes covered with a bamboo pole and hooked at each end, hung from the ceiling—a *jizai*—holding an iron kettle over the fire in the ancient, traditional way of cooking.

A more contemporary touch in the corner of the room was a refrigerator containing beer and soft drinks.

Off the entry hall was another tatami-matted room with a television set where guests gathered to smoke, nibble at small snacks, drink and watch television.

Japanese artifacts of one sort or another decorated the rooms. Paintings, old farm pieces, a grandfather clock.

Japanese quaintness aside, an equally appealing feature was its modern plumbing, recently installed, with Japanese and Western toilets upstairs, including tiled washrooms. Downstairs was a new *furo* for evening baths and also a shower.

My room was a neat, six-tatami mat room. I didn't realize it until later but outside of my sliding windows was a clothesline to hang out rinsed-out things.

Takako, the diminutive lady of the house, had short-cropped hair and sparkled. She danced me through the amenities.

Dinner, she said, by indicating the hands of the grandfather clock in the entry hall, was at six-thirty. Downstairs. Family style.

Late that afternoon everybody in the minshuku took turns in the furo in pairs. I was the last one in and settled for a private shower.

Note: a razor in one of the ankle-high soap dishes in the furo room made me wonder if this is where men shaved in the evening. I didn't see them shave in the upstairs washrooms in the morning where there was only cold water.

All furo-boiled or shower-clean, we gathered in the television room, dressed in our house yukatas including the three Japanese businessmen who had arrived in a big, black car dressed in black suits.

When dinner was announced, we all trooped through the main room to a large, sit-on-the-floor dining room with a single long table. I was the only Westerner and at the head of the table was one seat cushion with a back. It was for the foreigner.

Near me were people who understood a bit of English. Our evening conversation was quickly eased by an air-conditioning engineer who went to his room and returned with an English-Japanese dictionary.

The engineer, working on a local building project, was a semi-permanent guest. The rest were one-nighters. I was there for two nights.

Besides the engineer there was an undergarment manufacturer on a sales trip, a student, a married couple, the three businessmen. There was a truck driver and his wife and his colleague, a noodle cook, and his wife. The truck driver, a nice young man, brought a half bottle of whiskey to the table for his party.

Dinner consisted of shrimp tempura, soba noodles, garganzola beans, bamboo shoots, a salad of wild greens that a member of the family had gathered from the forest that afternoon—(one news item I read on arriving in Japan was of a woman gathering greens in a forest who was mauled by a black bear)—rice, tea.

Beer, sake and the truck driver's whiskey flowed freely and by the time dinner was over, we were a rather loose crowd, at which time Nakajima-san turned on a stereo and produced a pile of musical tapes, two microphones and a book of lyrics.

It was my introduction to *karaoke,* or literally translated "no orchestra", another original development in the new Japan and a tremendously popular fad in the nightlife entertainment in many bars. There is a stereo, a stack of taped songs and for a nominal charge, like fifty cents a song, a customer sings to the musical tapes using the book of lyrics.

Same thing in Sohsuke. Everybody sang. No Japanese bashfulness here. People were eager to take the microphone. The noodle cook's voice was of exceptional quality. He was *good*.

It was a late night by my standards but what fun after dining alone for so long.

The next morning at breakfast the cook and the truck driver were moaning, not singing.

We had a delicious local speciality for breakfast: *hoba-miso*.

Bits of charcoal impregnated with lighter fluid were ignited in a hand-sized *hibachi* (iron grill) in front of each guest. Over the grill was placed a large dried leaf and the center of the leaf was filled with miso paste. When the paste started to bubble, I was instructed by the engineer to chopstick bits on top of my bowl of rice and eat the hot paste and rice together. Fantastic. It tasted like warm raisin chutney, sweet and delicious.

The leaf never burned through. What was the leaf? *"Ho,"* the engineer said. The dictionary didn't define "ho."

On the bulletin board of the minshuku was a pictorial brochure showing the most interesting places to visit in Takayama. Nakajima-san had numbered and keyed the pictures to an accompanying map.

On arrival I had indicated to my host that I wanted to rent a bike for the next day. The non-stop proprietor indicated that he would take care of it and within a hour there was a bike parked in the entry hall for my use.

Takayama proved to be an excellent cycling town and for six hours, from mid-morning to mid-afternoon I went from one end of Takayama to the other. Admittedly I was on the outskirts of town in the very beginning because I was lost but a friendly by-stander looked at my map, turned me around and pointed me in the correct direction. By the end of the day I was tail-tired, but I knew Takayama thoroughly.

First stop: the Festival Hall at the Hie Shrine, a most important shrine, and the starting point of one of the grandest festival parades in Japan in April featuring twenty-three huge, ornate vehicles which pass through the streets of Takayama.

Four of the vehicles used in the festival parade are on display

in the glass encased area in the immense Festival Hall.
When you first enter the room, you stop—almost in shock. Facing you is an army of mannequin attendants in festival dress, grey silk robes over black tunics wearing wide, flat, straw hats.
The vehicles are astounding. Twenty to thirty feet high, two-wheeled and four-wheeled, elaboratedly decorated in black lacquer and gold and red, intricately carved, belled, tasseled, and canopied. Some of the vehicles date back to the eighth century.

Takayama is divided by a river, and I biked to the river bank where there is an open market. Fresh fresh vegetables and fruits of the area were for sale. Asparagus and hot-house strawberries were among the offerings.

Like Kyoto the venerable city has been laid out in a grid pattern making it easy for a biker or pedestrian to find the points of interest, like Kami-san-no-machi Street, lined on both sides with old houses and shops—poster and picture material. Here you have the feeling of the way Japan used to be, the Japan of yesteryear. Some of the old houses are shops, restaurants, inns. Several of the buildings are sake wineries, the rice wine providing a rich odor.

On the outskirts of the southwest quadrant of the city—easy to pedal to, tough to walk to—is a concentration of old houses and thatched-roofed farmhouses which have been restored and made living examples of the past architectural culture.

Hida Minzoku Mura is the first gathering point of houses but a few hundred meters further on, and part of the same cultural park, is the Hida-no-sato where there is a more extensive collection of restored antique buildings including several live craft exhibits. A nice touch is that in each house a wood fire is kept smoldering in an open pit which adds a pungent incense to the air, and the hint of smoke gives the visitor a feeling that the house is still occupied.

It was a hot spring day and the snowy alps could be seen in the distance, looking refreshingly cool. Inspirational. The scene inspired me to cool off by buying an ice cream cone at one of a long line of souvenir and fast food shops. I turned away from my ice cream parlor and started towards my bicycle. A man ran after me across the street and handed me a fifty-yen coin I had inadvertently left on the counter. I could have left a gold watch and the same thing would have happened.

Pedaling back to town I visited the impressive gates of the Jinya, the former location of the local government in front of which there is an open-air flower market.

In the back streets I found a string of antique shops and stopped in one and bought sections from a 100-year-old kimono which Honolulu seamstresses use to make into one-of-a-kind lounge jackets and vests. Two pieces: $20. The same shop had a colorful, hand-drawn poster of a horse by the door, but the proprietress refused to discuss selling it. Strange.

Pedaling on I found a mama-san in a window making *shiosembei,* a rice cracker with a pleasant salty taste. One bag: 70¢

Enough. I pedaled back to Sohsuke and took a nap.

That night at dinner the cast of characters had changed completely except for my dictionary-wielding engineer.

Four older men were seated at my end of the table; at the other end a married couple, a young lady fashion coordinator from Osaka, and two government officials who acted like superior government officials.

That night there was no *karaoke* performance but the evening was not lacking in the consumption of beer and sake.

Next to me was a 71-year-old Shinto priest with fists of iron which he demonstrated by massaging my shoulder muscles—oh, Lord it hurt.

"This man is tired," he said. "Look at his eyes."

My eyes were red with tears caused by the pain from his massaging.

Sake flowed, and I copied an example set by another guest, encircling the table with a fresh bottle of sake to fill each cup. Polite, yes, but I sometimes neglected to kneel with my head below that of the recipient, as good Japanese manners dictate.

My priest-massager, seeing that I was not eating the small, white river fish on my plate, asked my permission, and with permission granted, chopsticked the fish off my plate and popped it head first into his mouth, bit off the head and swallowed it, rolling his eyes indicating what a great delicacy it was.

I was glad to turn my attention to the cute fashion coordinator who had moved up the table to practice her English.

In the course of our stumbling conversation she asked my room number.

Stop. Did she want to practice English later on, I wondered? It was a Walter Mitty wonder. She was just asking a polite question.

Kanazawa and Takayama 169

The next morning at breakfast at each place except mine was an egg in the shell and a bowl of rice. My Shinto priest-masseuse took an egg from another place and showed me how the egg was broken into a bowl, mixed with a bit of shoyu and then poured over the rice. He placed it in front of me to eat.

At that moment Nakajima-san, who did all the cooking, appeared out of the kitchen, snatched the raw-egg rice mixture away from my place, removed it to the kitchen and returned with a fried egg and a fresh bowl of rice. He knew the Western world, his gesture said.

The minshuku had a horse poster similar to the one I had seen in the antique shop, and I indicated to Nakajima that I wanted to buy one.

Not this one, he said with his hands. But when he took me to the train station at noon he would take me to a shop where I could buy such a poster.

Great. Could we stop at a sake winery? Yes, we would do that also.

The last two hours before train time I took to the bike again and leisurely pedaled around Takayama, now my favorite Japanese city, even better than Hagi. Down the backstreets, down the Kami-san-no-machi, the street of the ancient houses, down along the riverside markets.

At a two-foot waterfall in the river small boys were throwing pieces of bread into the water where carp and trout swam lazily.

On the way back to Sohsuke I stopped at the flower market and bought Takano-with-the-laughing-eyes a small potted plant.

My bill for two nights including breakfasts and dinners plus all the beer and sake I had ordered was Y12,000. There was no charge for the bicycle. Nakajima-san tied a wooden good-luck piece to my hand luggage. It will never come off.

On the way to the train station Nakajima detoured in order to pass a small lumberyard piled with large logs. "Ho," he said.

He then turned and twisted down several other blocks until we reached a crossroads where, in the yard of a residence, he pointed to a tree with large green leaves. "Ho," he said.

I didn't recognize either the timber or the tree.

He then drove to a clothing store, parked the car, ducked inside and then reappeared and gestured for me to come inside.

The proprietor was an artist of horse posters called *ema*. They are good luck charms when placed in the home with the horse's head facing the door.

(That's why the lady in the antique shop had refused to discuss the sale of her poster. I had pulled a gaff.)

I bought an ema ($7.50) and the artist signed my name in Japanese on the bottom.

Next stop was a large sake shop. There I indicated to Nakajima that he had his choice of any of the sake he saw in front of him. He refused. No amount of pleading, cajoling, gesturing would make him change his mind.

At the station he grabbed my bags, placed them on the sidewalk, shook hands quickly, bowed once and was in his car roaring off. Quite a genial, hard-working gentlemen.

My cultural education on the married life of the Japanese received another lesson en route to Tokyo. A young lady from Philadelphia and I fell into a conversation at the station. She was taking her parents around Japan and she volunteered the information that she was married to a Japanese gentleman, lived in Tokyo, and belonged to the Foreign Wives Married to Japanese Club which, she said, has about five hundred members.

How many of these marriages are succesful?

About the same number as in the United States, she thought. Some wives felt the imposition of the Japanese family on their lives too smothering but, she said, it was just the parents' way of trying to be intimate.

She understood when her husband went out and drank with his colleagues a couple of times a week because that was the custom and if he did otherwise he wouldn't be considered part of his "commercial family."

Back in Tokyo I spent a couple of conversational hours over a bottle of Scotch with a Japanese friend in the tourist business.

"Drinking in Japan is a means of communication," he said. "If my superior says to me, 'Let's go have some drinks after work', I go even if I have a dinner party scheduled with my wife and other friends. It might be a chance for him to say something to me that he wants to say or a chance when I can tell him something I want him to hear. I couldn't afford to miss that chance.

"Also when I ask a new friend if he *banshakus,* I'm asking if he takes evening alcohol before dinner.

Kanazawa and Takayama

"If I feel after six or seven times with a person that he would be a close friend, I say, 'Let's go drink sake.' And we will sit on a tatami and pour each other sake and talk to each other seriously."

My friend's wife was due to have a baby in a few months and he confessed to wanting a boy.

"I lost my father in a railroad accident when I was fifteen. I missed never having the chance to sit down with him and drinking sake and talking.

"If my wife has a boy, well, when he gets to be an adult, I can see myself and my son sitting down together, drinking sake and talking seriously to each other."

What was the "ho" leaf used in making hoba-miso?
"Magnolia," the authorities told me.

In the guest book of the Minshuku Ikedaya in Hiroshima I found the names and address of a couple from New Zealand.

On a subsequent trip to Auckland, I called the couple, Richard and Norma Mashlan, in Hamilton, a hundred kilometers away.

Norma answered the telephone. I asked her how they had found the minshuku.

"We wanted to see Japan close up," she said. "Not just as tourists. We thought that the little family-run inns would get us closer to Japan."

"How did you know about them?"

"We made contact with the Japanese Embassy where we first learned about the minshuku, and, when we got to Japan, we went to the minshuku association office in Tokyo, and they made reservations for us in Tokyo, Kyoto, Nara, Morioka, Aomori and Hiroshima where you found our name."

"Did you have a rail pass?"

"Yes, we had fourteen-day Green Car passes."

"How did the Japan trip go, taking it all together."

"We just loved it. Everybody said we were crazy to spend so much time in Japan. They said there wasn't that much to see or do. How wrong they were! We just didn't have enough time, and now we are planning to go back in two years."

I felt the same way and slightly smug with the knowledge that I was going back in a couple of months with the Lady Navigator when we would work our way from Hokkaido back and forth across northern Japan down to Tokyo.

10. Hokkaido the Non-Japanese Northern Island

Hokkaido is different.

The island, second in size only to Honshu, is comparatively primitive, dominated by tall mountains and deep forests, rivers, lakes and rich plains, rare animals and flowers.

This was the home of the Ainu, an aboriginal people who looked more Caucasian than Oriental and whose religion reflected a belief in the trees and the beasts that were part of their lives.

The spirit and the mystery of the Ainu still tinges the historical atmosphere with tribal place names and legends.

Although the Japanese from Honshu drifted into Hokkaido from an early date and were firmly established in the fifteenth century, the island remained culturally removed from the rest of Japan until the nineteenth century.

The weather, too, is distinctively different being comparatively cool in summer while the rest of Japan suffers from humidity and heat. Winter dumps vast amounts of snow, particularly in the west facing the Sea of Japan, and is its own reason for visiting Japan's most northern land.

Although Hokkaido has twenty percent of the country's total land area, the island holds only five percent of the total population, creating another distinction from the southern prefectures: space.

And as is true in Western America and New Zealand and Australia, where there are fewer people there is more openness, more hospitality, more friendliness. It's true, too, in Hokkaido.

Five national parks and eight prefectural parks preserve seven percent of the total island for recreation.

All of these elements combine to make a delightful visitor destination. In the summer it is a vacationland of good hiking, mountain climbing, fishing and swimming. The autumn with the changing leaves is magnificent. Skiing in winter is so good that it attracted the Winter Olympics in 1972. In spring the island is reborn in flowers.

Hokkaido with its space is attractive to permanent residents as well and its mushrooming growth makes it an important part of the new Japan.

The August day we went from Tokyo to Sapporo, rushed to a museum and went to dinner involved five taxis, one monorail, one JAL 747 (a two-hour flight from Haneda Airport in Tokyo to Chitose, Hokkaido's international airport), two subways and two busses. Eleven pieces of transportation.

Did we get lost? Several times.

How many times did people come to our assistance?

Seven. Three times on the subway, twice on the bus system, twice in the street. And I didn't even count the button-cute stewardess on the JAL flight.

Although in Sapporo there are almost 500 English-speaking Goodwill Guides who wear a small blue medal badge on which is embossed a world and a small white dove and who are ready to answer your questions, none of our assistance came from Goodwill Guides. Just good people willing to take care of strangers.

That is typical of Hokkaido hospitality.

Our only mission before the end of the first day in Sapporo was to get to the Hokkaido Historical Museum, not easy to reach being sited in the middle of suburban Nopporo Forest Park.

By the time we arrived at the museum via taxi, subway, bus, it was four o'clock in the afternoon and, having been on the road since dawn, we were slightly travel-tattered and transportation-torn, but the museum was worth it.

Nopporo Forest Park is a respectably sized park (5,000 acres) harboring a rich lowland forest and a conservation area for plants, birds, and small animals.

Set back from green lawns and trees and encircled by white paving stones is the park's principal attraction, the Hokkaido Historical Museum a handsome modern, two-story building of red brick.

We were late. At the entrance a uniformed guard crossed his hands in front of his face to signal "closed."

Fortunately we had telephoned before leaving the hotel and had the name of our contact written on a piece of paper: Yasushi Akakawa. The presentation of his name took us past closed doors and to an administration office where Mr. Akakawa, a young, af-

HOKKAIDO

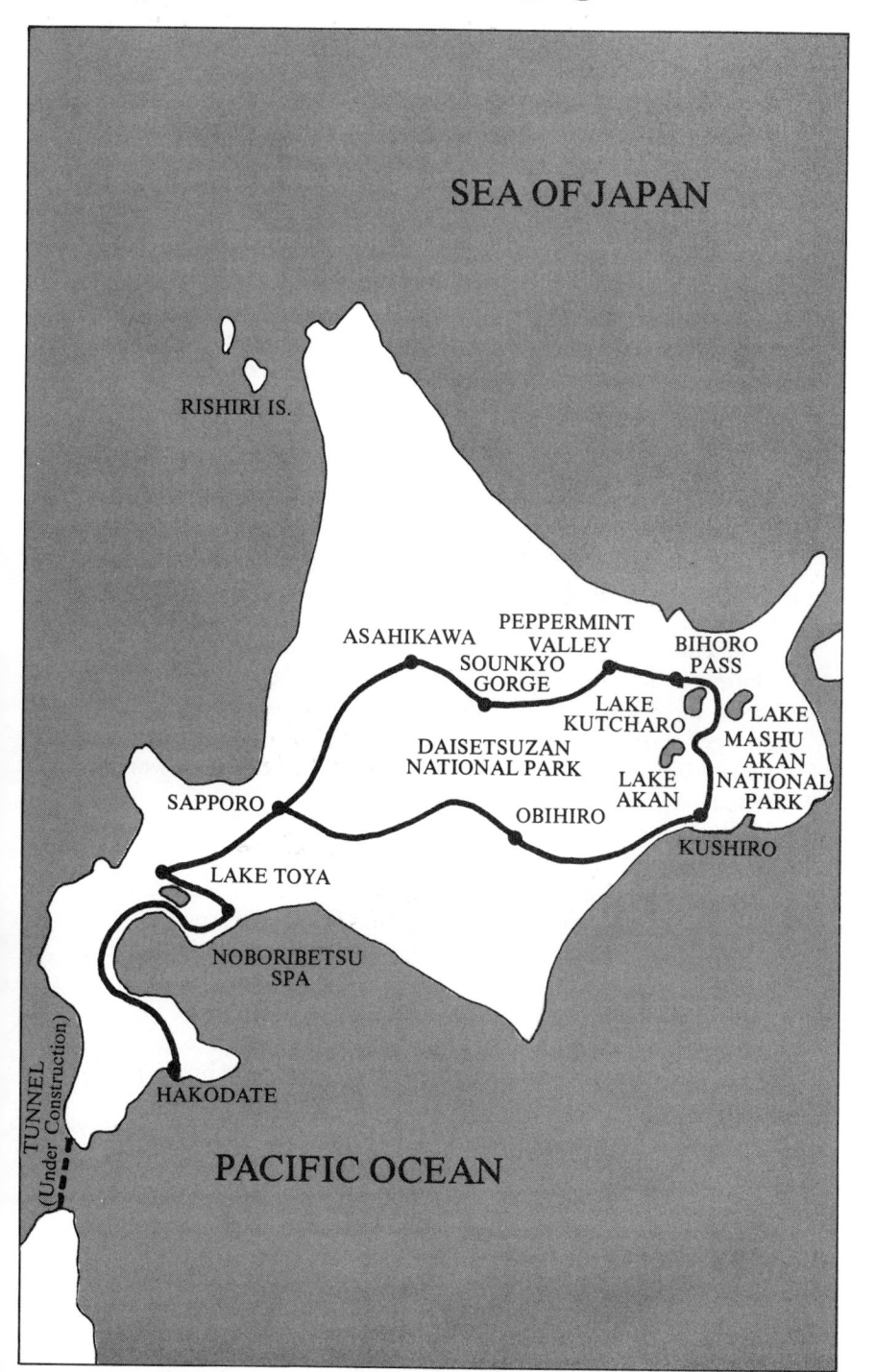

fable, slightly built, bespectacled gentleman plied us with English pamphlets and conducted an hour tour through the now closed museum.

It's a beauty.

Built to celebrate the centennial of Hokkaido in 1970, little expense was spared to create a first rate museum. No dollar or yen figure was given in the brochures concerning the construction cost but it had to be formidable.

The entry hall has a three-dimensional topographical map in back of which is a two-story satellite photograph of the island.

The first exhibit hall traces the history of Hokkaido from the Ice Age to the Hokkaido of Tomorrow.

Some 20,000 years ago the ice land-bridges to Siberia permitted animals to cross into Hokkaido. A species of elephant, the giant elk, man walked in.

Animals who survived the glacial period became known as "living fossils" and included the wolf, the marten, the red fox. And man.

The culture of the local Ainu tribes was known as the "jomon culture" named for the Jomon clay pottery used by the natives. Across the Tsugaru Straits the Honshu Japanese used iron pots and were classified as the "yayoi culture."

The Ainu exhibit is most absorbing, particularly their worship of the bear.

A young bear was kept caged in the village until the time came for the annual hunt for wild bears in the mountains.

Then the captive bear was strangled between giant logs, its meat eaten, the blood drunk and the head and skin worshipped.

Early drawings done by the Ainu depicting the ceremony are part of the exhibit.

Crowded by the density of the population on Honshu, the victims of war or famine, the castaways of Honshu began to push into Ezo or Yezo, as Hokkaido was then called, beckoned by the promise of untouched land and fish-filled seas.

A rebel Ainu chief fought back but was subjugated in the fifteenth century.

By the seventeenth century, Yoshihiro Matsumae, a supporter of Ieyasu Tokugawa, had established forts and fisheries supported by catches of herring and salmon.

The fall of the Tokugawa Shogunate followed the opening of

Japan by Admiral Perry.

Hokkaido's port at Hakadote became an open port in 1859. Less than ten years later the Tokugawa Shogunate fell and the new Meiji government changed the name of the island from Ezo or Yezo to Hokkaido. In 1871, the head of government for the island was moved to the newly created capital of Sapporo.

By the time the Meiji government was established the Ainu were all but finished, suffocated by the economy and military might of the Japanese.

Immigration moved forward. For example, two hundred unemployed samurai were sent to Hokkaido in 1875 to establish new homes. By 1904, when ex-military families were no longer encouraged to migrate to Hokkaido, there were over 7,000 ex-military families.

Forestry, mining, fishing, manufacturing became part of the island's commercial development. Scientific agricultural methods were encouraged through the importation of Western technological teachers.

Roads, shipping lines, railroads soon followed. The twentieth century had arrived.

The last exhibit at the museum is a multi-screen slide show "Hokkaido Tomorrow Aiming at Harmony Between Nature and People." (That's what the Ainu believed all the time.)

Put it in your "don't miss" travel schedule. The Hokkaido Historical Museum, the best regional museum we were to see in Japan.

Sapporo, with a million and a half in population, is the cultural, educational, political and economic center of Hokkaido.

It has it all, including the best noodles in Japan according to the publicity.

Eating ramen in Sapporo is one of the delights of the city.

Ramen, the Chinese noodle, is found throughout Japan but the ramen dishes in Sapporo have the reputation for being spicier and more flavorful.

Sapporo, as a new capital, was laid out on a grid and divided into north and south by the main avenue, Odori. Roads running east to west are called streets and roads running north to south are avenues.

Between two streets, South Five and South Four, at West Three is "ramen alley", a colorful, hundred meters of hole-in-the-wall, sit-at-the-counter noodle shops, each one with its own ramen speciality.

The taxi stopped on South Five. A noodle shop was facing the street and, luckily, we spotted two empty stools at the counter. We jumped on them like children playing musical chairs. The Lady Navigator stared hungrily at the large bowl of noodles being served to a lady next to her. The lady turned and said, "Pork."

By pointing and gesturing it was indicated to the counterman that we would like two of the same.

Two plastic glasses of water were placed in front of us. The request for beer was refused! Our lady translator explained that no beer was served until after 9 P.M. on Sunday.

Five minutes later two huge bowls of steaming, garlicky, noodle-filled miso soup arrived. Following the observed custom, we sprinkled black pepper generously from a large can, added a touch more garlic from an adjacent bowl, and with chopsticks and ceramic spoons demolished the contents.

The sheer enjoyment was added to by the lines of salivating, hungry people standing behind us ready to claim a musical noodle stool.

The tab was about Y600.

Add to your Don't Miss list: ramen noodles in Sapporo.

On the second floor of the City Hall is an information office where you can get a kit full of material (in English) on attractions and accommodations in Sapporo.

You can also request a home visit experience which had been arranged for us that evening.

We filled out the home visit form and received instructions on how to reach our hosts' home and also a profile on the family.

> Note: the left-hand wall of the lobby in the new City Hall looks as if it is disappearing in the distance. Go look.

The City Hall faces Odori Park and is near a TV tower in the park. The tower is a good place to start a city tour. The elevator automatically takes you to the third-floor level where you buy a ticket to the top of the tower for Y500.

Hokkaido 179

From the top you get a 360-degree orientation of the city. You can look up and down Odori Park, originally planned as a firebreak when the city was laid out and is now a green, narrow, twelve-block long park filled with fountains and flowers, grass and benches—and pigeons.

In the late summer and autumn the park is dotted with carts attended by little old ladies selling corn barbecued on the cob—another Sapporo specialty—basted in a butter and shoyu sauce. One dollar each and delicious.

The pigeons grow fat-fat on the kernels of corn fed to them by children.

In February Sapporo celebrates the annual "Snow Festival", an international ski event utilizing the facilities built for the Winter Olympics in 1972, and Odori Park becomes stage-center for a unique display of snow creations.

In 1950 students from six high schools contributed to the spirit of the festival by carving six snow statues in Odori Park. Fifty thousand people came to look, making the statues a smashing success.

In 1983 there were thirteen giant statues—some three stories tall—and 177 smaller statues with themes varying from the whimsical to the historical. Disney characters, palaces, forts, etc. In 1983 the attending crowd was estimated at 1.83 million. In 1984, snow sculptures from ten participating nations were featured.

We went to the top of the tower and then walked the length of the park, and, when it started to rain, explored the immense underground shopping complex beneath the park. Many stores and restaurants.

We stopped at a Sapporo-beer pub. The table menu was only in kanji but by taking the waitress outside and pointing to two dishes in the window we solved the food problem. Ordering beer was more dificult.

I ordered two beers—*ni birru*—but I received in return a spate of questions in Japanese.

A neatly dressed Japanese gentlemen at the next table leaned over to help.

"The waitress wants to know what type of beer and what size beer you want," he said.

Gratefully, we told him we would like two medium-sized lagers which he translated to the waitress and, shortly, she placed two

180 *How to Get Lost and Found in New Japan*

immense chilled mugs of cold, pale lager before us. Excellent beer made in Sapporo.

"Do you mind if I talk to you?" our neighbor asked.

Our helpful friend was with the University of Hokkaido in the research department where his specialty was investigating the results of low temperatures—"like the tundra in Alaska", he explained. Pursuing his specialty he had spent two years at Cornell University in Ithaca, New York.

When he learned that we were planning to go to the Sapporo Brewery for the noted Genghis Khan barbecue the following night, and that we had no friends in Sapporo, he asked if he and his wife could join us, if he could get the approval of his wife—showing that wife approval is international. Of course.

The mist outside had now turned to heavy rain.

A time comes in extensive time-zone travelling when a clear signal from up above says: "let go, relax, read, rest."

We slept all afternoon and awoke only in time to get ready for our home visit.

Our instructions told us that we were to take a certain commuter train leaving at a precise time, go two stops and get off where we would be met by our host family.

Buying a commuter train ticket was not that easy. Everything was in kanji. However, showing our instruction sheet to a friendly ticket seller solved the problem. He left his window, came out into the station, took us to a ticket-vending machine, took our coins, bought us two tickets and indicated with his fingers the platform number.

The same sort of thing happened in the sushi bar underneath the station where there is another entire city of shops and restaurants.

The sushi bar staff spoke only Japanese. We were bewildered. Sushi, as we knew it, is rice wrapped around a sliver of fish and then encased in the thinnest piece of seaweed. If not fish, then a pickle or cucumber.

In this restaurant a sliver of fish was placed *on top* of a roll of rice.

After sitting at the counter and staring back at the counterman and exchanging English-for-Japanese and Japanese-for-English, a kind-faced rotund gentleman heaved himself out of his counter chair, walked over to us and asked softly, "May I help you?"

Yes, yes, tell us how and what to order.

He advised us to try the red tuna, which we did. Two portions of sliced red tuna atop rice rolls appeared which we tried to pick up with chopsticks. It SPLAT on the plate.

"No," said our counselor. "Pick it up in your fingers, dip it into the soy sauce, pop it into your mouth."

Voila. Success. Next?

Our helping friend pointed to the glass case running the length of the counter which contained all the different kinds of fish available.

The Lady Navigator loves sushi and was as happy as a child in a candy store. She went down the case pointing at this, pointing at that. She had sushi of red fish, shell fish—lobster, shrimp—cuttlefish, white fish.

We barely made the train.

Two stops from Sapporo Station at our destination exit we were met by Mr. & Mrs. Toyofumi Kanatsu. After bowing, shaking hands, exchanging cards, they put us into their car for a five-minute drive to their suburban home.

Both were slight, dark of hair, in their mid-forties. The wife, Yoshiko, wore spectacles and our first impression was of a bashful, modest, passive Japanese housewife. Wrong. As the evening unfolded it became very evident that she was a lively, humorous and strong-minded lady.

Yoshiko spoke no English. She didn't have to. Toyofumi was a senior high school English instructor with an excellent technical command of the language, although his only contact with verbal English was a morning, fifteen-minute English newscast.

During the evening's conversation he maintained a running translation for Yoshiko. Their teen-age son in high school joined us. A teen-age daughter was away with her grandmother on vacation.

First Toyofumi volunteered to show us the house, a neat, two-story, mostly Western-styled home, four years old and the first the Kanatsus had ever owned.

We had gathered in a Western parlor and from there toured the dining room and kitchen equipped with an electric rice cooker and a giant-sized hot water thermos for tea. Off the kitchen was a small room with a new washing machine, a separate room for a deep furo-type bath, another room with a Western-style toilet.

The only traditional tatami-matted room downstairs was the bedroom for his father and mother. Upstairs were Western bedrooms for each of the children. The adults had a tatami-matted bedroom. Toyofumi's den blended East and West. A Western-style desk vied for spatial dominance with the traditional floor table around which were zabutons, Japanese cushions. We spent the evening on the zabutons around the table... and never stopped talking.

A home visit, according to the literature, is to last an hour or so. Food or refreshments are not, supposedly, involved but, of course they are, and our visit lasted over three hours.

We took macadamia nuts and candy from Hawaii and an Air New Zealand bird etching.

Yoshiko served a cold repast. Toyofumi served sake.

Yoshiko came back with grapes and Japanese candy and then, while the Lady Navigator was looking at wedding pictures, she brought in a box of her sewing and presented her feminine guest with a home-made apron, a delicately embroidered cloth for covering food and an oyster-white textured pillow cover on which she had embroidered a classic geometric design.

Toyofumi, who had been to the United States once and to Europe once, was now teaching English in his fourth school, a new senior high school with 450 students in each of his three classes.

"Is learning English difficult for your students?"

"Yes. Very. The university entrance examination is based on a written English test. Nothing orally. Therefore teaching concentrates solely on written English. There are many Japanese teachers who teach but who cannot speak English."

He showed us a typical university English examination. It would be a tough examination in any American university.

"With the emphasis on television, on stereo music, on manga, is it harder to teach English today than it used to be?"

"Yes. Much harder."

Takashi, the son who ate all the macadamia nuts, wanted to be a barrister. If he failed the first university test, he would go to a prep school and study for the next year's examination. This could go on as long as his parents could afford it.

They drove us back to the hotel. We parted warm friends.

The Lady Navigator rang Yoshiko on the telephone the next day and they had a long conversation—the Navigator in English,

Yoshiko in Japanese.

"We knew what we were saying," said the Navigator when questioned. Men can never state with certainty that they understand women.

Sun poured into the window the next morning. Not one grey cloud scarred the sky. Not a day to be wasted.

After a fast breakfast in the room (plump peaches bought at the station the night before, coffee and tea, and biscuits) we caught a taxi to Okurayama Jump Hill, made famous in the 1972 Olympics with its 90-meter ski jump and stadium accommodations for 50,000 spectators.

On a bright morning, bald of snow, the sight of the jump—so high!—the spectator stands, the official judging stands, is altogether quite impressive. A chair lift takes visitors to the top of the jump.

From Okurayama we had a clear view of the city.

The taxi driver pointed out Maruyama Park, the Zoo and the Hokkaido Shrine en route to our next destination, the Hokkaido Museum of Modern Art.

It is worth going to the museum just to admire the exciting mobile art in the garden, a superb collection of toys made by grown-ups for the amusement of grown-ups: wind-driven revolving paddles, arms, sails, twirling metal spirals. Delightful to the eye and proper for a city which is an outdoor city—until it goes underground in the winter—filled with park and gardens and surrounded by forested hills.

Next door to the museum is the spacious park surrounding the Governor's House. The grounds were dotted with playing children and picnicking families. A dozen blocks away in the middle of Sapporo is the Botanic Garden containing some 5,000 varieties of plants, including a rock garden of alpine plants.

On the grounds of the Botanic Garden is the Batchelor Museum, located in the former residence of Dr. John Batchelor (1854-1944), a minister who lived among the Ainu people and published books about the disappearing aboriginal race of Hokkaido.

Nearby is the Old Hokkaido Government Building also surrounded by gardens.

On the top of the "not-to-be-missed" list however you have to put the Clock Tower, a symbol of the beginning of modern Hokkaido. The classic Western building in the heart of the city looks as if it were shipped from New England. Once part of the Sapporo Agricultural College, it is now a city museum.

But let's turn the clock back to 1875.

When the Japanese opened the gates to Admiral Perry and soon after changed governments, the new regime adopted Westernization with typical Japanese thoroughness.

People were sent abroad to study. Foreign instructors were brought to Japan.

One school was opened in Tokyo by the Hokkaido Colonization Commission (Kaitakushi) whose faculty was comprised of foreign teachers from countries with the same weather and land characteristics as Hokkaido. Instruction in the school was entirely in English.

In 1875 the school was moved to Sapporo and renamed the Sapporo School. At the same time an idea was approved of establishing an agricultural school, and Dr. William S. Clark, president of Massachusetts State Agricultural College was brought in to be the first dean of the Sapporo Agricultural College.

Part of the charter of American state schools after the Civil War included mandatory military training for the students, and so it was instituted at the new agricultural college, the first such training in Japan.

Dr. Clark not only taught agricultural principles, in English of course, but Christian principles as well, despite objections. He installed a hard-rock New England discipline in his eager students. When he left after one year, his students rode with him as far as they could, reluctant to see their teacher go. He turned to them in their final parting and said, "Boys, be ambitious."

Several of the ten students in the first graduating class went on to become national leaders—indeed, the whole nation seemed to take his words as a national motto.

Dr. Clark's statue stands on the grounds of the former agricultural school, now the Hokkaido University. His immortal words are inscribed on the base of the statue.

Our helping research professor from lunch, Dr. Kaoru Horiguchi, called to say that he and his wife would join us for dinner at the Sapporo Brewery, and that they would meet us at the entrance to the old brewery at six o'clock.

At ten minutes to six our taxi deposited us at the brewery but our friend was already there with his wife, Kyoko, and two sons, Kenichi and Koji. (Japanese are always prompt.)

In a glass case near the entrance we examined replicas of dinners we could order.

I had read that for Y4,000 you could have all the Genghis Khan barbecue you could eat and all the beer you could drink during a two-hour period. We didn't go that route, electing to follow our host's suggestion.

Three buildings were crammed with diners; our dining room was in the old malt house. "I called for reservations because when you have this kind of weather with a clear night and a full moon the place is full and you need them," said the doctor.

We sat at a bare wooden table in the middle of which were two gas burners topped with heavy, slotted, round, convex, black-iron grills that looked like squashed helmets.

The doctor ordered.

Two giant platters filled with slices of uncooked lamb and onion and bean sprouts appeared.

Kaoru took care of the two sons while Kyoko was our chef. She first placed a piece of suet on top of the hot grill to grease the cooking surface. Then slices of meat, onion and bunches of bean sprouts were positioned carefully on the hot dome. When grilled to our preference, each morsel was pulled off with chopsticks, dipped in a special sauce and washed down with tankards of cold lager.

"Oishi." Delicious dinner with attractive intelligent companions. It is an added experience to be adopted, if only temporarily, by a local family.

"Where do you go from Sapporo?" asked Kaoru.

"To Noboribetsu," we answered.

"Oh, I envy you the hot baths," said this specialist in low temperatures.

From Sapporo you can take day trips to surrounding points of interest.

One such tour takes you through a southwest swing past lakes, hot springs, volcanic mountains, Ainu villages and back to Sapporo. We were going to take only half of the tour, getting off at the hot springs spa of Noboribetsu.

186   How to Get Lost and Found in New Japan

At an early morning hour, we rolled our luggage around the corner to the ANA Hotel Sapporo to join the Ace Bus Tour and were assigned reserved seats on a modern air-conditioned bus with a uniformed driver and a uniformed hostess.

The hard-working hostess was a petite young thing, pretty, demure in manner; she had a running commentary in Japanese that went on without a break for four hours—including one song—and she also had a whistle to direct the bus when it was in reverse. At every stop she bowed passengers on and off the bus.

We were the only non-Japanese tourists.

The bus left promptly at eight and took an hour to clear the outskirts of constantly growing Sapporo before reaching the mountains.

At the first stop on top of a mountain pass a young lady leaned forward to translate the announcement made by the hostess. "You have ten minutes before you have to be back on the bus."

We had found another new friend. Michiko Araki. She was from Osaka and was taking the day tour while her husband attended a biogenetic seminar at the university.

Michiko could have come out of the same stable as my Kyoto student guides. Vivacious, honest-friendly, without any assumed manners, jean-clad, black hair. A love.

The stop provided a view across the mountain range to the perfect cone of Mt. Yotei, called the "Fuji of Hokkaido."

Also at hand was a string of souvenir shops and food stands selling corn on the cob *(tomorokoshi)* and roasted potatoes *(jagaimo)* three on a stick for a dollar.

From the mountain top the bus descended to another view-stop overlooking Lake Toya, slightly hazy in the morning sun, round in shape, with a thickly wooded island in its middle.

Although Hokkaido is known for its cold winter weather the large lake is so deep (179.2 meters) that it never freezes over.

After everyone had shot pictures of the lake, their travelling companions, the bus, the bus driver, the hostess, and the shopkeeper's cat, the tour continued down to the lake front.

> Note: you are almost never refused if you offer to take pictures of couples travelling together with their cameras. Much bowing and thank yous in English and Japanese.

The lake region is rich in agriculture. Fields of corn and asparagus, two Hokkaido specialties, and miles of vines of beans from which pastry shops make the black paste filling for little cakes.

From the lake we cut inland to Mt. Usu which had uncorked molten rock, steam and gas in 1910, 1944 and 1977.

The bus stopped along with a fleet of others opposite Mt. Showa Shinzan, formed during the 1944 eruption, and at the foot of Mt. Usu which last blew in 1977.

You wonder what you are doing here as you lick a chocolate ice cream cone and look up at the slopes of Mt. Showa—you would like to think that a "new" mountain would be nice and pretty, polished, cellophane wrapped. But this mountain was gray-ugly, white-scarred at the vents where steam escaped reminding you that the mountain was not only "new" but it was alive. Broken cement walks leading up the mountain and former barriers pushed aside were further evidence that Mt. Showa was also still growing. It was rather ominous.

New wire barriers had been erected to prevent the unthinking doing the unthinkable, i.e. climbing higher on the flanks.

Adjacent to the bus stop, souvenir shops were hawking carved bears—tiny bears, huge bears, bears holding giant trout in their mouths, cute bears holding whiskey bottles. Bear carving is a major industry in Hokkaido.

The bus headed over another mountain range, past apple orchards, down a gravel highway under repair known as "massage road."

Soon after twelve we arrived at a cluster of hotels nestled between the mountains: Noboribetsu Spa. After lunch the tour would continue on to Sapporo but without us.

At the Daiichi Takimoto, a modern tourist hotel with Japanese rooms and a reputation for the best hot springs in Hokkaido, (forty baths and ten types of mineral water) we checked our bags and had a Japanese box lunch (bento) with the group.

After lunch Michiko led us in a five-minute walk to the Valley of Hell—an acreage of white and yellow hills with many steam vents and boiling water bubbling in hot pools, running down the mountain to be piped into the hotels' hot baths.

Shop keepers in the village were putting up prettily decorated bamboo poles holding lights and streamers of colored paper in preparation for the annual festival to be held over the next three days.

There would be a parade, street stalls selling edibles, entertainers imported from Sapporo and sporting events.

At the bottom of the street Michiko had to turn back to catch the on-going tour bus.

We parted in the middle of the street, shaking hands in the Western fashion, bowing in the Japanese fashion, and finally embracing in the international fashion.

I think back to the scene and to Michiko with tenderness because she had been a stranger a few hours before, then, volunteering her help, had become a close friend, and as she left us, her eyes brimmed with tears.

One of the Noboribetsu Spa's attractions is "Bear Ranch" at the top of the mountain, reached by cable car.

Here in sunken open cages is the world's largest collection of black bears—some 150 animals. One area is for cubs, another for giant males, another for females.

You buy a box of "Bear Cubes" at Y100-a-box and throw the morsels to the bears below, even the cubs, who are sitting on their haunches, clapping their front paws together begging for food.

From the "ranch" you can see into a lake formed in a volcanic cauldron, and, in the distance, the ocean and the town of Noboribetsu, some twenty minutes away from the spa by car.

Back at the hotel we were shown into our eight-tatami-sized Japanese room with Western bathroom, poured tea, given registration forms and asked what time we wanted dinner served in our room. Breakfast, we were told, was a Japanese breakfast and was served "Viking Style", meaning buffet, in the dining hall.

Negative. Western breakfast, please. Consternation. Huddle. Solution. Go to the coffee shop in the morning at the hour named. Smiles all around.

The Lady Navigator had never been in a hotel spa but went off bravely in her hotel yukata to investigate the mineral baths while I did notes.

In an hour she was back, flushed, relaxed but twittering.

She had followed the procedure of peeling and washing down—scrubbing her toes for an unnecessarily long time in order to "research" the system—before proceeding into three different pools. "I had read that no one pays any attention to your body. Well, there was a male attendant, and he seemed to be paying a lot of attention to mine. Do I look that different? There were all kinds of bodies, young, old, sagging, pretty. A mother and daughter came in wearing bathing suits. They looked funny. I want to go back and do it again."

Later I went to the men's baths. In the dressing room I removed my yukata and slippers, put them in a wicker basket and, clutching my washcloth as if it were going to prevent my catching cold in the crotch, proceeded to one of the several rows of six-inch stools in front of tiled troughs of fresh running water. With a plastic yellow bucket I dipped out water and soaped down and sluiced off.

Many Japanese men take a sybarite delight in minutely cleaning each toe and each finger studiously and completely, washing each square of flesh painstakingly, scrubbing and soaping and rinsing and then starting all over again.

I didn't count forty pools but out of at least ten pools I tried three. Over each pool was a sign written in kanji telling what its mineral content was and listing its cures. I finished slightly wrinkled but ignorant of the extent of my new health.

Oh, in one corner, three separate streams of water poured down from a height of about six meters and, having witnessed others, I went and stood under a stream and let it hammer the nape of my neck. A fine massage and much better than the "massage road."

At dinner time, Ume, our mama-san, brought stacks of trays to our room and on the floor table laid out a traditional Japanese dinner—vegetables, fish, pickles, miso soup—and as a concession to the Westerners, a covered bowl with meat balls and potatoes. Hot rice came as a last course.

A room refrigerator held soft drinks, sake and beer.

After dinner, as Ume made up our floor bed, we ventured somewhat timidly into the street dressed in our yukatas and, with wooden clogs provided at the entrance to the hotel, joined the other similarly-clad Japanese tourists taking an after-dinner stroll.

In addition to the shops selling sticky candy and pastries and carved bears, the village had two girlie shows hustled by sidewalk pitchmen—evidently a standard part of the Japanese spa-vacation-convention scene.

Whether it was the bus ride or the mineral baths or the combination of massages, we were curled up on our futons and fast asleep by eight-thirty.

The next morning at dawn, the Lady Navigator stretched and said, "Now I feel like I'm in Japan."

At the coffee shop at the appointed hour a single table had a sign in kanji; we correctly guessed it was reserved for us. A huge salad, ham and eggs (!), two two-inch slices of delicious buttered toast and a cup of strong coffee were served. A gold star breakfast.

Our destination for the day was Asahikawa, the second largest city of Hokkaido, located in the middle of the island.

The morning was wet.

The taxi ride from Noboribetsu Spa to the Noboribetsu train station took twenty minutes. The Lady Navigator got involved in a winking contest with a doll-child, age three, culminating with the young lady toddling over to us and giving each of us a stick of gum.

The journey marked the first day usage of our 21-day rail pass with a three-and-a-half-hour ride to Asahikawa via Sapporo with no change of trains.

The sun came out as the train sped northeast passing lush fields of rice, grain, corn and onions.

All of the rice on Hokkaido is mechanically planted, cultivated and harvested in a relatively short season.

Travelling as usual during the mid-day period and not having found a sandwich shop in Noboribetsu, I told the Lady Navigator that we would have to eat out of the rolling food-and-drink carts that the girl attendants kept pushing through the train.

I stopped one attendant to see what was available and asked, "Sandwich?" She replied in the affirmative and said "Katsu."

I bought one soft drink, one beer and one bento of "katsu."

Six neat sandwiches, cellophane wrapped, were in the box. What the sandwiches contained was a mystery. The meat was numbed of any flavor by the tomato sauce but we thought it was pork. Wrong again. It was bonito.

Asahikawa, Timber Town

At the station was Hiro Imamura, a city executive in the Department of Economic Development who had been taken off his normal duties to show us Asahikawa, because he spoke

English. He was an excellent guide. In his early thirties, broad shouldered, handsome in his way, he walked with a slight samurai swagger as he led us through a fast-paced look at the many facets of Asahikawa, a city serving as a commercial center for the surrounding rich agricultural and forestry country, four major railroads and as many national highways. A major airport puts Tokyo within 100 minutes of the city.

When the city was established by a handful of Japanese settlers there were an estimated 5,000 Ainu people in the area.

Today the population is 355,000 Japanese . . . and a handful of Ainu.

Facing the station is a relatively new shopping mall, a half-mile of traffic-free shopping.

From the mall Hiro took us to Asahiyama Park outside of the city. The park's elevation provided an airplane view of the two rivers bordering the municipality, and the surrounding green fields and the dark green, tree-covered mountains in the distance. A pretty picture.

Next stop was the Yukara Ori Folkcraft Museum, a highlight of Asahikawa, a large, new, hilltop building, almost Nordic in design with red-brick foundations and white washed walls.

Yukara Ori is a hand-woven fabric featured in the craft center and its motif reminded us of Nordic color and design. Breathtaking stuff. The prices are somewhat breathtaking, too.

The next stop was at an Ainu village where mixed-breed remnants of a once proud forest people who couldn't conform to a society—they refused to learn to read or write—are now sustained in a squalid livelihood by selling trinkets and carved bears.

"With all of these carved bears," said the discerning Lady Navigator, "there has to be a carved bear factory."

"Ah," said Hiro.

The next stop—the bear factory—presented nine men and three women roughing out, finishing, staining and polishing another ranch of black bears. One sculptor was using a pneumatic carver.

A good bear, one even twelve inches high, is expensive.

Pre-studied literature claimed that because of Asahikawa's pure water it was known for its fine sake.

Questioned about the veracity of the claim, Hiro had us almost immediately in the halls of the Otokoyama Sake Company where rice is converted into white wine. The distillery was not in production because the new crop of rice was yet to be harvested but we saw the machinery, a graph of the process, many artifacts of old-time sake distilling—beautiful ceramic jugs—and a boutique museum of sake cups and serving flasks.

Both the bear factory and the distillery are open to the public.

More important than agriculture as the mainstay of Asahikawa's prosperity are the forests which yield timber for giant pulp-paper manufacturing plants and furniture making.

After only two questions regarding the furniture industry, *presto,* our Hiro-hero of Economic Development had us in the Interior House Company (trade name: Hook) where we looked over a showroom of contemporary western furniture of Japanese-American-European design, the majority of which goes to Japanese home buyers. But the company is aggressive ("Boys, be ambitious.") and has a showroom in the Furniture Mart in San Francisco.

"Hiro? Today's Japanese interior housing is all western. Western beds, western kitchens, western living rooms, bathrooms. Is there no longer any use of tatami mats and shoji doors?"

"Ah, yes," he said. "When one builds a new house in Japan today, it is as you say, all western interiors. But, always one room is traditionally Japanese."

Across the street from the showroom and offices was the mill and construction part of the company, a computerized operation including a robot milling machine.

Enough, enough.

Hiro took us back to the hotel for a quick shower, a quicker siesta and was back at 6:30 to take us to dinner.

The restaurant, according to my notes, was called Bottom Restaurant, a teppan-yaki, Benihana-type of operation where a chef with slashing and flashing knives cooked steak and vegetables on a counter hot-plate in front of the customers.

We had steak, vegetables, onions, eggplant, shrimp. Three kinds of sauces for dipping: miso sauce with mustard, garlic and shoyu, and a "secret" white sauce for the eggplant.

Included was a seaweed and taro soup—*kon-nyaku*—which sounded frightening but was, in fact, fantastic. Rice, of course.

The cost of such a dinner was under $20 plus the beer. And peo-

Hokkaido 193

ple still ask us every day, "Japan is terribly expensive, isn't it?" After dinner Hiro strolled us through the "entertainment district", the Sanjo Rokuchomo, where visiting farmers, salesmen and residents come to have a good time. In one seven-story building he counted over thirty nightclub-hostess bars.

Our constant bombardment of tourist-oriented questions were sometimes outside the area of Hiro's day-to-day expertise and the next morning he appeared with Mr. Watanabe, the head of the Asahikawa Tourist Department.

Q. How many hotels and inns do you have in the city?
A. Over 1,000 rooms in 66 hotels and inns.
Q. How many annual tourists?
A. Over 2,000,000.
Q. How many overseas visitors?
A. About 2,000.
Q. When do the overseas visitors come?
A. Primarily for the Winter Festival which is scheduled to take place about two weeks after Sapporo's Winter Festival. More and more visitors are coming in the autumn.
Q. What is projected for the next five years?
A. Five million visitors and five new first-class hotels.
Q. So few hotels for so many visitors?
A. Within an hour's drive from Asahikawa are many other fine tourist hotels, including Sounkyo Hot Springs.

That's where we were heading—to a leading destination near Asahikawa called Sounkyo Hot Springs.

We would drive a rental car.

We wanted the experience of driving in Japan because everyone told us not to do it. The safest choice seemed to be this remote region with a small population at what we assumed to be a lull in the tourist season. It was not the most economical choice.

Taking a medium-sized car for four days at about $50 a day plus petrol when we had already activated our rail passes was not the smartest budget move but the experience, we hoped, would make it worthwhile.

It was.

A car had been reserved before leaving Tokyo and Hiro took us to the rental agency in Asahikawa where I had to show my Inter-

194   *How to Get Lost and Found in New Japan*

national Drivers License issued in Honolulu which I had obtained before leaving. It is mandatory to get such a license before leaving home because states' licenses are not recognized by Japanese authorities and obtaining an international license in Japan is very time-consuming.

Hiro decided to go with us as far as Sounkyo the first day, only 67 kilometers away. In fact he drove. It would have been interesting to navigate ourselves out of Asahikawa—how many times can you get lost?—but with Hiro it was no problem and we soon cleared the city.

Surprisingly the speed limit was never more than fifty kilometers an hour. Everyone passed us of course but we stuck to fifty kilometers an hour.

At one point an on-coming car flashed its lights as a warning signal, indicating, Hiro said, that there was a policeman in the vicinity. "Telling each other that there is a policeman around is good for our morale."

The two-lane highway entered a gorge sidling along a river. On each side were steep cliffs carved from rocks and covered with trees. An occasional spike of rock would stand out like a stark, pointed statue from the sloping background.

We left the river and drove to the base of Mt. Kurodake where a 100-passenger cable car carried us up 670 meters to a lookout. From there chairlifts took us on a delightful forest ride to the top of what is a formidable winter ski run.

The chair lift is modified in the summer season by lowering the cable from a top arm on overhead pylons to a mid-section arm. The result is that the passenger's feet float barely above the grassy, flower-dotted mountain floor.

The morning was perfect. Sunny. Not too warm. The mountain air clear in the lungs. A happy-to-be-here-and-be-alive morning.

From the top of the chairlift, the surrounding mountain tops of the Daisetsu Range were visible. Great hiking, tramping, climbing country.

Heavily loaded, back-pack hikers were on the chairlift embarking on three-day trips through the mountains.

A pair of mountain climbers laden with sacks of climbing rope, pilons and other mountaineering gear was getting ready to assault one of Daisetsu's peaks.

Many of Japan's leading mountaineers come from Hokkaido

because of the easy accessibility of good mountains on which to train.

At the bottom of the second lift a food stand was selling corn-on-the-cob and potatoes-on-a-stick. It was potato-tasting time. Three potatoes per stick, each covered with a doughnut-flavored batter and deep-fried. Good. Like all sweet, greasy, fattening things are.

Back in the car and back to the river, Hiro drove a short distance to two spectacular waterfalls with exotic Ainu names. One straight, towering waterfall was called "Shooting Star." Next to it a second waterfall, "The Milky Way", spread out a lacy white curtain over an expanse of rock on its descent.

After a ramen noodle lunch, a city staff car picked up Hiro and took him back to his civic duties.

The Sounkyo Kanko Hotel was empty but a bulletin board at the entrance held ten placards announcing in kanji the tours that would be checking in later that afternoon.

By six o'clock the lobby—dark at midday—was lighted and boiling with Japanese tourists. Their busses bore license plates from Osaka and Tokyo and other Honshu cities.

Japanese dinner was served in a large mess hall on long tables. Fair at best. A three.

Breakfast was served in the same room, "Viking Style." You should try it once. Egg cake, seaweed, candied peas, tiny plums, pressed meat, vegetables, beans and the standard miso soup, rice and tea. Interesting, but another three.

The tours flood out of the hotel on the morning tide—busses already in formation, engines running, hostesses whistling, a line-up of hotel staff to wave goodbye.

I checked out and went to the car not waiting any longer for the Lady Navigator to come down. Her promise of "in-two-minutes" is not measurable by mortal clocks. Surprisingly, while I paid the bill, she had preceded me to the car and, dressed in white shirt, white slacks and a hot pink jacket, had already been seized by a Japanese tour group for a group picture with much laughing and posing beside our car.

I can hear them now in Osaka saying as they showed their prints, "And in the Sounkyo Gorge we found *this!*"

It was a great day. Rolling along in our own car, stopping and gawking, taking pictures, going faster, slower.

Masters of our own schedule.

Thankfully, we were on our own because from Sounkyo to Kawayu Spa we enjoyed at leisure one of the prettiest corners of Japan—a garden of rivers, rocks, forests, rich farms, scenic mountain passes, magnificent lakes.

The Sounkyo Gorge is 24-kilometers long, part of the Daisetsuzan National Park, the largest of Japan's twenty-seven national parks.

(I found Daisetsuzan an impossible name to remember. Then a ridiculous 'name reminder' came to mind. The park was named after the famous television actress—mythical of course—Daisy T. Susan. The Lady Navigator nearly fell out of the car—but it worked. More of this later if you can stand it.)

Now in our own car and guideless, we soon discovered a simple rule: stop where the tour busses stop.

Being in a car and not on a train or plane made us realize how big the internal travel business is in Japan. There were fleets and fleets of tour busses.

We stopped the first time behind a fleet of busses to see an accordion of overhanging rock, pleated like a cheerleader's skirt, on the cliff facing the road. We would have missed it if it hadn't have been for the tour busses.

We would have missed Obako, a pretty canyon of bare granite if we hadn't seen the tour busses turn off. The visual of the river running into the canyon entrance was one scene. Another was the scene of Japanese tourists buying handfuls of key-chains, flags, bear carvings, corn-on-the-cob, barbecued fish and ice cream cones. Obako was a number ten bus stop. Full of action.

From Sekihoku Pass to Bihoro Pass in the Akan National Park, a three-hour drive, we crossed a farm-filled plain lush with rich crops. It might have been the bright summer-bordering-autumn day or our freedom-on-wheels but those fields fat with produce encompassed the most beautiful farm land in Japan.

Rice, corn, potatoes, onion—and most of Japan's peppermint—is grown here. The Lady Navigator called it Peppermint Valley and that is what it is still in our memory, although technically, the plain is called Kitami.

After making one false jog in a switch of highways (Lost), we soon found where we had missed the directional sign and were back on the proper road (Found) to Bihoro Pass which we conveniently reached just in time for lunch.

The Pass has a sweeping view overlooking Lake Kutcharo, the largest of the three principal lakes in Akan National Park, considered to be the jewel of all the parks in Japan.

After dutifully climbing to the best lookout and taking pictures, we retired to the large restaurant on the second floor of the souvenir-noodles-candy building and ordered, by pointing to the food being eaten at the next table, a Genghis Khan barbecue.

Fine lunch.

The ideal weather continued—a perfect day, clean, airy, a touch of coolness in the air and a touch of color now in a few trees as they prepared their autumn wardrobe.

Our "tour-sheet" schedule suggested that we go directly to Kawayu Spa for the afternoon and spend the following day at the spa attending the local festival, then the third day drive to Lake Mashu and Lake Akan.

Lake Mashu, however, has two reputations. One, it is the clearest lake in Japan with a visibility through the pure water to a depth of over forty meters. Secondly, the lake has a reputation of being the "Invisible Lake" due to frequent fog and inclement weather blown in from the nearby coast, closing the area to visitors. The Emperor, we were told, had been to Lake Mashu ten times and had only seen it twice.

Why should we peasants ignore the fine weather that the gods had laid before us?

We raced to Lake Mashu.

At the end of a winding, inclining highway, was a visitors' parking lot. From there it was a short climb up an embankment and—pow!—there was the magazine cover. Glorious.

In the cauldron of an extinct volcano, without any inlet or outlet, the almost perfect circle of undisturbed water of Lake Mashu was a vivid cobalt blue.

The volcanic cliffs rising one hundred meters in most places discourage the spoiling touches of mankind. No boats. No houses. No people swimming at its shore. A simple, uncluttered piece of nature. A masterwork.

A second, larger, twenty-bus Observation Point a few minutes farther on was a disaster. The smorgasborg of fuming bus engines, the whistles of bus hostesses, the smoking barbecues of corn and cuttlefish, paths of stepped-on cigarette butts, trash cans overflowing with beer bottles, souvenir shops junked to the rafters—what a contrast to the pristine peace of Lake Mashu below—a ring of utterly simple beauty.

Between the lake and our hotel at Kawayu Spa is Mt. Io, a fuming, rumbling mountain with yellow sulphuric scars (solfataras) emitting puffs of steam. People climbed up the flanks of the mountain amid the ash and the steam as though they were going on a picnic.

Kawayu Spa nearby takes mineral water off Mt. Io. It is a popular Japanese resort built, not on, but behind Lake Kutcharo. Many small inns and larger hotels line the streets and every sign was in kanji. We were lost again. Which one was our hotel?

Finally, after driving through the village three times, we stopped by a gardener working on a municipal garden beside the road, showed him our schedule with the name of our hotel written in Japanese characters, and asked him directions in English. You never know.

He was an older man, his forehead wrapped with a scarf, lacking several teeth, solidly built, keen of eye. He looked at our schedule, dropped his shovel and pointed to the locked back door. He wanted in. We unlocked it, he got in and pointed the way through the streets to our destination. Once we were in the hands of the hotel staff, he got out, refused a ride back to his garden and walked away without a wave.

Our room was a combination of Western-Japanese with tatami mats, low table, and tokonoma alcove in the front half of the room and in the back half, next to the windows, was a regular coffee table flanked by two Western sofa-cum-daybeds.

Would we like to sleep Western style on the sofas or Japanese style on the floor mattress futons.

Futons, please.

There was still much light left in the day and at the festival area they were preparing the booths for food and games and trinkets, tiny carp, bonsai and alpine plants, Japanese pottery. The games were already drawing crowds.

This was the starting place the next morning for the festival parade when the *mikoshi,* or portable shrine, of the village would be carried through the streets.

In big cities the mikoshi will be sizeable and carried by many men who perform elaborate drills while carrying the shrine,

another example of do-it-together discipline.
Large, elaborate floats, *dashi,* will follow the shrine.
The Kawayu festival however was quite small.

The parade was led by a solitary policeman, followed by white-robed acolytes carrying banners on bamboo shafts. The Shinto priests in pointed black hats and soft silk robes preceded the shrine. At intervals the men would go through a frantic whirlwind routine accompanied by a pounding drum.

The children, next in line, were wonderful in their festival regalia. The spectators were not tourists—they had already left on busses—but the mothers of the children and the townfolk.

> Note 1: most of the time in Japan we spent admiring and pointing at adorable children.
> Note 2: there were also several adorable mothers but I refrained from pointing.

After the parade we drove to Lake Akan, an hour and a half away from Lake Kutcharo, where the hotels front the lakeshore and the main activity is to cruise around the lake for an hour or so, stopping at a small island where there is a different sort of aquarium.

What you see are not fish but samples of *marimo,* a green ball of lake grass, as big as a tennis ball, which grows on the lake bottom and comes close to the surface only on sunny days.

Pretty, forestry shoreline.

The next morning was overcast, and we were happy that we had moved our schedule forward and had seen the lakes on clear days. (Actually, we were *smug.)*

The car was to be turned in at Kushiro on the coast, not far away, but we took a short-cut, defying lack of maps in English, a short-cut that worked (now we were really smug) and we were in Kushiro by ten o'clock. The original schedule had us leaving Kushiro at five in the afternoon which would have put us back in Sapporo after ten. By taking a noon train we would be back in the New Otani Hotel in time for dinner.

At the station we went into the Green Car office to change our reservations.

It happened again.

A strangely attired man with tinted spectacles in a red-striped shirt, a towel around his neck, carrying a black satchel stepped to our side and inquired, "May I help you?"

Always happens.

We explained what we were doing, and he said, "There is a train at ten-thirty. It takes an hour less to get to Sapporo than the noon train."

The man behind the window informed our new friend there were no Green Car seats left on the ten-thirty train. He made out new tickets for the noon train.

Good Samaritan said, "But there are lots of other seats on the train."

The idea had to be declined because our rental car still had to be returned. We opted to check our bags at the station, turn in the car and sightsee Kushiro on foot.

Our G.S. left.

The luggage was retrieved from the automobile and we were going to the lockers to put the bags away when our friend reappeared.

"I checked," he said. "Lots of seats. You can use your Japan Rail Pass and sit in the reserved section and after Obihiro move into the Green Car."

"But the rental car?"

"The Information Booth will take care of your car. Here, come with me."

A few steps away, at an Information Booth, he talked quickly to the young lady inside who seemed to take it all in stride as we dumped keys, parking ticket and rental car papers on her and ran for the train.

What had we committed ourselves to?

The last time we had done something like this was at the Fort Worth-Dallas Airport where a bell captain had forgotten to pick up a rental car and we were shocked later with an extra $400 bill.

"We Japanese, you know, are flexible. We take things as they come," said the G.S in the strange costume.

Our fears about his character soon disappeared. His name was Hajime Sasaki. He was returning to his home in Obihiro after a hiking expedition at Lake Akan, hence the garb.

Respectability? He was a recently retired high school principal and was president of the Obihiro Volunteer Language Club.

We conducted a two-hour English conversation lesson all the way to Obihiro where Sasaki-san got off. Most informative and pleasant gentleman. We moved into the Green Car and continued on to Sapporo in the rain.

Our conclusion about driving in Japan that night over dinner, as we did our notes, was that it wasn't that difficult in the country where you can stop and ask directions. I still, however, wouldn't want to drive in any big Japanese city.

Japanese drivers are more polite than their European counterparts. They are not trying to prove their masculinity.

The driving speed is slow. That helps.

Principal highways are marked in Roman numerals. The road signs conform to internationally accepted graphics.

The Lady Navigator recommended having an English map together with a Japanese map. On the English map you know where you are. When you stop and ask directions, you can use the Japanese map for pointing and for cross-referencing.

The Japanese map will come with the rental car. For an English map, there is an excellent sectional series published by the Japan Guide Map Company available in hotel bookstores.

We refilled the petrol in Kushiro and did exactly what we were told to do when driving into a filling station. You say, "Regular—fill it up." And that's what happens. The cute, eager, uniformed girls at the station filled a nearly-empty fifty-liter tank which was all our entire trip had used. Good mileage.

We never saw a road accident in our four-day excursion.

Driving on the left for an American driver presented no difficulty.

Our car had an English-written dashboard and was equipped with the latest gadgets—cruise control speed, tape deck, warning lights for seat belts, changing oil, even rotating tires.

The paramount requirement is to acquire an International Drivers License before leaving home. It takes three weeks to obtain one in Japan. The automobile club in Honolulu issued mine in ten minutes, including a polaroid photo.

Driving in Japan? A piece of cake.

Our last adventure in Hokkaido was a two-day stay in Hakodate at the tip of the island before returning to Honshu by ferry.

The train from Sapporo to Hakodate takes four-and-a-half

hours. The latter part of the trip along the coast is another view of Hokkaido. Mountains and forests and lush farms are replaced by fishing villages, boats, nets, floats.

Hakodate is the center of the marine action.

Ferry boats connect the port to the mainland of Honshu at Aomori and for many visitors who come by rail from Tokyo and then ferry to Hokkaido, Hakodate is their first glimpse of the island.

Fishing boats ply the harbor waters leaving their catches to be canned or frozen in the food processing plants, a major local industry.

Historically, Hakodate became a coaling station for the American fleet in 1855 under the American friendship agreement forced by Admiral Perry.

In 1859, still under the Tokugawa Shogunate, Hakodate became an open port to other nations along with Nagasaki, Kobe, Yokohama and Niigata.

New churches and consulates became part of the cityscape in Hakodate which is one reason for finding a Greek Orthodox church founded by a Russian prelate in 1862 and a Trappist monastery founded by French-naturalized Japanese in 1895. A Trappist convent was established in 1898.

In the same year as the opening of the port to other nations, the Tokugawa leaders ordered the construction of Hakodate's most famous landmark, the Goryokaku Fort, a five-pointed, star-shaped fortress constructed according to Western principles.

It took eight years to complete the massive fortification.

Shortly after the Meiji Restoration in 1868, a vice admiral in the Tokugawa navy, Takeaki Enomoto, dissatisfied with the crumbs left to the former holders of power, mounted a revolution and with a fleet of ships and commando units took the fort in Hakodate and held it for a month before finally surrendering. It was a time of high drama.

You can still walk the grassy ramparts of Goryokaku, a ten-minute taxi ride from the station, feed the giant carp in the moat or hire a rowboat and paddle around in the moat waters.

Inside the fort is a branch of the Hakodate Museum. When we were there, we saw an exhibit on the second floor devoted to a series of amusing drawings depicting the visiting ships from other nations in the nineteenth century.

All of the Western sailors and officers are drawn with the same

faces—"They all look alike to me"—including gross noses.
Next to the fort is the Goryokaku Tower. From the top you get panoramic views of the city and harbor.

Pension Kokikan, our abode in Hakodate, was our first pension, an inn styled somewhere between a traditional ryokan and a minshuku.

The price of $80 for the two included breakfast and dinner—dinner being served in a restaurant owned by the proprietor of the inn a block away. However, breakfast was served family-style in the pension at a long table next to the open kitchen.

Dinner was Japanese with chopsticks but breakfast was Western with knives and forks to eat salad, melon, hard-boiled egg, corn-on-the-cob, a boiled potato, two pieces of giant-sized toast, fresh milk from a giant pitcher, and strong, black coffee.

Our tatami-matted room was large—eight tatami in the main room and another three tatami in our private entrance hall. To watch television cost Y100 an hour.

The toilet facilities, both Japanese and Western, were down the hall as was a tiled shower room and a large furo where, at an appointed hour, we had a funny communal bath.

The pension was filled with college girls on vacation—lovely-skinned black-haired birds of gentle modest manner.

At breakfast they would sit with eyes down, eating silently.

Not for long with the Lady Navigator.

Between her fractionalized Japanese and her English coaxing, she soon had the whole table giggling behind hand-covered mouths and the school-trained English words gradually emerged from first one girl and then another.

Chatter while eating is not a custom with the Japanese but it was a custom broken that morning.

Our first impression on arriving at the Pension Kokikan was that we were on the back-end of nowhere but actually we came to find that we were on the edge of the Motomachi District which is the sightseeing area of Hakodate.

We were also within easy walking distance of the Mt. Hakodate cable car, a good place to start on a sunny morning. The Y600 ticket to the top of the mountain was a better buy than that to the top of the Goryokaku Tower. From the mountain top we looked down on the ferries heading across the Tsugaru Straits to Honshu.

Near the foot of the cable car we could make out the Greek Orthodox Church, the St. John's Anglican Church, the Motomachi Catholic Church and a number of Shinto shrines and Buddhist temples.

Near one railing was a marble-slab monument and a bas-relief bust of Thomas Wright Blakiston (1832-1891), one of the first traders in Hakodate and a student of bird life who discovered that birds were different on either side of the Tsugaru Straits. Zoologists refer to the imaginary line in the middle of the straits as the Blakiston Line.

Also interesting was a large sign—in English—protesting the U.S.S.R. take-over of four islands off Hokkaido following World War II.

"The Habomai, Shikotan, Kunashiri and Etorofu are Japan's inherent territories. The Northern Territories realize their return through our national will.

(signed) Hakodate City"

The walk through the Motomachi District, once the site of wealthy residences and consulates and government buildings, gives you small glimpses of life in the earliest days of the "open" port. An excellent series of street signs in English clearly directs you to the points of interest, even indicating the distance to the next one.

We inspected the exterior of the Greek Orthodox Church and the Anglican Church which are back to back, walked past the old houses of the district to the former Public Hall, a gracious wooden, Georgian building painted blue-grey with butterscotch trim.

Just below the Public Hall is the Corinthian-styled building—a rare style in Japan—of the former Hokkaido Prefectural Government, now a government tourist office and a small museum recalling the history of the city.

The original Japanese fort-castle built on the site in 1454 looked, from a distance, like a box, hence the name of Hakodate—"Boxed Castle."

The Western world made its first intrusion in 1792 when the Russian ship, *Ekaterina,* became the first foreign ship to anchor in the harbor, part of a Russian demand to open trade relations, a move which was refused, repeated in 1804 and again refused.

In April, 1854 Admiral Matthew Perry, after having signed a friendship pact with Japan, brought an American squadron to the

Hakodate harbor a year later. The residents, petrified of these monsters with large noses, stayed behind closed doors.

The Russians followed in August and established their own friendship treaty.

The prosperity of Hakodate resulted in substantial international trading and an early establishment of foreign consulates. In 1864 the city received 131 foreign ships.

All of this is documented with paintings and photographs of places and people in the little museum.

The morning had almost escaped us. We didn't want to miss the famous Morning Market adjacent to the station where fresh produce is sold so we hurried by taxi to arrive before the morning action was finished.

The two-block area of the Morning Market is a grand canvas of color and action.

Vegetables are sold by bright-eyed, smooth-cheeked, little old ladies who sit on the ground in their allotted squares surrounded by produce both familiar and strange to the overseas visitor: corn, onion, lettuce, mushrooms, tomatoes and daikon, gobe, Chinese cabbage and strange rooted things.

Fruit ran the gamut of citrus, bananas, peaches, pears, black plums, grapes, raspberries—including kiwi fruit from New Zealand.

The fish market section is immense given mostly to the display of silver-sided salmon, glistening in rows, often with a sample fish sliced in half lengthwise to show the firm deep red flesh.

Salmon eggs and salmon parts are part of the displays.

Crab, cuttlefish and seaweed are offered in profusion.

Or you can also buy shoelaces, toothpaste, sweaters, shoes, dresses and tons of white chocolate, a specialty of the area.

After checking the Morning Market off of our list, we moved on to the next *must-do* recommended by our friends in Tokyo: take a horse-drawn covered wagon tour of the city. The tour takes two hours and starts from the east side of the railroad station most afternoons at two o'clock.

We were there.

The wagon held a dozen people. The exuberant elderly guide with rumpled grey hair flowing over his temples and rumpled grey clothes over his thin frame must have come out of Japanese vaudeville. He did a two-hour performance in Japanese. He told jokes, kidded the girls, sang songs as the poor old sagging horse clip-clopped over much of the same ground we had seen that morning.

When the horse did something naughty in the street, the driver would stop the wagon, get out with a broom, clean up the deposit, put it in a bag and drive on.

The Japanese passengers did the same thing they do on all moving vehicles. They went to sleep.

The weather started to turn black. Then it was black. It rained. It poured. Thunder rumbled and lightning flashed. The Japanese slept on. The guide never stopped performing.

Very funny, very wet, very miserable afternoon. But we picked up two sights we had not seen: the foreign cemetery where two sailors from Perry's squadron are buried and the waterfront filled with ships from Hokkaido's fishing fleet.

From the waterfront we could see, close to the shore, a curious, large concrete enclosure. What was it? Later, we were told, it was the first element of the base for an immense bridge which will cross the harbor. Completion date: 1986.

Another project, incredibly daring, is the Seikan Tunnel connecting Matsumae, Hokkaido with Cape Tappizaki. The borethrough of the tunnel, 52 kilometers in length, is completed, but, in 1987, the tunnel was not yet in use.

At breakfast the next morning the proprietor quoted a Japanese saying for the kind of fast-changing weather we were experiencing: "Ladies' hearts and autumn skies."

A new group of co-eds were at breakfast, from a university in Kyoto, members of the Samaritan Guides of Kyoto, and friends of my guides in Kyoto and Nara.

The day before they had gone to Onuma Park, outside of Hakodate, and had had a fun afternoon riding rental bicycles. They missed the rain.

Our Sapporo-Hakodate train had stopped at Onuma Park. We could see the lakes that dominate ninety percent of the park's site and also the winter-time ski lifts. Although a park outing was recommended, we had run out of time, and we still hadn't bought the famous products of Hakodate, Trappist cookies and white chocolate candy.

The college girls were finishing an eleven-day holiday on Hokkaido. (The Japanese travel their own country more thoroughly than any other nationality we know.) They thought each part of Hokkaido was more beautiful than the last.

The most scenic, according to their concensus, was Rishiri Island off the northern tip of Hokkaido.

We put it on our list for the next visit.

Hokkaido is a place you want to go back and explore again and again.

TOHOKU
North of Tokyo

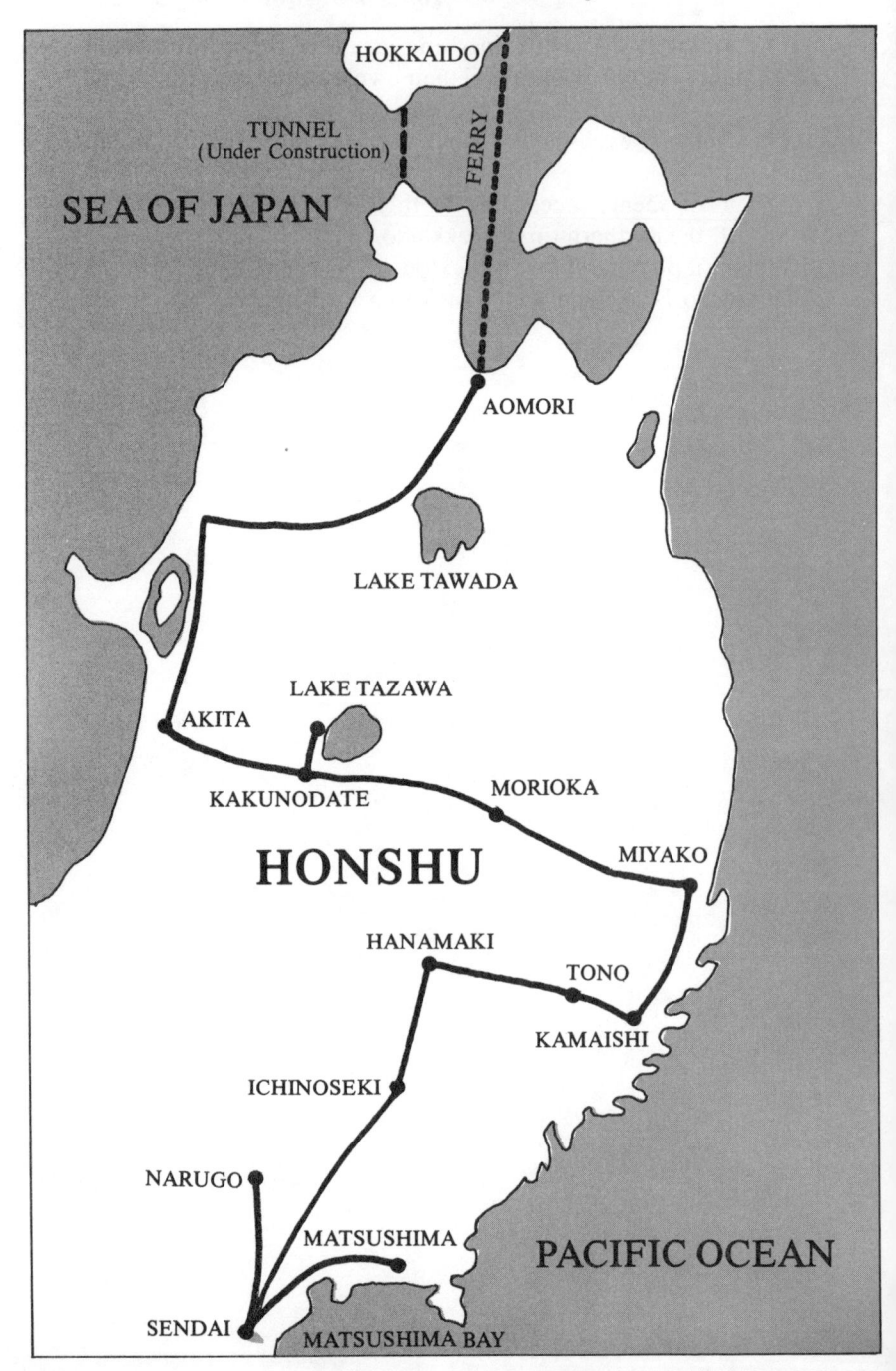

11. North of Tokyo: Tohoku

South of Tokyo is the production muscle of Japan.
North of Tokyo the scene changes. Farmlands replace factories.
A rural atmosphere replaces the industrial city atmosphere.
   Here half a dozen prefectures comprise the Tohoku district, an area with a hint of Scotland. It is a place of beauty: mountains and rivers and pretty lakes and fields of grain—in this case, rice.
   Our game plan was to start at the top and zig-zag from East Coast to West Coast down to Tokyo visiting the ocean towns, the lake towns and the cities that comprise the spine of Tohoku and are connected by the vertebrae of the Bullet Train, bringing these central spine cities within reasonable proximity of Tokyo businessmen and visitors.

   The Tohoku adventure started by taking the government-owned ferry operated by JR from Hakodate to Aomori on the north tip of Honshu, a trip that takes four hours.
   Our Green Car railroad passes were good for reserved seats on the ferry.
   The seats resembled sleeperettes on a first-class section of an airplane, although not as wide, but fully reclinable with extra leg support.
   A Green Car "non-reserved section" was aft and divided into regular seats on one side and slightly elevated bedroom-sized squares on the other where passengers could sit Japanese-style on the floor or stretch out and sleep. Show me a moving vehicle in Japan and I'll show you sleeping Japanese.
   There was a separate enclosed bar between the two sections with deep-cushioned seats.
   The deck below for Ordinary Class was similarly divided. Instead of a bar, there was a cafeteria.
   The reserved Green Car section with a capacity for a hundred passengers was virtually empty. We had a quiet crossing catching up on notes, finishing a difficult Japan Times crossword puzzle and napping.

> Note: the best beer buy in Japan is from a vending machine in the Ordinary Class which sells a large can of Sapporo beer for a dollar.

One of the major attractions in Tohoku is Lake Towada, a popularity attested to at the ferry terminal in Aomori by the number of English directional signs reading: "Bus to Lake Towada." The signs are fortunate because the route to the bus is circuitous: downstairs to a railroad platform, upstairs to another passageway, downstairs to the terminal, outside to the bus station. Killing if you are over-baggaged and lost.

The JNR bus takes three-and-a-half hours to reach Lake Towada, first having to clear the considerable traffic of Aomori, a prosperous port town for shipping and lumber and apples. Four stops en route, at ski resorts and mountain spas, make it an easy, pleasant trip.

The last half hour is one of the most scenically satisfying drives in Japan.

The bus descends into the Oirase Valley and follows the Oirase River to the headwaters at Lake Towada—and it is spectacular.

The river, small by New Zealand standards, is formed by outlet waters from Lake Towada and it bounds and rushes through deep woods and around giant boulders, augmented by frequent waterfalls from surrounding cliffs. It is the poet's idea of the perfect river.

At the little village of Nenokuchi, passengers change busses and proceed along the shore to the larger village of Yasumiya. (Memory clue: "You summoned me, yah?") A hotel bus collected us and drove another fifteen minutes to the Towada Prince Hotel, a first-class hostelry with a first-class kitchen and a first-class location on the lakefront.

It had been a long travelling day. One taxi, one ferry, three busses.

Excellent dinner. Early bed.

The Oirase River had to be explored on foot.

The prettiest part of the river valley can best be appreciated by walking up river from Kumo-no-taki Falls to Nenokuchi.

Reversing our bus routing the next morning we returned to Nenokuchi and went down the Oirase River to Kumo-no-taki Falls, then hiked the 6.3 kilometers back to the lake. "Hike" is the wrong word. Stroll. Meander even.

It was another ideal morning.

Sun filtered through the tall trees to dapple the water, the bushes, the rocks with splashes of soft yellow.

At times the river was a booming, raging torrent of white foam contrasted against the green moss-covered rocks as it tumbled through a steep descent—and then the water would be flowing calmly clearly through a level stretch lapping gently at the pebbled river bank.

Every hundred meters would be another picture-taking vista.

At one point I remember a tree on the opposite bank. Two giant trunks from a single root formed a huge set of Viking horns and between the horns, in the distance, could be seen a small waterfall, shielded by dense ferns, splashing down the mountain.

The well-designed path along the river occasionally crossed the water over wooden bridges. Along the riverbank thoughtfully placed benches encouraged the walker to stop and enjoy the scenery.

It was a hand-holding, smell-the-flowers morning.

Back in Nenokuchi where the river starts and after a lunch of soba noodles, tea and beer, we boarded a twin-hulled lake cruiser to take us back to Yasumiya.

Lake Towada was formed by two volcanoes making a double caldera.

After the first eruption subsided the first lake was formed. A second eruption occurred inside of the first lake and a second caldera was formed. When a wall of the second volcano collapsed, water rushed in from the first lake.

The boat cruises through the blue-green water of the outer volcanic basin and, when it enters the inner caldera, the water changes to a deep-sea blue, reflecting the depth of over three hundred meters.

On the second caldera cliff walls you can see the volcanic crust and beneath the crust the red, iron-oxidized earth of the second eruption.

One tip of the second volcanic rim is swollen like an injured thumb. The swelling was caused by a much smaller third volcano. In the middle of the lake, just below the surface, is the remains of a fourth volcano.

One of the few lake trips we'd recommend.

Yasumiya was preparing for a weekend festival. Pink lanterns separated by garlands of artifical pink flowers were being strung outside the shops. Food-vending booths were being erected alongside the street.

In Yasumiya you should see the museum, the shrine, the famous statues.

The museum is an interesting-but-small science museum with exhibits depicting the development of the lake and descriptions and samples of the local flora and fish and fauna of the area.

In an especially appealing setting, next to the village, the Towada Shrine is guarded by peaceful, herculean trees that look as if they have been arranged by a stage designer, a torii gate and two large metal lanterns. The shrine is on top of a small cliff reached only over primitive steps carved out of the dry, stone-based creek bed.

The ancient wooden structure, grey-weathered, elaborately carved, stands alone, a quiet, spiritual shrine.

At the lakefront, a stroll away from the shrine and the village, are two figures of girls sculpted by Kotaro Takamura (1883-1956), one of Japan's leading poets and sculptors. The women are ample in their proportions, strong, forthright, hardly symbolic of the demure, petite Japanese lady.

Below Lake Towada on the west coast facing the Sea of Japan is the major city of Akita, capital of Akita Prefecture. Our routing was by one taxi, one bus, and two trains and the luggage transfers were making me an old man before my time. The roller on one bag continuously stuck. Another bag constantly keeled over unless the packing was precisely balanced. Joyless.

However, the punctuality of the bus which took us from Yasumiya to our first train, a ride of one hour and ten minutes, gave me happiness.

To keep to the bus schedule, the driver had posted next to the steering wheel ten checkpoints with minute-by-minute arrival times.

> Note: Such enviable punctuality I associate with mental purity, organization of purpose, discipline of objectives, sainthood and a straight ticket to heaven.
>
> The Lady Navigator associates the same punctuality with sterility—both mental and spiritual—blank-blackboard mentality, over-starched collars, too-tight underwear and a greased chute to hell.

Akita and the Kanto Festival

Coming into Akita by train from the north, we saw the largest continual rice planting we had ever seen in Japan, stretching for several level green miles in every direction.

Later we were to learn that the new rice fields were made possible by the reclamation of the giant-sized Hachirogata Lagoon. Before the reclamation, the lagoon consisted of 225 square kilometers of sea water, the largest such body in Japan. By 1975 the reclamation project had filled in twenty-three percent of the lagoon to create fifty square kilometers of new rice paddies.

Akita is known for its food, its spectacular lantern festival, for its craftsmen and for the famous Akita dog.

We saw everything but the dogs. Akita dogs are bred everywhere in Japan but Akita.

After checking into the Akita Castle Hotel, we accompanied Matsue Fujimoto and Kurumi Marunouchi of the prefectural tourist office to the Akita Citizens Market where a visitor is overwhelmed by the wealth of food produced in the area.

About 220 stalls in a great covered hall sell virtually every necessity of life—fish, meat, chicken, vegetables, eggs, fruits and many speciality items.

Over 12,000 people visit the market daily to replenish family larders.

We had never seen such a variety of product from the sea—large fish, tiny fish, pink fish, red fish, salmon, octopus, cuttlefish.

At a stand specializing in dried items we stocked up on almonds and peanuts.

At a vegetable stand we bought a giant-sized nectarine and two succulent peaches and a fresh Sunkist lemon from California at about twice that we pay back home.

The largest eggs cost Y140 for a package of ten.

From the market we went to the "new" Festival Hall, a former bank edifice built in 1909 and given to the city in 1981 for display of items related to the *kanto,* the nuclei of the annual Lantern Festival.

Imagine a forty-foot bamboo pole with multi cross-arms bearing forty-six paper lanters. This is a kanto. The adult version weighs 100 pounds.

During the festival these candle-lit kanto will fill the evening streets as individual men demonstrate their skill in manipulating the kanto. Not only do they hold the kanto aloft on the palm of one hand—that's 100 pounds, remember—but they then demonstrate the technique of passing the pole from the hand to the forehead without assistance and then to the shoulder and then to the hip without losing balance.

Boys of seven begin kanto training with a pole sixteen-feet long weighing ten pounds. Juniors of fifteen graduate to a kanto of sixty pounds. It takes another seven years to hold and manipulate a senior kanto.

Thirty-six kanto festival clubs meet and compete each year. Each club's lanterns bear the club's distinctive symbol.

When the men carry the kanto in the streets in the evening parade, it is said that the swaying lanterns resemble wind blowing through a field of golden rice.

Each kanto is accompanied by a booming drum and a piper which, along with the shouts of the participants, make the Akita Lantern Festival one of Japan's most unusual, spectacular, and popular August events.

Our tour led us to an arts and crafts exhibits hall where the Lady Navigator filled a notebook with shopping ideas and then to a silversmith, one of ten such shops in Akita where approximately fifty silversmiths follow their ancient craft.

Kawabata Street is the nightlife area of Akita. Here bars, restaurants, hostesses, etc. are concentrated.

Among the amusement-entertainment emporiums is the Dai-Ichi Kaikan, a fine restaurant where we sampled the local dishes. For example a dish of mashed white yams mixed with egg yolk and added shoyu. Piquant and delicious.

An outstanding specialty was the *inaniwa udon* noodle dish that came in individual pottery dishes divided into four parts. The four-part pottery is called *tokuri*.

The small cup on the lid held a sauce made of shoyu. The middle section held a mixture of mushrooms and chopped onions which was added to the noodles in the larger, bottom portion. A tasty treat. Oh, yes, the fourth piece of the tokuri is a saucer.

"You are now going to have a true Akita speciality," said Kurumi with the authority of a lady who knows her kitchen. "Actually there are two unusual dishes. One is the *kiritampo*, a chicken stew. The other is *shottsuru*, a fish stew.

"You are going to have kiritampo. We selected this for dinner because the shottsuru can be too strong, smelly, especially when it is made with the hard-finned *hatahata* from the Sea of Japan.

A waitress brought a large glazed bowl filled with special rice, Japanese leaks, mushrooms, carrots, beancurd, and richly seasoned chicken.

The rice was pressed around a cedar stick and barbecued. Lovely food.

Next came tofu. Akitans take pride in their tofu when it is covered with bits of onion and shoyu sauce.

"How do you say 'enough'?"

"*Onaka ippai,*" said our guide.

I said, "Onaka ippai, onaka ippai." It didn't matter. Food continued to arrive. Fresh fruit came. A dessert came. Sake continued to be poured.

You can get over-fed in Akita.

Kyoto of the North

Between Akita, capital of Akita Prefecture and Morioka to the east, capital of Iwate Prefecture, is the village of Kakunodate, known for its samurai houses and cherry blossoms and called the "Little Kyoto of Northeastern Honshu."

Also a half an hour away is Lake Tazawa, the deepest lake in Japan.

Our schedule recommended checking into the Ishikawa Ryokan, leaving our luggage, using our rail passes to go to Tazawako and then taxiing to the lake.

It was a hot September Sunday afternoon and, after following instructions, we found our lakeside destination filled with tour busses, taxis, motorcycles and family cars. Sunday by the lake is popular.

Groups took turns having their pictures snapped against a sign reading: "Lake Tazawa—426 Meters."

The restaurants were overflowing, and the lake was covered with foot-pedal-powered boats that came in the shape of swans, helicopters and multi-colored canvas-topped boats that looked like floating ice cream stalls.

There was a scattering of wind surfers, water skiers and the constant buzz of self-propelled water sleds.

Occasionally, cruise ships took off for hour and a half round-trip crossings of the lake, an experience we missed because our scheduled crossing was sold out. It didn't dent our morale. With rare exceptions lake crossings produce little exciting copy unless the ship catches fire or is boarded by pirates or sinks with the loss of all hands except those of the reporter and his navigator.

When we cruised Lake Akan in Hokkaido, we passed the time playing a "I-can-recall" game: "Parades We Saw Together."

On another cruise we played, "Rivers We Have Cruised, Swum or Rafted."

Try it the next time you cross a lake.

Back in quiet Kakunodate, walking the streets, looking at old houses, we agreed that the time would have been better spent enjoying "Little Kyoto" rather than take half a day, two train rides, and two taxi rides to see the deepest lake in Japan.

Kakunodate (memory clue: "Mr. Kaku doesn't have the dates.") was a castle town in the seventh century, protected on three sides by hills.

The local feudal lord was also protected by a band of loyal samurai who lived on the north of the town on a wide tree-canopied avenue. At the time the village was founded in 1620, there were eighty samurai in residence.

The southside of town was reserved for merchant shops estimated to be around 350 in the seventeenth century . . . . and it still looks to be the same size.

A bustling community.

The avenue of trees in the samurai quarter still exists as do a half a dozen of the classic residences preserved as a major visitor attraction.

The residences are expansive but simple. The Edo Period style was simple. Tatami-matted floors. Shoji doors. Uncluttered. Only in the carvings of the eaves or the wall screens were art forms more complex.

At the far end of the avenue three small buildings comprise a museum, preserving a potpourri of memoribilia from different eras—old phonograph players and posters to handsome samurai swords.

Elsewhere in town old treasury houses or store houses, *kura,* with bank-vault windows, peaked roofs and thick, solid, white-washed walls posed in the sun for the photographer.

In the spring Kakunodate is a beauty spot of blossoming cherry trees. Some 150 graceful cherry blossom trees are protected as "precious national products" by the government.

During our strolling we were witness to the feverish activity of the townspeople getting ready for their harvest festival less than a week away.

Lights and paper lanterns were being strung along the street, fake flower bouquets hung from the eaves in front of shops.

At the main intersection and also at the main shrine, giant *yama* or mountains were being created out of scaffolding and cloth. The simulated mountains would hold life-sized kabuki figures during the festival.

Our curiousity was aroused by the unusual floats being prepared. Strong timbered structures, rolling on small, wooden wheels, also decorated with simulated mountains and kubuki figures were being made ready.

"Ready for what?"

"Ready for battle!"

At the height of the festival some fifteen floats would meet in individual head-on combat on the samurai avenue.

The float that pushed the other float back or, better still, toppled it over would be the winner.

Another festival to put on the list.

A ryokan stay was in keeping with the Kakunodate experience. The Ishikawa Ryokan lived up to—even surpassed—our expectations.

We had the second floor of an isolated wing to ourselves with a ten-tatami room, tastefully decorated and traditionally furnished.

Next door, behind shoji doors, a six-tatami room served as our bedroom after the maid laid out the futons and covers for sleeping.

Across the hall was a lounge—a room we never used—with Western-style table and chairs. Around the corner, a private toilet, Japanese style—with toilet slippers—and a washbasin.

Bathing took place downstairs. A tiled shower room was used for the ritual preparation of the deep furo in which we soaked until we were spaghetti-weak.

Dinner was served in our air-conditioned sit-on-the-floor room by our maid Emiko—she had the demeanor of a saint and the hands of a ballet dancer. Each dish was served on a porcelain plate or in a pottery bowl of harmonizing colors, shapes and textures, the food dictating the type of dish used. Dining in Japan is an exercise appealing to all the senses.

Emiko-san's table was a tableau of art.

Among the memorable dishes were kiritampo, the dish we had in Akita, and probably the best miso soup in Japan and a wonderful serving of eggplant, *nasu,* stuffed with mushrooms, miso, onions, garlic, chicken skin, seasoned and fried in salad oil.

Fantastic.

Ishikawa Ryokan is operated by Hitoshi Ishikawa, a constantly grinning, bowing, eager, nervous host who bounds around serving guests to the ultimate, even to crossing your shoelaces neatly after you have changed into house slippers at the inn's entrance.

His family has operated the inn for over one hundred years.

The Lady Navigator gave it five stars for cleanliness, including an impeccable, clean-smelling bathroom. At Y15,000 a day, including breakfast and dinner for two, it was a "best" buy.

(Emiko refused my proferred thousand yen note. I did it wrong just trying to hand it to her. I should have placed the bill in a white envelope and unobtrusively left it for her to find.)

Morioka, Soba Stuffing and Sake Sipping

Morioka is a pleasant city and a "spine" city on the Bullet Train track.

It is an important city, too, as the economic center of the surrounding agricultural country and as capital of the Iwate Prefecture with a population over 200,000.

We stayed at the Morioka Grand Hotel with the advantage of having a large junior-suite overlooking the city and the disadvantage of being a taxi trip from the middle of town action where taxis are not easy to find.

The excellent staff provided us with a hand-drawn xeroxed map of the city with the names of places of interest keyed to numbers, including *three antique shops.*

Whoosh, the Lady Navigator pulled a brush through her hair and flew out the door before the girl bellboys (bellgirls?) had set down the luggage.

I played notebook catch-up.

At mid-afternoon the telephone rang. It was Yoshimasa Taguchi of the city's tourism section and a friend of a friend in Tokyo.

He said in halting English, "I will be at your hotel at four o'clock and take you to a sunset dance."

Sunset dance?

Promptly at four o'clock Mr. Taguchi, a slight nice looking young man drove into the porte cochere of the hotel.

"I will take you to a coffeehouse. My favorite."

Evidently I had misunderstood what he had said about a sunset dance.

He parked by an old building, two stories high. "This building is two hundred years old. Its architectural style is known as kura. Just like you've seen in Kyoto," said Mr. Taguchi.

Downstairs was an art gallery. Upstairs at long tables and round tables, people were reading books, writing papers, talking animatedly. A menu on a wooden paddle was offered, and we ordered iced coffee.

Mr. Taguchi pulled a clutch of colored pamphlets and maps from a briefcase describing and depicting Morioka in Japanese and in English.

"The coffeehouse is called Issaryos and is on Kaminohashi Street, just over the bridge," he said pointing it out on a map.

"Thanks" I said. "I need your advice and recommendations. Our schedule tomorrow calls for a city sightseeing tour at mid-morning to see the Prefectural Museum, a cattle-stock farm far out in the country, Lake Gosho, Hara Takashi Memorial Hall, the Nambu Iron Factory, the Iwayama Observatory, the castle ruins and a park." I paused. "And more. The tour doesn't end until five in the afternoon, and that means six and a half hours of a guide's non-stop Japanese monologue. I don't won't to do that."

Over iced coffee we changed the bus tour to a hired car with driver-guide and four stops in three hours. Much better.

"What about the famous cherry tree that has split the boulder which I have read so much about. Where is that?" I asked.

Mr. Taguchi looked at his watch.

"I'll take you by it on our way out into the country. Come."

Out in the country?

We passed the cherry tree called Ishiwari-Zakura, or stone-breaking cherry tree, growing out of a gigantic block of granite in front of the district courthouse.

"It is three-thousand years old," said Mr. Taguchi.

As we drove we talked about tennis (he was taking lessons),

about music (he played the guitar and sang in a band), and about summo wrestling (he was lacking about two hundred pounds to qualify for summo). Mr. Taguchi had graduated from the highly respected Waseda University in Tokyo—very impressive for a boy from a village an hours drive from Morioka.

By now we were in rice field country and Mr. Taguchi turned off the highway into a side road.

"The dancing is at a very small, very old temple near here."

We were going to a sunset dance after all!

"The *sansa* dancers are all farmers and their families who live in the area around here."

"SANSA" not sunset.

"During the August festival there will be ten thousand dancers parading through the streets of Morioka."

He parked near a small temple tucked into a small grove of trees with nothing else in the vicinity but rice fields. The exciting, rhythmic beat of many drums could be heard.

We walked up to the weather-greyed building.

What a delightful spectacle.

In the temple yard more than twenty colorfully costumed drummers, mostly men, were dancing in a circle beating their drums, rotating around an inner circle of fifteen dancing ladies who were similarly robed.

They wore red hats resembling royal crowns, white robes sashed with multi colors that trailed a rainbow of ribbons, black gauntlets on their hands, and white tabi socks and straw slippers on the feet.

Friends and family stood in the background applauding the dancers.

The temple was piled high with gifts: bags of rice and bottles of sake. During one break in the dancing a pile of envelopes containing contributions was acknowledged one by one.

At another intermission, a styrofoam cooler was placed in the middle of the circle and the anciently garbed dancers refreshed themselves with Coca Cola and Sprite.

"Sometimes they dance until midnight, and then they drink sake. They know about fifty dances. I only know about two."

Flimsy bamboo side booths gave a carnival atmosphere to the small village festival: barbecued meat sticks, cakes, candy, pastries, flavored shaved ice, sticky candy floss, and toys—lots of toys—and tiny goldfish which the tiny new owners proudly took away in plastic bags half-filled with water.

The sunset was almost gone and we had to leave.

A colorful, joyous experience.

Our next rendezvous with Mr. Taguchi was for a *wankosoba* lunch at Azumaya Soba on Nakanohashi Street (upstairs) where people play an eating game which we dubbed "Piggin' Out On Noodles."

You sit on zabutons and are tied into a bib and served a cup of tea, a towel to cleanse your hands and half a dozen bowls of delicious condiments. Chopped walnuts. Mushrooms. Fried chicken skin bits. Grated radish. Seaweed. Pickled vegetables.

Malicious, mischievous, sadistic waitresses bring a box of matches, empty the matches off to one side of each diner. A bowl containing a bite-size of noodles is placed in front of you and a waitress stands beside you with a tray full of bowls containing more noodles.

The game is to see how many bowls of noodles you can consume.

As soon as you finish one bowl, you move a matchstick over from one side to the other to keep count and the waitress quickly empties another bite-size amount from her tray of noodles into your bowl.

You are advised in the English instruction pamphlet to go lightly with the condiments. Interferes with the volume, you are told.

Soon it becomes clear that there is another game. It is between you and the waitress. The rules are that you must finish your bowl of noodles, and the only way to stop is to place the lid on the bowl. It is not that simple.

You can't say "Enough" because the waitress will continue to fill your bowl. Before you can get the lid on the bowl, she has deftly put in another portion of noodles.

She has had years of practice. You are an amateur.

You weep with laughter. You get more noodles. You cry for mercy. You get more noodles.

The whole restaurant is watching you. Laughing.

I finally managed to get the bowl and lid underneath my nose and, with a last scoop of the chopsticks, get the lid on as the waitress put the last portion in my lap.

I finished at twenty-two bowls. The Lady Navigator at a puny thirteen. Our host had twenty-eight.

Later in the afternoon an English-speaking tennis player told me his average was fifty. The record in the restaurant is a hundred and fifty.

This style of eating wankosoba is more than a tourist gimmick. Most tourists never find wankosoba.

The tradition goes back to a time when the country was poor and the only decent food of the farmer was a buckwheat noodle (soba).

The most gracious sign of hospitality was to stuff a visitor with bowl after bowl of wankosoba even though the guest tried to stop the serving. Thus was the tradition of the game was born.

Today the locals go maybe once or twice a year, the tennis player said, especially when they have visitors in town.

We didn't take the hired car either.

We took a day off instead. The Lady Navigator went back on the Great Antique Hunt. I walked the neat city . . . . Iwate Park in the center, formerly the site of the local castle . . . . the department stores, especially the basements. Later I played tennis and even had a nap.

Loved Morioka.

That night we went to an old country inn, Nanbu-Robata, in the entertainment district of Hachiman-cho where in a large, darkly panelled, smokey room we sat around the edges of a large, low stage with the firepit in the middle attended by a comely, kimono-clad maiden who served sake in lacquerware buckets.

I don't recall what we ate and the scribble in my notebook is undecipherable but I know we drank unrefined sake—white sake—*doburoku or nigori zake*—also called "White Horse"—in copious amounts.

The next morning I felt like the cherry tree was growing out of my split skull.

Avoid white sake.

One of the well known local dishes in Morioka is *nambu-hittsumi*, a grain-and-chicken stew. We were told one of the best places for the dish is the restaurant Tanaka in the shopping-restaurant complex underneath the railroad station.

Miyako on the Pacific

The first local train from Morioka to the east coast fishing center of Miyako leaves at 9:10 A.M. and takes almost two and a half hours, stopping at every little hamlet on the way. The rustic wooden stations make you think that you are on a country line in a Russian province.

The train windows are open in the late summer, and fishermen and farmers, coming home from a big night in the big city, are sprawled across seats drinking beer and hot tea and smoking cigarettes.

At Miyako we took a taxi out to the local harbor and the small Funaki Hotel, across the street from the wholesale fish market and surrounded by fish processing plants.

The odor left no doubt about our location.

However the principal tourist activity in the area is a visit to Rikuchu Coast National Park, a seacoast park of unique beauty where sea-eroded cliffs poke white limestone fingers from a jagged hand into the ocean. It is a short ride from the Funaki.

Our taxi driver, solemn-faced, English-less, took us to the center, let us out, then got out himself and preceded us to the ticket window to make sure the boats were operating and that we bought the correct tickets. It happens all of the time.

We ate ramen noodles from a counter, and then walked down to the ocean and along a paved-path shoreline to the dock and boarded our cruise boat just as the first drop of rain splat on the deck.

As the ship left the dock the drops of rain turned to a sprinkle, then a drizzle and finally a full throttle deluge. We saw the Rikuchu Coast Park and the cliffs and beaches through a curtain of water. The famed Jodogahama ("Joe, give that dog a hammer.") Beach was an empty dismal sight in the rain, save for the colorful umbrellas.

By the time we returned to the hotel the rain had stopped, and I walked down to the boat-filled harbor, now empty of people.

Fishing harbors are eye-pleasing, spirit-lifting havens for the painter or poet. The variety of boats, their shapes, their honestly earned scars and colors are satisfying to inspect. And fishing has a romantic appeal to it even though you know, in reality, it is a tough, demanding, stinking, dangerous business.

At the little harbor I could see the gradation of boats.

Beached were the comparatively small, open boats propelled by Yamaha outboard engines and wrapped in rain-wet canvas.

Out in the harbor riding at anchor were larger wooden boats with enclosed cabins.

Across the harbor at dockside were rows of metal-hulled, deep-sea fishing ships which roam international waters to bring home frozen catches to the processing plants of Miyako.

That night the dinner served in our room included ten different kinds of fish. All guaranteed fresh.

At breakfast I became aware of another Japanese touring custom.

The breakfast was served on ankle-high floor-trays in a large, tatami-matted banquet room. There must have been over a hundred places set.

But in the floor plan of the hotel I had counted only thirty-seven rooms.

During my walk the night before I had counted at least ten small tour busses at the hotel.

The conclusion was obvious and correct. Passengers on Japanese tours sleep family style, i.e. several to a room. (That's one way to meet new people.) However, JTB does not do that with overseas visitors who also pay the difference for being exclusive.

Breakfast, on the standard Japanese menu, included a raw egg whipped with chopsticks into a tablespoon of shoyu and poured over a bowl of rice. I was beginning to like it.

The Legends of Tono

Between the coast cities of Japan and the spine cities that run up the middle of the country, there are many remote, isolated mountain villages with a special flavor and old-time appeal of their own.

One of these is Tono, advertised as "the home town of Japan", which we reached by train, first going down the coast to Kamaishi and then cutting inland. Tono lies halfway betwen Kamaishi and Hanamaki, a spine city.

The reputation of Tono is enhanced by a famous book called *The Legends of Tono* by Kunio Yanagida (1910) in which the stories of the mountain people are recorded. The emphasis of the legends centers on their animistic belief that all things of nature—

stones, trees, animals—contain spirits.

For example, the horse in old-time Tono was highly prized and in some instances worshipped. One of the most famous stories in *The Legends* concerns a young girl in love with the family's white horse. The father learns of the love and kills the horse. But the girl marries the reincarnated animal and they go to heaven.

Symbols of the horse and the girl together are found throughout Tono. A motion picture was made about the legend.

The horse in Tono lived under the same roof as the family in a structure called a *magariya,* an ell-shaped building with the horse stabled in one wing.

We checked into the tourist section of the village government, always a good place to go for information. In the tourist section in almost every city the visitor can count on finding a fresh university graduate who speaks English and who can give advice and help.

We arrived in Tono at noon and conferred with the tourist chief and a pretty interpreter, Rumiko Tada.

Rumiko was not a recent graduate but a recent bride married to a man from the district a couple of years younger than herself— unusual. She had worked as an interpreter guide for the Mellon Bank in Tokyo earlier and was another in our collection of sparkling, adorable Japanese ladies.

Our new friends took us to the Yoshinoya Restaurant for a local specialty, *hitsuki soba.*

A stack of four bowls was brought to each person. The top bowl contained condiments: onion, chicken bits, mushrooms and seaweed. The other three bowls held soba noodles.

To the side was a raw egg to be broken into a mixture of shoyu, water and sake and whipped with chopsticks and then poured over each bowl of noodles as it was consumed. Included with the lunch was a bowl of miso soup and a bowl of rice to assure the visitor that starvation was not a threat.

Another *oishii* meal.

From our companions we learned that Tono has 250,000 visitors a year who come mostly in the summer for climbing, fishing for rainbow trout, camping. Most of the young people see Tono on a rented bicycle—$2 a day.

Eight hotels and ten minshuku take care of the tourists. Our bed was to be at the Minshuku Magariya, the best of the minshukus, we were told, five minutes by car from the station.

The newest hotel in Tono is the Suikoen, a government sponsored hotel on the outlying hills of town where we went after lunch. The hotel has only eleven private guestrooms but accommodations—several large tatami-matted rooms each with the sleeping capacity of thirty—for over two hundred.

The foothill location of the hotel is also the source of the city's water supply. The hotel gardens feature a profusion of waterfalls, bubbling brooks, fountains and ponds.

Several buildings comprise the complex which is really half hotel and half museum and tourist attraction.

All of the walls are filled with folk art treasures, the likes of which lighted the Lady Navigator's greedy eyes.

From this "half" museum we went to a full museum in the middle of the city. The Tono Museum has a full display of historical objects, folk craft—the girl and the horse appear as dolls, in paintings, in films—agricultural tools of yesteryear.

A major highlight for us was a venerable collection of horse votives painted by farmers for placement in shrines to bring good luck and perhaps eternal life to their cherished animal. The sophisticated lines and colors of the horses were quite incredible.

Another highlight was a charming, wide-screen, cartoon-slide presentation of three *Legends of Tono,* all done with local talent and backed with haunting music.

The "heritage museum" on the outskirts of town, Denshoen Park, is a magariya which has been moved from a distant valley and restored.

In the ell of the farmhouse is an indoor oven—an *umagama* or. "horse stove"—a four-foot tall bowl of clay which provided heat to the freezing barn in the winter and hot water for the animals and family.

Every Sunday a grandmother comes to the park to recall the folklore of her earlier days for children and visitors.

Next to the restored magariya is a workshop where village women work at old-time crafts.

The purpose of the park is to keep old traditions alive in a valley which still has about one hundred magariya. However, thirty of the classic buildings are unoccupied and unless an active program is set in motion there could come a day when the magariya would be only a memory.

The Minshuku Magariya, our abode, was on the side of a hill in the middle of an apple orchard, rich with ripe fruit. Intermittent shotgun shells were set off around the orchard to keep the bears back in the mountains and away from the apples.

Our tatami-matted room was large and private. (We suspect that JTB books the largest, nicest rooms for overseas visitors.) "Facilities" were down the hall.

The room was also known for *azashiki warashi,* a boy-child spirit whose patter of little feet could be heard in the night but who was never seen.

Meals were served in the main room on a long low table that backed up to the smoky *irori* (firepit) that was always burning, giving the air a smell of wooden incense.

Our ten table companions were all university students from Tokyo, half boys and half girls. (Girls speak better English than boys.)

After dinner the atmosphere of the *Legends of Tono* was recreated by a local author/storyteller. He sat with his back to the wall on the other side of the irori, poked occasionally at the fire with a stick and recounted the tales.

Dressed in a white western shirt and a short jacket, calm of face and easy of manner, the middle-aged writer had the captivating magic of a consummate storyteller.

He wore a slightly amused expression but not a superior smile on his face. With one leg propped before him, he used the knee as a fulcrum for an arm whose hand was used to illustrate the story with small, orchestrated gestures.

The university students sat enthralled.

His legendary stories reflected the basic animistic spiritual backbone of a farming community, largely shut-off from the rest of the world where the fears of the inhabitants were relieved or kindled by the creation of good and evil spirits, the spirits taking many forms.

The storyteller continued his spinning of legends in Japanese but I sneaked back to my room and fell asleep, twitching slightly at the periodic sounds of exploding shotguns, listening for the patter of little feet, fighting off bears and dreaming of our daughters marrying white horses.

The next morning we climbed a mountain creek bed where we

saw a few of the five hundred faces a Shinto priest carved into river boulders in memory of the many victims of a long-ago famine.

We visited the largest "working" magariya in the area whose builder once owned all of the land in the expansive valley. The treasury-storehouse on the property was large—three windows— and on display there were samples of its treasures: fabulous lacquerwear bought by the rich farmer who didn't have anything else on which to spend his money.

For the Lady Navigator the village of Tono was memorable because Rumiko found for her a loot-loaded antique store.

Do you know the most disgusted look in the world? It is the one a wife gives a husband after she has bought a second-hand iron cookie mold to make Japanese pasteries filled with black bean paste in the shape of a lotus leaf, and he asks, in all innocence, "What are you going to do with it?"

Rumiko thought the whole antique antic hilarious.

At the station Rumiko, by now as dear as a daughter, gave us a carton of local goodies to eat on the train. We gave her candy from Hokkaido. She cried. We cried.

It was getting to be a habit.

Hanamaki: The Poet, The Sculptor, The Spa

Hanamaki, a spine city on the Bullet Train line, is a small city of 70,000 but popular with visitors who come to bathe in several spas in the western foothills.

Also it was the birthplace and workplace of a most unusual person, a true renaissance man, who, while teaching agriculture at the local high schol, gained fame as a poet, a composer, an astronomer, a fine artist, an illustrator of children's books, and a confidant of young people.

His name was Kenji Miyazawa and he lived only thirty-seven years, (1896-1933) burned out, it is implied, by trying to cram several lives into the space of one.

When I first saw his photograph, I thought him a terribly homely man. (He was.) But when I had concluded a tour through his museum, the same photograph conveyed the spirit of a saint.

The museum dedicated to Miyazawa is a handsome, modern edifice, located on a wooded, idyllic hilltop overlooking the city.

The exhibits devoted to the life of this remarkable man are substantial—unfortunately all of the written material is in kanji.

Shown are his cartoon stories with the whimsy and the humor of a Disney, manuscripts of his music, films of symphony orchestras playing his music, books he wrote, stars he studied, children's books he illustrated.

Miyazawa went to Tokyo when he was a young man to become a writer but the death of his sister brought him back to his home in Hanamaki.

His creativeness and curiosity were twin fires. He ceaselessly produced works covering many art forms and at the same time poured himself into diverse studies: Zen Buddhism, organ and cello, astronomy, Esperanto and typing, mathematics and calligraphy.

His poetry gained international recognition, and, besides his own volumes, international poetry anthologies included translations of his work in English, Italian, German, Swedish, among others.

"Twigs of a ginko still reflecting
Cypress blacker and blacker
Sparks of a cloud pour down."

With all his multi-interests and accomplishments, his life was really dedicated to helping his farmer friends improve their crops and being a compassionate counselor and advisor to young students.

A most unusual man.

In the foothills surrounded by rice fields there are handsome new houses everywhere. Our guide said, "Farmers make much money." Obviously.

In contrast to the upper-income housing of the farmers, we went to a small, lonely cottage in the woods, the *atelier* of Kotaro Takamura, sculptor of the two robust women on the shore of Lake Towada.

The humble, simple, one-room cottage was his creative nest for many years. He lived here through the Tibetan-cold winters. In summers he would go to sweltering Tokyo. A man made for suffering.

His rustic abode, now a national treasure, is enclosed in a protective, encompassing building. Inside, a second enclosure of glass wards off the damaging hands of visitors.

One of the principle spas in the area is the Hotel Hanamaki which, together with the surrounding hostelries, is owned by the Osano family, who also owns the Sheraton-managed hotels in Waikiki and Maui as well as San Francisco and Los Angeles, among a host of other leisure-industry properties.

Quiet by day, the popular Hanamaki spa is the nesting place for evening tour busses that arrive as the sun sets. The safety whistling by the hostesses as the busses back into parking places sound like birds coming home to nest.

Next to Hotel Hanamaki is the Ryokan Kasho-en—a delightful and quite expensive Japanese inn whose monied Japanese clientele wouldn't be seen near a tour bus.

The ryokan is not a rustic, old-fashioned inn but a new building with much polished wood and glass and green lawn and tasteful furnishings throughout. Very posh.

From the inn a twenty-minute walk takes the guest alongside a nearby river and a five-star waterfall.

We had a major domo who smothered us with attention.

He took us to our Japanese-style room with the sound of the river in near proximity, and only after he had the maid serve tea did he produce registration forms for us to fill out.

He then took details for dinner and breakfast times, and the time to have a taxi at the door the next morning for our departure.

When we took a walk, he was there to point the direction.

When we had dinner, he sat kneeling anxiously through four of the thirteen dishes like a worried father.

When I pointed out what to me was a new vegetable, he said something I didn't understand in Japanese and finally, after a pause, his face lit up and he said, "Pop ai. Pop ai."

What?

"Pop ai," he repeated and then flexed his arms to indicate he had muscles, "Pop ai."

Popeye! Spinach! Of course.

The next morning at the appointed hour for breakfast, he was back to clarify that breakfast was not served in the room but downstairs. He looked at my yukata disapprovingly. His expression said, "that won't do", and he hastily rearranged my robe to the correct Japanese code. He pulled the collar back off the nape of the neck. He straightened the edge of the robe into a perfectly straight perpendicular line. He retied the sash into the acceptable knot. He stepped back and inspected his work, gave a short nod of approval and only then did he lead his properly dressed children down to breakfast.

At departure, he was beside the taxi along with three others to bow us farewell until we were out of sight.

Can you imagine that happening anywhere else in the world? And it happens all the time in Japan.

Ichinoseki and The Golden Hall

We came down the spine of the Bullet Train to Ichinoseki, and a ryokan with funny memories.

(Ichinoseki memory clue: "I have an itchy, dry nose." French for dry is *sec*. Sorry.)

Our written itinerary informed us that to reach the Takemoto Ryokan we only had to walk two minutes from the station.

Two minutes in which direction when it is raining?

How far is two minutes when you are over-loaded, over-bagged and your companion is carrying an iron gismo which will make Japanese pastries filled with bean paste in the shape of lotus leaves?

It's too far, that's how far it is.

The taxi driver laughed when we showed him our itinerary with the kanji name of our inn, pointed down the street, indicating that it was very close—but also indicating that he would take us if we wanted. For $3, we wanted.

The ryokan, it turned out, was less than 300 meters away, and the taxi driver was almost rolling in the street when he delivered us.

No matter. As I told the Lady Navigator, we would walk back to the station the next morning for our departure which would break down to 75¢ per person for each leg of the transportation.

She said I had gravel in my budget brain.

Ichinoseki is the starting point for a host of unusual attractions within half an hour of the city, the most famous being Konjikido, a small, black lacquered structure containing three altars elaborately decorated with much gold and inlaid mother-of-pearl.

To tour the area, you can take a city-operated sightseeing bus to four important attractions.

The cost is Y2,100 plus the admission fees and transportation back to the city because the tour terminates at the Chusonji Temple, site of the Konjikido, half an hour away from the city.

We were on the bus promptly at 13:05, just as the instruction sheet scheduled, clutching our luncheon sandwiches and picnicked on the way to Gembikei Gorge, our first stop.

The scene is spectacular. The river gushes in a torrent of water through a giant, narrow canyon of bare boulders and is fringed with thousands of Japanese tourists taking pictures of each other.

A safety line marks the edge of the canyon. To the Japanese photographer the line is a challenge, and he is constantly sending his subjects beyond the line to get a better shot. The number of lost wives who took one step too many backward is not recorded.

The second stop is at a temple where a giant face of a Buddhist spirit is carved on the side of a cliff.

The third stop is at the Motsuji Temple.

To appreciate Motsuji you have to go through a mental timeframe change and use all of your imagination.

Cast yourself back to the pre-Edo Period of the twelfth century when the Fujiwara family dominated the district and built here one of the most splendid, flourishing groups of temples of the time.

Imagine how exciting it must have been. The elaborate temples exquisitely carved and lacquered, the attendant priests and servants, the nobles gorgeously robed. The smell of temple incense would have filled the air. The temple drums sounding their rhythmic cadence. What a tableau.

The buildings have long since been destroyed by fire. What still remains are the garden grounds and paths connecting the former temples. On a small lake float two boats with dragon heads, the last vestige of the playthings of the feudal lords of the Fujiwara family.

The Motsuji Temple was only one of the family's ambitious temple projects. Not far away is the Chusonji Temple built on a wooded hill that at one time held more than forty buildings on its hilltop domain. All have been destroyed by fire with the exception of the Konjikido and another small building holding Buddhist sutras.

Our instructions indicated that the Konjikido was a five minute walk up the hill from the village of Hiraizumi where the bus left us off. Make it a puffing twenty minutes.

But through the woods and past other buildings erected since the Fujiwara time, past lookouts over the countryside, through lanes that wander through the forests, Chusonji is a place to spend much or little time.

Its treasure is imprisoned in a white, modern concrete cellblock. The Konjikido—the Golden Hall—is very small, only 5.5 meters square. The exterior encasement is black lacquered, originally leafed with gold. The main pillars are inlaid with mother-of-pearl.

The inner chamber holds the three altars where, on each altar, there are eleven symbols of Buddha. Underneath the main altar lie the remains of three rulers of the Fujiwara family.

Konjikido's strikingly elaborate decoration is what makes it a "National Treasure."

It takes five minutes to walk down the hill.

We were back in the city by four o'clock thanks to one of the Japanese passengers on our bus who politely told us during the tour—in English—how much time we had at each stop.

After descending the hill of Chusonji, he sought us out and pulled us out of a local bus line and took us around the corner to the express bus stop.

Back in Ichinoseki when we parted at the train station where the express bus stopped, he said, "I hope you have a good voyage."

"We will," the Lady Navigator said, "because people like you always help us."

That night at the Ryokan Takemoto, our thoughtful hosts served us only a small portion of sashimi, which the Lady Navigator appropriated and devoured, and two large portions of the best, rarest, juiciest steak we had in Japan.

The next morning six members of the family bowed us out the door, watching and bowing as we rolled our bags down the street to the station to catch the train for Sendai, a short distance to the south. It was the biggest send-off we had for the most ignominious exit.

Sendai and the One-Eyed Dragon

Sendai is a major city, capital of Miyagi Prefecture, with a population of over half a million.

Flattened during the war, the city has been rebuilt with wide, tree-lined, gridded streets, modern buildings, covered shopping malls and much industry.

It could be just another big, modern city to an overseas visitor but for three Americans who teach in Sendai. They decided to share their discoveries of their adopted hometown's many attractions in a book in English entitled *In and Around Sendai,* an easy-to-read guide book.

Included in the book is practical information, a calendar of events, places of interest in Sendai and the surrounding district, facts, history, restaurants, hotels, even an explanation—but no recommendations—of love hotels.

Like Ruth Steven's book on Kanazawa, it is a fine reference piece to increase greatly the pleasure of a visitor. Also like the Steven's book, we were told that it is easier to buy in Tokyo than in Sendai.

We were lucky in that we were given a copy by the management of the Hotel Sendai Plaza—fine people.

With the amount of territory we had to cover in such a short time, we were fortunate in having help from prefectural people in both Sendai and the Yamagata Prefecture which we toured following Sendai.

It was Sunday when we arrive at Sendai Station. A stocky, bespectacled young man, Shiro Nakano, holding up a placard with our name on it, met us at the train exit. His driver took over our luggage. Shiro took over our lives. We were so grateful.

First we huddled over a bowl of noodles and agreed on an itinerary that included cruising, temple-museum-castle hopping, a tour of the hill country and craft shopping.

Our first objective, as it is for most visitors to Sendai, was to take a boat trip on the nearby scenic bay of Matsushima, one of the "Scenic Trios" of Japan. (The other two are the floating temple and torii at the Itsukushima Island near Hiroshima, and Amanohashidate, in the middle of Honshu facing the Sea of Japan, which is a sandbar appreciated, the guide books say, if you look at it through your legs. We caught the first; missed the second.)

The fishing port of Shiogama is about thirty kilometers east of Sendai, the departure point for the tour boats.

One sight, on the way, was a Buddhist priest in traditional black and white robes wearing a white crash helmet as he maneuvered a black Honda motorcycle through city traffic.

Another sight was the blinding action of the Lady Navigator who spotted an antique store, talked Shiro into stopping, spent two minutes buying a lacquered soba soup pot and a lacquered cake bowl. Which we badly needed.

Pierside at Shiogama we boarded a cruise boat decorated to look like a peacock—the entire bow was a peacock's head and the rest of the ship had painted peacock feathers as a motif. Later, cruising the bay, we saw ships resembling dragons and viking ships, and I was reminded of the pirate junk-cruisers I saw at Lake Hakone. Masquerading is a thing in Japanese cruise boat promotion.

The boat trip from Shiogama through the Matsushima Bay to the resort-shrine village of Matsushima takes one hour. The charm of the cruise is the 260 small islands that dot the bay, carved by the waves and currents into many strange shapes with caves, see-through arches and tunnels.

The white sandstone walls of the islands are topped with tufts of grass and stunted pine trees, wind-twisted and contorted, all most scenic and camera-grabbing.

What makes Matsushima so famous? The reputation comes from the harmony, the blending of island and water and sky. Its beauty is different but not less inspiring in rain or snow, sun or fog.

Matsushima means pine island. *Matsu*—pine. *Shima*—island.

With our host's help we reviewed Japanese names related to water: *wan* is bay, *ko* is lake, *minato* is port, *umi* is ocean, *kawa* is river.

Adjacent to the pier at Matsushima is the tiny temple of Godaido on a picture-postcard island jutting into the bay. Two short, arched, red-lacquered bridges connect the island to the mainland.

The wooden temple, guarded by pine trees, wears a patina of soft ocean-weathered grey. Carved under the eaves of the roof are the twelve symbols of the Chinese zodiac. The rat designates the north point, followed by the cow and the tiger. The rabbit is at the east point followed by the dragon and the snake. The horse marks the south point with the sheep and the monkey leading to the cock at the west point. The dog and the boar bring you back to the rat.

Behind the beach is the important temple of Zuiganji founded in

828 A.D. at a time when the followers lived in caves carved out of cliffs. (There was even a jail for bad Buddhists.)

The present temple was erected by Masamune Date, the fierce "One-Eyed Dragon" and the great lord of the surrounding lands and the leading character in North Honshu's history in the seventeenth century.

He held court in the Peacock Room of the temple where, behind sliding screens, a small troop of faithful samurai stood guard over their master. One door allowed Masamune to escape to the protection of his warriors if need be.

Nearby is a museum with the seated statue of "The One-Eyed Dragon." The statue has two eyes in accordance to the master's request in his will, replacing the eye lost as a child to chickenpox.

Masamune first gained prominence as a minor chieftan when he avenged the assassination of his father. He became a retainer to Toyotomi Hideyoshi, the first conqueror of Japan and the builder of Osaka Castle. At the death of Hideyoshi and with a good nose for winners, he then switched loyalties to Ieyasu Tokugawa, founder of the Tokugawa Shogunate.

Ieyasu appointed Masamune, a daimyo, feudal lord of the territory of what is now Iwadeyama in northern Miyagi.

After helping Ieyasu win an important battle, Masamune was given permission to build his own castle.

(The shoguns were wily. Building castles took time and money and reduced the ability of the daimyo to finance an insurrection.)

South of Iwadeyama, Masamune selected a hilltop site for his castle where he was protected by a deep ravine on one side, a river on the other and a thickly wooded montain on the third side. On the fourth side was a great plain which extended to the Pacific.

No enemy ever approached the fortress-castle during the reign of Masamune.

When he moved from his former headquarters to the new castle site he brought with him an army of 50,000 warriors and retainers. The subsequent city became known as Sendai.

Masamune was more than a spear carrier in Japanese history. Not only did he rule over the largest fiefdom north of Tokyo but he also initiated the action for one of the most unusual adventure stories in Japanese history.

As seen in Nagasaki, there was an appreciation that Christianity and trade went hand-in-hand and Masamune, always ambitious, obtained permission from Ieyasu to send a delegation to Rome to petition the Vatican to send missionaries to Japan.

Masamune obtained the release of an imprisoned priest, Luis Sotelo, to be the negotiator/interpreter, and appointed a minor samurai, Tsunenaga Hasekura, to lead the expedition.

A small galleon was built modeled on a wrecked English ship and set sail on September 15, 1613 with a contingent of one hundred and fifty men and a letter from Masamune to Pope Paul V.

The ship managed to reach Luzon in the Philippines and then sailed to Acapulco following the trade route established by the Spaniards.

The ship was the first Japanese ship to cross the Pacific reaching landfall at what is now Mendocino, California and sailed down the coast to Acapulco.

Hasekura and Sotelo crossed Mexico by foot and donkey to Vera Cruz dismayed by the bleakness of the countryside and the poverty of the natives.

Another ship took the expedition to Havana and then to Spain, France and eventually Civitavecchia, Rome's port.

On September 12, 1615 they had an audience with the Pope and presented Masamune's letter.

Back home, however, Ieyasu had had a change of heart and had shut the doors to the country, attributing much of the evil in the land to the bad influence of the Portugese and Spanish missionaries. Christians were persecuted and martyred. The papal petition was refused but Hasekura was baptized, his portrait painted and given gifts.

The party returned to Japan via Manila and Nagasaki after a seven-year absence but not to a hero's welcome. Sotelo was martyred and Hasekura disappeared.

The portrait of Hasekura, wearing long Japanese robes and carrying two swords, hangs in the Vatican.

Matsushima and the temples are popular visiting areas. One measurement is by the number of souvenir shops, noodle shops, restaurants. High. A second measurement can be the number of foreign visitors. Many.

Across the road from the Zuiganji Temple on a rocky cliff overlooking the bay is the royal teahouse, Kanrantei (Wave Viewing Pavilion) the largest early-period teahouse in existance, a gift

238 *How to Get Lost and Found in New Japan*

from Hideyoshi to Masamune Date.

The "wave-viewing" pavilion is known for its painted sliding screens. Behind the teahouse is a small museum with magnificent robes on display.

On the return to Sendai we stopped at the Shiogama Shrine, a forest-filled, hilltop enclave, guarded by giant cypress trees and imposing pines.

The day had almost gone. It was twilight and, at the main shrine, a Shinto priest in gorgeous silken robes and high peaked black hat crossed the gravelled courtyard followed by a sweet-faced feminine acolyte in an elegantly simple robe.

It was time for evening prayers. Incense wafted through the air and the steady air-filling rhythm of a slowly beaten giant drum took up its booming cadence. Impressive.

As we descended the hill to return to the twentieth century and Sendai and its half-million people, we noted at the bottom of the hill, a rectangular area marked off for a dozen parked cars. The area was decorated overhead with plastic bunting.

"What's that?"

"It is where you go to get your car blessed."

"Really? How does it work?"

"You go to the Shinto priest in that building, make a donation and then you take your car to the sacred area and you and your car pray together for your safety."

"Do you get a certificate or anything?"

"You get a memento with a little bell in it to put on your dashboard or key-ring."

"How much is the donation."

"Oh, anywhere from $16 to $40."

"That's expensive."

"Not if it works," said Shiro.

We arrived safely through the evening traffic back at the Hotel Sendai Plaza. Our driver had three jingle-belled safety mementos on his dashboard. It's worth it.

Note: the service at the Hotel Sendai Plaza is without fault. It was the smilingest hotel I remember in Japan. Everybody smiled. The major domo was Mr. Katakura, the smiling leader.

(Katakura memory clue: "cure a cat." The next morning I

addressed him as Mr. Kuracata. You have to be careful with your memory clues.)

Masamune first reigned over his fiefdom at Iwadeyama, an hour and a half north of Sendai by car.

A day trip was scheduled to the area because it is the locale of an historic school, a rare museum and a scenic wonderland.

I went alone with Shiro-san and Yamada-san, the driver.

The Lady Navigator had scripted her own adventure: an all-important rescue mission. The night before in Ichinoseki she had tallied our daily expenses in her Finance Book—a year's worth of tax information—and had left it in the chair at the ryokan. A devastating loss. Worse than losing a passport.

She enlisted the aid of Mr. Katakura who telephoned the inn. They found the ledger! The Lady Navigator took the Bullet Train back to Ichinoseki where a member of the family was at the station when she stepped off the train, handed her the ledger and she stepped on the next Bullet Train back to Sendai, all on her rail pass. All within two hours.

But we were already on the road, driving north and talking about women.

"The Shiogama shrine that we visited yesterday. Besides blessing cars, is it a special shrine for any other reason?"

"Yes. It is a favorite shrine for expectant mothers praying for a safe delivery."

"Are there many shrines like that?"

"Yes, but the most popular shrines are devoted to the Shinto spirit *dosojin* invoking fertility. The Tagata Jinjya Shrine in Nagoya is famous as a fertility shrine." Shiro turned and said something to Mr. Yamada in Japanese. Mr. Yamada took one of the jingle-belled mementos from the dashboard and handed it to Shiro who in turn handed it to me.

"Open it."

It was a small sack with a bell attached. I opened it and drew out—a small, wooden phallic symbol.

"This isn't for the car at all."

"No, Mr. Yamada visited a fertility shrine."

"And now?"

"He has one daughter."

I wanted to ask him how long he intended to keep the memento on his dashboard but decided it might be indelicate.

Near the town Iwadeyama we stopped at the historic school of Yubikan, one of nine schools left in Japan which was established for the education of the children of the daimyo.

The Yubikan "school" is now a museum and garden. The school itself consists of just two buildings; its rooms true to the simple lines of the Edo Period.

The garden, an oasis of scenic beauty, is worth the drive. In the middle of a large pond several small islands please the eye: Tea Island with a teahouse on it, Helmet Island, Crane Island and Tortoise Island.

A path encircles the pond offering fresh vistas from every stop.

Alongside the path are the three trees associated with good fortune: the pine, the bamboo, the plum.

Flowers and tree blossoms are planted to provide color throughout the year. In September the flowering crape myrtle trees with delicate pink and white blossoms were in bloom.

The pond holds an estimated 2,700 carp of every color, size and age. One monster, the museum director pointed out, was fifty years old.

The collection of carp, or *koi*, are valued according to their combination of colors, the most prized being equal portions of the purest black, scarlet red and cloud white.

A slight mist veiled the Yubikan. Not a tour bus in sight.

A most pleasant stop.

From the ancient, thatched-room school we drove to a modern, white, tile-roofed museum, the Nippon Kokeshi-kan, holding the best of the kokeshi dolls in Japan.

The simple, limbless dolls date back to the Edo Period when farmers, having nothing to do in the winter, whittled out playthings for their children. Those living near spas sold their work to the visitors who came to take the mineral baths; thus began a national hobby of buying and collecting kokeshi dolls.

Because the northern district of Tohoku receives more than its share of snow, the long winter season encourages the cottage industry of kokeshi carving. Ten centers teach ten distinctly different styles in the district. The museum's collection offers an opportunity see all the styles in Japan side by side and to study the subtle differences.

In the area of Narugo, where the museum is located, the dolls have distinct shoulders, painted flower patterns on their kimono and heads that squeak when turned.

In another center, Kijiyama in Akita Prefecture, the style is for a shoulderless doll with the kimono always painted in vertical stripes. The head does not turn.

Dolls from Tsugaru in the Aomori Prefecture are easily identifiable by the face of a *daruma* (spirit) painted on the front of the kimono.

Two major private collections donated to the museum have added hundreds, perhaps thousands, of the kokeshi dolls to the permanent collection.

Each September during an annual Kōkeishi Festival, craftsmen from all over Japan donate the best examples of their work to the local shrine.

Next to the museum is a training institute for doll carving.

From the painted dolls we drove into a painted gorge, the Narugo Ravine Gorge.

In October when the air is crisp and clear and the days are sunny, the yellow leaves and red leaves of the changing trees are intermingled with the evergreen pines, and it is a place of great beauty. The area is packed with visitors.

Narugo is also a popular hot spring spa and ski resort with ten hotels and seventy ryokan.

En route back to Sendai, we stopped in the suburbs at a *tansu* factory that makes the classic furniture chests of Japan. Sendai is famous for its tantsu, made of elegant woods and laced at the corner with hand-wrought iron. Each iron corner or handle carries a design pounded out by hand. Each piece of wood is hand lacquered ten times and dried ten times and polished ten times with powder made from deer horns. Only wooden pegs are used.

The owner of the shop, Hiroshi Kumano, is a deeply involved artist who obviously loves his craft. He supervises the felling of the timber he buys, he cures it outdoors, dries it in special rooms of varying temperatures, hand matches pieces for grain.

A small tansu, a piece of art, can cost from $5,000.

If the Lady Navigator had not gone to Ichinoseki, she would have bought one on the spot.

Mr. Kumano has a display shop in downtown Sendai. I didn't tell her.

The site of Masamune's fortress in Sendai was called Aoba after the hill on which it was built. Like so many castles in Japan it was destroyed by the Meiji forces in the nineteenth century.
The main gate survived only to be obliterated in the 1945 bombings.
At the corner of the castle site overlooking the city is a statue of Masamune on a horse—with two eyes. On top of his helmet is a slice of metal shaped like a crescent moon.
The "One-Eyed Dragon" died in 1666 at the age of seventy, the most powerful daimyo in northeastern Japan.
On an adjacent hill a magnificent mausoleum was built—also destroyed by World War II bombers. It was reconstructed in 1979.
Prior to the rebuilding, an exploration of the underground vault in 1974 found his bones in perfect condition along with many grave accessories that had been buried for 338 years, including European items Hasekura might have brought back.
It is a striking, dramatic tomb. Black lacquered wood and embossed gold under a tiled, pagoda-styled roof with much elaborately carved and colored wood under the eaves.
To the side are twenty stone monuments for the twenty samurai who committed harakiri, sword suicides, to protect their lord when he crossed the Buddhist river to the next world, a custom later forbidden by the powerful Tokugawa.

On the road to the top of the castle a new museum was under construction. It will undoubtedly exhibit artifacts from Masamune's tomb and other memorabilia of the trip he initiated to the Vatican.

That night we picked out a restaurant from the *Sendai* guidebook featuring barbecued chicken basted with shoyu sauce. Confused by the location, we were led—literally—to the restaurant by the executive vice president of the hotel. He smiled all of the time.

12. Yamagata and Fukushima... Back-of-Beyond Prefectures

The names of Japanese cities are confusing enough for an overseas visitor without adding prefectures and districts.

But, after two weeks in northern Honshu, we finally came to appreciate that nearly all of the north is known as Tohoku.

The names of prefectures became more important as they took on shape and characteristics. Aomori, Akita, Iwate and its capital, Morioka, Miyagi and its capital Sendai.

Yamagata is a good example of our ignorance. We had never heard of Yamagata Prefecture and yet we were scheduled to spend the next three days in the prefecture. We knew from the map that it was below Akita touching the Sea of Japan with a large mountain range in the east.

We were to learn after a fast, thorough tour that Yamagata is a remote, unspoiled area made up of green valleys with navigable rivers, most unusual shrines and temples, miles of rice paddies, fruit orchards and vineyards, spas and ski fields.

One attraction of Yamagata is that the prefecture is non-touristy, unvisited by overseas tourists. It invites leisurely exploration by car—little traffic, a simple net-work of roads, few traffic lights—to experience an unsullied part of Japan, back of the back-of-beyond. Such a trip, we found out, makes an unforgettable adventure.

From Sendai to the mountain resort village of Yamadera takes less than an hour on an express train. *Yama* means mountain. *Dera* means temple.

We were met at the train station of Yamadera by three people from the prefectural office of tourism, two newspaper reporters, one photographer and two television cameramen.

We were stunned. Having groped our way blindly, anonymously around much of Japan, such attention was overwhelming.

Our leader was Toshiyuki Saito, head of the Yamagata Tourist Office, who was responsible for the battle campaign planning and scheduling of the next three days. A serious, lean administrator who spoke no English.

Our interpreter was Midori Saito, no relation, who worked for an English language school and who fell into the mold of our previous lady guides: vivacious, cuddly-cute, black hair and laughing eyes.

The driver completed the trio.

Both Saitos wore tee shirts emblazoned with the English words: "Yamagata Fun—Winter and Summer." The driver wore a black suit.

After a street-corner interview with the press, we visited the shop of a local craftsman, Kazuo Ishiyama, who carved and painted kokeshi dolls. A table had been set up outside the shop where the Lady Navigator was seated next to Mr. Ishiyama and asked to copy his swift skill in painting a doll. She was still on the hairline when he finished, five minutes after beginning.

The two small dolls were presented as a gift along with a large kokeshi.

Gift-giving became part of every stop in Yamagata.

If we admired anything, it immediately became a present.

After the craft store we visited the main temple of the Tendai sect in northern Japan built in 1057, one of thirty on the mountainside. A young, serene-faced Buddhist priest showed us through the temple, one highlight being a lamp which has burned continuously for over 1000 years.

The top-most temple is reached by 800 steps. Our battle plan didn't call for us to climb 800 steps, fortunately, but we did go high enough to reach the most photogenic spot.

It was another world being in the mountain temple grounds and climbing stairs that existed before many countries were founded, dwarfed by tall, evergreen, seemingly immortal trees.

When we returned to the bottom again, the young priest appropriated a book of photographs from a souvenir stand and presented it to us.

Basho, the famous Haiku poet of Japan, visited the temple in 1689. A statue of the poet was erected in the temple grounds and a poem he wrote is inscribed in English: "Silence. The voice of cicadad (locust) penetrates the rocks."

From Yamadera we descended by car into the town of Tendo and visited the private museum of Tendo Mingei Kan.

The museum is a bewildering mixture of trash and treasure

YAMAGATA & FUKUSHIMA
Back-of-Beyond

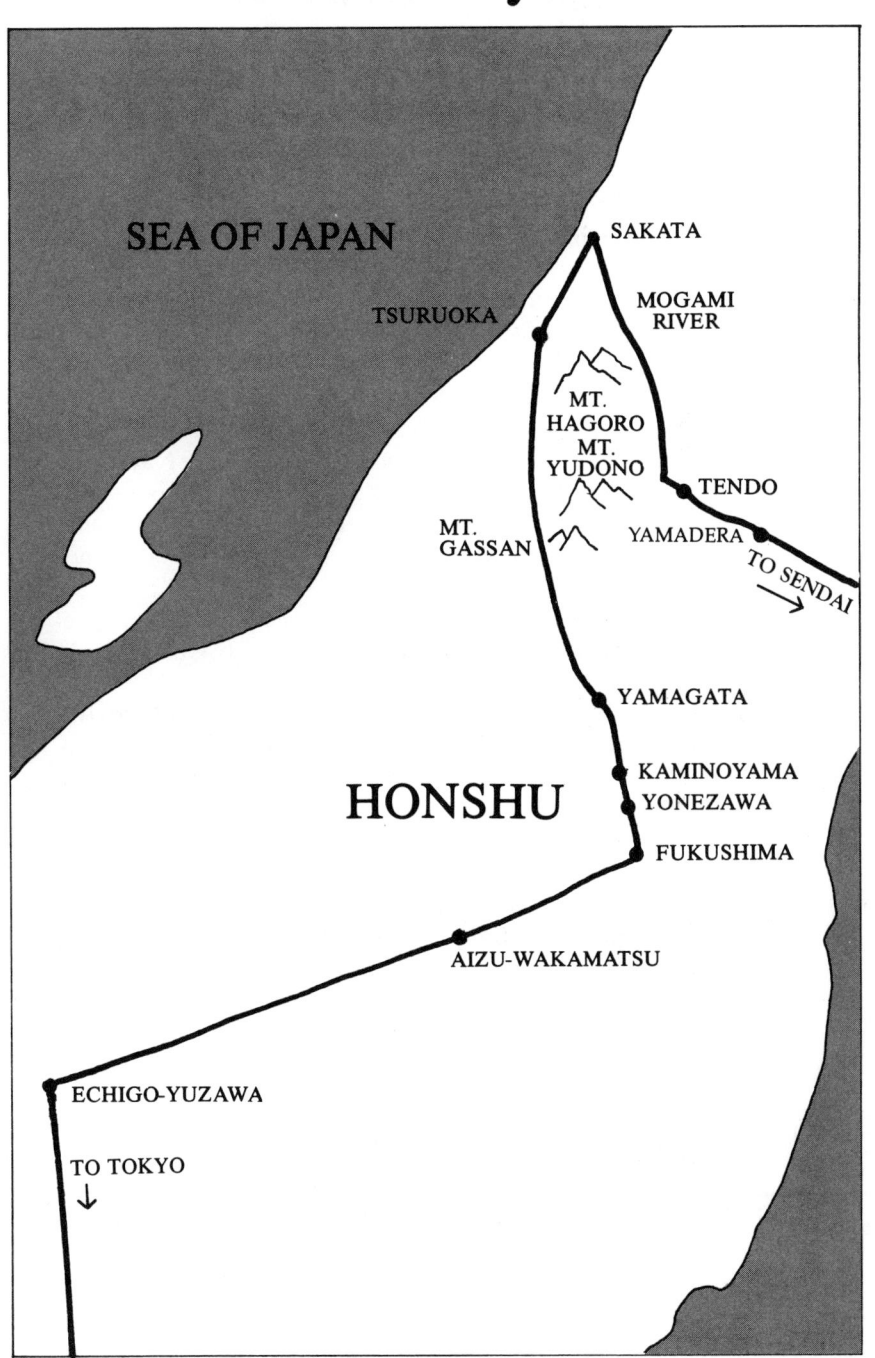

including memorabilia of Chiako Sato, Japan's first female recording star. Musical instruments, wood block prints, food utensils, lacquerware, rice buckets and a vast collection of valuable kimono—it goes on and on. Part of the museum is an old farmhouse which was moved to the site and renovated.

Next door and part of the museum is a souvenir shop where craftsmen were painting Japanese characters on wooden chess pieces of varied sizes.

The shop also sold safflower oil in large and small tins because safflower is a traditional product of Yamagata used originally as a dye source and now as an important cooking oil.

The Lady Navigator said she would try to find safflower oil from Yamagata when we returned to Honolulu. With that the proprietor of the shop presented her with a large tin. Did the Lady Navigator take it and ship it home? Yes, she did. All three pounds of it.

Fifty meters down the street from the museum is the Okubo Soba Shop in another moved and renovated 150-year-old farmhouse where Kazuo Mori, the owner-chef sat on his heels beside me to watch me eat soba noodles with chopsticks. He had the happy expression of a parent watching a child eat its spinach without dropping it all over his bib.

The expedition then headed north. We never asked where—or why—we were going but just let Mr. Saito's battle plan unfold. We did exchange puzzled looks when the driver turned off the highway and headed towards the foothills alongside a river, through a small village to eventually stop at road's end.

Mr. Saito beckoned us to follow him down towards the river, down a steep flight of stone stairs—and there in the river was the the world's damndest fishtrap.

Imagine this: below a two-foot waterfall stretching across the broad, fast-flowing river, a giant platform, the size of a large living room, had been built of slotted wood, strong enough to withstand the current and to hold the fishermen who manned it. The upriver portion of the deck near the waterfall was submerged. The downriver portion was elevated on support poles.

Small river trout called *ayu* swimming downstream over the falls would be pushed by the strong current up the grate. When the water dropped through the slots, the fish were left high and dry.

If they tried to wiggle back down the slanted elevated platform, the current pushed them back up again. The fisherman netted the

wiggling, flopping fish and plopped them into a water-filled tank.
The season for such fish trapping is August, September and October.
Seven such fishtraps on the Oguni River are permitted. The average daily catch is only fifty fish a day. Many days there are none. On one memorable occasion the trap we visited caught 2,000 fish.
The trap also catches crabs, other river fish and eels.
Below the village of Funakata a small restaurant serves ayu smoked over charcoal. Tour busses stop for a special treat of barbecued sweet fish.
We were offered a barbecued fish on a stick to sample. Still stuffed with soba noodles, I declined. (Bad manners.) The Lady Navigator, always hungry thankfully, accepted hers and nibbling daintily pronounced the fish delicious.
Midori ate everything, head, bones and all.
Two boxes of barbecued fish were presented to take along with us. They were the only things the Lady Navigator didn't ship home.
The Oguni River empties into the Mogami River, the major waterway of the prefecture. The economy and culture of the region developed around the Mogami River basin and the river, as a result, is considered the "mother" of Yamagata Prefecture.
The car stopped by the river at a large Japanese-styled building with restaurants and souvenir shops. A loud speaker blared across the gravel yard, and we recognized the word "Hawaii." We were being welcomed.
What now?
"Now" we were told, was a trip down the river rapids in a long flat-bottomed boat.
However, the recent rains had lifted the river waters too high for safety and instead of the rapids we were programmed to cruise the river for half an hour in a thirty-foot-long open boat, one of a fleet of twenty-five owned by the Sato brothers, who accompanied us.
We were also accompanied by a huge bowl of crab soup, fresh crabs on the side and bottles of sake.
Passengers take off their shoes on boarding the boat and sit on a tatami-matted bottom.
The crew consisted of a young man who served sake, a most attractive young lady who looked like a kokeshi doll who served

soup and crab, and a boatman who sang river songs.

But Kiichi and Nisaburo Sato were the joys of the cruise. Short, grizzled, faces of rivermen, creased by outdoor weather, strong in character and still humorous in mien, they radiated strength. Kiichi, 65, had been sailing on the river since he was fifteen at a time when bigger boats used to take rice, timber and safflower down river to the seaport of Sakata.

The trip then would take ten days down, and thirty days to sail back if the winds were favorable, using a single sail and keels set on the sides of the boat as needed.

The usual tourist trip today goes down river through the small rapids—not through any Colorado River-sized rapids—to a pull-out point where there are more restaurants, of course, and where the tour busses pick up their passengers. Boats operate all year long. In the winter the open boats are covered with all-enclosing, clear-plastic canopies permitting passengers to view the snowy landscape.

Sitting in the boat, sipping sake, listening to the river songs proved a most pleasant interlude.

After the cruise, as we went up the river bank, we saw gourd plants.

What did they do with gourds?

Kiichi explained that the gourds were picked, dried, painted with spirit faces—*darva*—and sold as souvenirs. Two examples were added to our growing bag of loot.

The loudspeaker said farewell to the visitors from Hawaii, the Sato brothers bowed *sayonara,* and we were off to the seaport of Sakata, running an hour behind the battle-plan schedule and near dark.

Sakata was founded as a shipping center for the rice grown in the river basin, said to be some of the best rice grown in Japan according to our hosts. It is called *shonai* rice or *shonaimai.*

The prominent family in the region was the Homma family, once the largest landholders in Japan in the early Meiji Period.

"How much land did they have," asked the Lady Navigator from Dallas.

"Thirty hectares," said Midori. "About seventy acres."

"That's tiny," said the Lady Navigator.

"You have to remember," said Midori gently, "That this isn't Texas."

The former Homma residence, large, simple, is now open to the public.

Nearby is the Homma Museum, actually two museums, one being a modern art gallery, the other an old fashioned museum in the Japanese tradition exhibiting objects of historic interest to the city and the region.

Of particular appeal was the small but exquisite Japanese garden called the "Garden of the Dancing Cranes."

Before leaving Sakata for our hotel in Tsuruoka, the Lady Navigator was promised a look at the Sea of Japan. She had flown over parts of it but had never seen it from the ground.

We went to Hiyoriyama Park, known for its commanding view of the sea.

The evening had gone absolutely black.

"Out there," we said pointing into the dark, "is the Sea of Japan."

She never said thanks.

Tsuruoka is the center of traditional arts and crafts.

First we visited the atelier-home of a candle maker/painter who was practicing a 300-year-old craft.

We sat on cushions around his work area in a peaceful setting with a Japanese garden visible through the room's floor to ceiling windows.

It takes five years to learn to make a candle properly, he said, and another three years to master its painting.

The candles are bought for use in ceremonies and parties.

Besides the traditional designs, he had a popular selling candle featuring a pretty geisha girl, a motif he developed for American military parties.

"The Americans always like girls," he said in an understatement.

The Lady Navigator received an elaborately decorated candle as a gift.

Next was a doll-making factory where a dozen women, watched by one cat, were making and dressing miniature dolls, to be wrapped warmly and set in a round basket. The babies-in-a-basket date back to a Northern Japan custom of mothers tucking infants into padded baskets to keep them safe and snug in frigid winters.

It was like being in a Tiny Tim dress factory as the women cut and snipped minute pieces from dozens of rolls of fabric, stitched and sewed the pieces together—extremely intricate work.

The Lady Navigator received one of the baby baskets as a gift.

Note: at every town on the Yamagata tour we were met by a local tourist official. If you want to see a candle painter or a doll maker, find the City Hall and ask for the tourist section and get the details.

Also in Tsuruoka is the Chido Museum, a major museum of the area with several exhibit buildings including two wooden structures with New England architecture resembling the Clock Tower in Sapporo.

Another building is a renovated, three-story farm structure. (I think there is a computer-run factory in Japan that makes antique farmhouses.)

Everything imaginable is on display at the Chido Museum from prehistoric animals to samurai armor, from old phonograph machines to burial mound figures similiar to the figures seen in Miyazaki, to battle murals and fishing equipment, to boats, real and duplicated, to agricultural implements.

Our route then cut southeast back to the mountains and the Three Mountains of Dewa or Dewa Sanzan—Mt. Haguro, Mt. Gassan and Mt. Yudono. All spirit mountains and dotted with temples and shrines.

On the entrance road to Mt. Haguro is a giant torii, the symbol of an entrance to a shrine, because Mt. Haguro itself is considered a holy shrine.

Under the eaves of the houses in Haguro hung *shimenawa,* the sacred straw ropes, to keep out evil spirits.

At the bottom of the mountain is the start of 2,446 stone steps leading to the top. We took about 100.

On the first part of the path, you can see the oldest and largest cedar tree on the mountain, a 1,000-year-old thing of beauty, in what is called *sugidori,* or avenue of cedars.

At one point is a waterfall where Buddhist students, young men and women, come and stand under the cascading water and pray for thirty-minute intervals.

Also in the vicinity is a most photogenic five-story pagoda, a uniquely high structure in this part of the country because of the devastating snow and winds.

Each story represents an element of nature: earth, water, fire, air and wind.

To appreciate the craftsmanship of the pagoda's construction, you are invited to stand under one corner of the building and look up at the perfect plumb-line accuracy of each of the five corners.

Topping the pagoda is a nine-ring decoration that looks like a TV antenna.

In Buddhism the odd number is always good luck. You'll never see a two-story pagoda with a four-ring decoration on top.

You can drive to the top of the mountain instead of hiking up 2,446 steps.

Here is the important Gosdaiden Temple.

We were greeted by a *yamabushi,* a mountain ascetic, a tall, stately and attractive young priest belonging to the Buddhist temple, who blew a giant conch shell in welcome as we approached.

What a marvelous costume. From bottom to top! He wore on his feet black-laquered *geta,* wooden platform shoes, black stockings, white bloomers over his legs, and his torso was covered with a loose blouse of bold black-and-white checks. On the top of his forehead was perched a small lacquered pillbox, a miniature version of a page boy's cap.

He walked with the aid of a long staff.

The yamabushi stayed with us until we had finished visiting the temple with a thatched roof supported by carved black figures under the eaves, and then waved us goodbye as we descended the path to another building for lunch.

We had the most delicious lunch of our northern tour. The vegetarian temple cuisine, *shojin ryori,* comprised fourteen dishes including shoots, various kinds of edible wild mountain plants, mushrooms, eggplants, and all kinds of unknown but interesting ingredients. The most tasty dish was a baked tofu stuffed with secret things. The recipe for the dish is guarded.

Even our prefecture guides said they had never tasted better tofu.

Mt. Haguro was one mountain and one temple. We had three more mountains of temples and shrines to go.

Temples and shrines intermix in these mountains because Shintoism and Buddhism were dual aspects of Shugendo, a sect of

Esoteric Buddhism, until they were separated by the Meiji government in 1871. The mountains today are under the custody of the Japanese government as Shinto shrines.

The next stop was at the sacred shrine of Yudonosan whose spirit dwells in a cone of stone emitting a cascade of hot water on Mt. Yudono.

Here we took off our shoes, were blessed by a Shinto priest. We then wiped our chests with small pieces of paper on which Japanese characters were written to cleanse our souls. The papers were placed in a small stream, and they floated away carrying our sins with them. (It's easier than a Roman Catholic confessional.)

Now purified, we descended a series of outdoor stone steps until we reached the "Rock God."

It was enough to make you a believer. Ever worship a rock?

There, surrounded by lantern decorations, was a massive, smoking cone, ten meters, or thirty feet high, out of which poured boiling water and steam. Spooky.

Was it alive? What this "thing" required was a Mr. Spock or Star Trek explanation. Certainly, it was eerie.

We climbed the flank of the rock through running hot water, followed the example of others and tossed coins on the top, and descended a few steps to the other side where we looked out over the valley below.

Between the yamabushi and the "Rock God" it was already quite a day in quite another world.

At the foot of Mt. Yudono, our third temple-shrine was called Dainichibo. Here both Shintoism and Buddhism were practiced under the same roof.

The feature of the temple-shrine was a mummy.

We were told that this mummy was once a holy man who *wanted* to be a mummy, studied to be a mummy, prayed to be a mummy and at a very old age retired to a cave, refused all food and drink and became a mummy. Which proves you can be anything you want to be.

An hour south of the park, we stopped at the last shrine, a Hachiman Shrine where the horse is venerated. Established in the Kamakura time of power, it also emulates Kamakura with an archery contest. Three arrows are shot by a galloping horseman at a stationary target during the annual September 15 festival. We were a day too early to see the real performance but we did see a dress rehearsal, sans arrows, but with the horsemen in samurai costumes making practice runs.

The destination for the night was the spa village of Kaminoyama. (Memory clue: "King Kamehameha doesn't like the yams.)"

The hotel was the luxurious Koyo Hotel, voted the country's third best resort hotel by Japan travel agents.

The travel agents might well have been influenced by the charm and beauty of the 31-year-old manager, Mrs. Yoshie Sato, a former Japan Air Lines stewardess, whose objective, with the help of a large staff, is to make guests feel cozied and loved.

We were smothered with attention.

First we had to paint a plate.

On the hotel site was found a *koyo,* an ancient kiln which gave the hotel its name. Today the custom is for guests to paint a plate—wildly, passionately or in our case, ineptly. It is fire-glazed overnight in a koyo and presented to the guest as a memento upon departure.

A thousand celebrity plates are on display throughout the hotel, most of them, we felt shamefacedly, showing enviable talent.

It was now after six. I by-passed the highly touted mineral baths—never after six in a hotel which accommodates 500 guests—showered and put on a starched yukata.

Our party gathered in a private, tatami-matted dining room for the second stomach-extending, eye-bulging meal of the day.

A pink cocktail was served called *shiso* made from a leaf that we couldn't get translated.

Bottles of pleasantly drinkable white and rose wines from Yamagata were also served.

Our first of fourteen courses (14!) was a seasonal stew made with fresh taro, an autumn potato, and beef. Excellent. (The Sato family also owns the Koyo Restaurant in Tokyo's Ginza District where taro stew is served during the autumn.)

One dish was a fresh fig covered with creamed chestnut sauce. The saliva wells up in the mouth at the memory.

Another memorable dish was thin slices of highly seasoned raw Kobe beef.

Yoshie Sato spent much time with us, mostly answering questions. She had two hundred employees. Yes, they could stay with the hotel after being married. Who knew a better way to take care of babies? Yes, she usually wore a kimono.

Why the travel agents didn't declare her hotel number one we didn't understand.

Whatever we had for dessert was topped by Mr. Saito.

Our serious, pragmatic tour general—was a magician! He was a ham. He obviously loved the stage.

His grandfather and his grandmother were magicians.

Two daughters and one son are magicians.

For an hour he entertained the party with stage-show tricks— the real egg appeared out of nowhere, the scarves, the disappearing cigarette, the cards, the dice. He had a bagful.

Each day with us his English became stronger and stronger, too. That was another trick.

We told Midori that if we were going to be on the road for another three days we wouldn't need her as an interpreter.

During dinner the Lady Navigator admired a small, wooden, square serving dish. She received the dish at departure the next morning.

Her bag of presents was now getting too large to pack in the car and too heavy to carry. The mailing cost to send her booty to Tokyo was $37 but, happily, that included the Tono iron mold to make leaf-shaped pasteries.

September is supposed to be a rainy typhoon season in Japan. We cannot attest to it.

September 15 was another perfect morning. In the distance we could see Mt. Zao, the winter sports center for Yamagata. With over thirty chairlifts and cable cars, it is a major ski resort with a good mix of runs for beginners, intermediates and experts.

Heavy snow in the winter completely drapes the pine trees, turning them into an army of white "monsters"— a favorite subject for winter photographers.

Long before Kaminoyama became a fashionable spa, it was a feudal castle town.

The castle was subsequently destroyed but the donjon (the main tower remember) was recently reconstructed out of concrete and is now a museum, a now-familiar story.

In September, adjacent to the castle-museum, an annual scarecrow contest is held to see who can construct the most imaginative strawman. The contest was now going on.

It was also the time of the local harvest festival and on the way to the castle, we encountered the start of a festival parade and jumped out to take pictures of wheeled floats pulled by uniformly dressed men. The float's load was a bevy of traditionally coiffed and gowned Madame Butterflies singing and dancing.

In the space of two minutes we met the mayor, were given a scarf to wrap around our heads, given a piece of dried fish to sample and a flask of sake to drink.

I gave the dried fish to Mr. Saito, kept the sake and used the polka-dotted scarf as a cravat—and still do.

The Scarecrow Festival was a delight.

Over fifty entries came in every size and shape.

The first prize went to a boar, eight meters tall, dressed like a man and smoking a pipe.

There was a giant-sized robot, an "E.T.", a tuxedo-dressed strawman, a stuffed horse with jockey, raggedy-anns, animals, plants, and a crane with a bandaged leg recalling the legend of the founding of Kaminoyama when a Shinto priest saw a crane curing its injured leg by sticking it into the hot, mineral-healing waters.

A fun festival.

We went into the donjon-museum next door, a very swept-up museum with expensively done, effective exhibits. The modern Japanese are quite good at this sort of thing. For example the multi-projector slide show of the city is done with outstanding photography and superior quality in the big soundtrack background music.

From the top of the donjon you get a sweeping view of the spa town and the peaceful, agricultural countryside.

"The reconstruction of the tower and the creation of the museum had to have cost more than a million dollars. Did the federal and/or prefectural government contribute to the cost?" we asked Mr. Saito.

"No, it was all done with local monies."

"Were taxes from agriculture and tourism the primary source of the income?"

"No, the city could afford it, thanks to a municipal racetrack

on the outskirts of town where there is weekend racing."
Headline: Bangtails Pay for Bang-up Museum.

One of the agricultural items in southern Yamagata is grapes.

On our way south we pulled off the main highway into an area of vineyards where hawker-owners were gesturing private cars and tour busses to pull into their parking areas and feast in their vineyards.

For about Y500 you are given a pair of vine-cutting shears and set loose in a vineyard where you can cut as many clusters of succulent grapes as you can eat. Some families bring picnics and sit in the shade of the grape arbors to have their lunch with grapes for dessert. Very pleasant.

You can pay for any grapes you want to cut and take with you or buy packages of grapes at the vineyard stands where bottles of wine are also for sale.

A large basket of superior table grapes of a variety they called Delaware, weighing perhaps a kilo, sold for about Y600.

Is grape feasting popular? Ten vineyards in the area, in the short grape-harvest season, will host 300,000 paying visitors.

We sampled excellent white and red wines. Strong, running thirteen to fourteen percent in alcoholic content.

A charming scene: four thigh-high children with joined hands, were dancing on top of an old wine vat playing "we all fell down." down."

Continuing south on good roads we stopped in a remote pasture near the village of Takahata. Would you believe a dog shrine— and a hundred yards away from it, a cat shrine?

Very much isolated at the edge of a wood is a small shrine dedicated to a strain of hunting dog now extinct but known in its time for giving easy birth to pups. It is now a frequently visited shrine by expectant mothers.

Nearby is the cat shrine. The legend dates back to the year 1100 and concerns a farmer who killed the constantly squalling family cat by decapitation. The head of the cat stayed alive, according to the legend, and managed to kill the snake (devil) which had been hiding in the family fields. That's why it had been squalling. The contrite farmer then built the shrine.

In the village of Takahata the people were preparing for their local festival at the Shinto shrine. At a three-story pagoda the Shinto priests purified the dancers and accepted the many offerings—envelopes of money, sacks of rice, produce, bottles and barrels of sake.

"Where is the most exciting festival in Yamagata Prefecture?" we asked Mr. Saito.

"The Flower Dance in Yamagata City. Over 10,000 dancers will participate in the three-day festival. They all wear the same kind of wide straw hat with red flowers on top and bells around the edges. We have a hat for you to take with you."

The Lady Navigator jingled all the way back to Tokyo.

We crossed a mountain range on the way to Yonezawa via a new expressway, a multi-million dollar highway recently opened.

Before the highway there was only a one-way dirt road. Adventuring in Yamagata in former days was difficult. Today, thanks to such new construction, it is easy.

Yonezawa is famous for its silk and rayon industry. In one silk exhibit we saw a kimono priced at $20,000.

The name Uesugi is known to every Japanese because of the victory of Kenshin Uesugi (1521-1572) in hand-to-hand combat against the villainous lord of Kai Province, a deed celebrated in the annual festival.

The castle town of Yonezawa was ruled by the Uesugi family. The former residence of the family is now a museum and restaurant, where after visiting the silk museum and the mausoleum of Kenshin Uesugi, the first lord of the district and the hero of the combat tale, we returned for a steak and red wine lunch.

It was late afternoon by the time we had finished and were taken to the train station. Midori, Mr. Saito, the driver, and the Yonezawa city official who accompanied us in his area, all bought tickets allowing them to go on the station platform. They carried our bags, put them on the train, and bowed and bowed and waved and waved, good-bye, good-bye. Good friends.

> Note: If one wanted help in planning a tour of Yamagata, or engaging an interpreter, write to the Yamagata Prefecture Tourism Association c/o Yamagata Ken Kanko Bussanka, 2-8-1 Matsunami, Yamagata City, Yamagata Prefecture, Japan 880.

Fukushima and The Spas

The *New Official Guide, Japan,* lists the three fashionable spas of Tohoku as Kaminoyama, where we had just spent the night, Iizaka near Fukushima and Higashiyama in Aizu-Wakamatsu.

We were now going to visit the other two "fashionable" spas.

The train from Yonezawa to Fukushima, a spine city on the Bullet Train line, took less than an hour.

It was raining and by the end of a twenty-minute taxi ride from the station to the spa town of Iizaka and the Ryokan Kasui-kan, it was almost dark.

Never stay in a high-rise ryokan . . . . excepting the Hotel Koyo. You are stuck for dinner and breakfast, having paid for both. In the case of Kasui-kan, both meals were terrible.

The bill was Y15,000 per person for the night and we left at nine the next morning for another twenty-minute taxi ride back to the station, having had no opportunity to explore, eat different food of our own choosing, or to meet people.

It would have been more fun, more adventurous and much less expensive to have stayed at a businessman's hotel near the station.

We almost had the same experience at the high-rise Higashima Park Hotel, a taxi ride from Aizu-Wakamatsu where we had a combination Western and Japanese style room with terrible maid service and food to match for $300 a day per couple.

One immediate sign of good service in a spa-hotel is when a maid spots a six-foot figure and immediately goes away and comes back with a "LL" sized yukata, big enough to reach below your ankles so you don't look like Lil' Abner going through a pea patch with ankles and knobby knees showing.

It didn't happen at the Higashima Park. Under one bed was a broken toothpick when we arrived. It was still there when we left. That sort of a hotel is unusual in Japan.

The city of Aizu-Wakamatsu (Memory Clue: "I told you, Sue, to walk on the mat.") deserved more time and exploration than we gave it.

An historic castle town, prosperous in the Edo Period, Aizu-Wakamatsu was the scene of the tragic last stand of the Shogunate loyalists. One band of teen-age soldiers committed harakiri when they thought their castle town was in flames. Women of warriors had themselves killed so that they would not be in the way of their men's fighting.

These moments are recalled in exhibits at the excellent Samurai Residence, a large compound with several buildings showing the life as it was in the Edo Shogun Period. (Life was pretty good if you were a samurai.) The collection of artifacts in the buildings is first-rate. Also on the grounds is an intriguing working water mill for grinding grain.

A short walk towards the city from the Samurai Residence and on the same side of the street is the Donga-ku Restaurant where you must try a speciality of the area: barbecued tofu. Very tasty. Recommended.

The castle of the town, Tsurugajo, was destroyed in 1874 but was restored to its original elegance in 1965. The expansive grounds of the castle and its museum in the middle of the city is an inviting place to explore.

We also visited a sake museum (fair) and found one antique shop. Antique shops get rated on how much time the Lady Navigator spends in them. This was a one-hour, eight-point antique shop.

I thought perhaps we were getting jaded due to weariness from one and two-night stands, a malady not uncommon among travel writers, but the local train ride from Aizu-Wakamatsu to Koide and then to Echigo-Yuzawa restored our faith in our enthusiasm for beauty and appreciation of the magnificent.

The entire, stop-at-every-station trip took five and a half hours. I wish it had taken ten hours, it was so satisfying.

The first leg, the best part, takes four hours in a rattling, open-window local train—and it is all lovely. The best train ride in Japan.

Much of the time the train skirts the Tadami River with many scenic river views opening up and then closing as the train goes through mountain forests.

The tiny, remote stations have a charm of their own where the train frequently took on or let off hikers and campers and local farmers going to and from.

The small rice farms of the mountains were being hand-harvested.

Throughout Japan I had been mystified by the sight of stacks of long poles alongside most of the rice fields. I could never get a proper answer for their use. Now I saw. Farmers were binding the poles together to make drying fences for the rice stalks.

What did they do with the dried stalks? Make thatch roofing for the houses? Tatami mats? Plow back into the soil as mulch? I don't know. I'm going to find out on my next trip.

How many times have we said the day was gorgeous, clear, full of sunshine? This was another one. The contrast of colors was emphasized by the sun. The texture of the green forests, the green water of the river and the white of the rapids, the now-yellow color of the ripened rice in the fields made for a five-star trip, ranking along with the drive through Hokkaido's "Peppermint Valley", the sea-coast scenery on Kyushu, and the walk along the Oirase River.

At Yuzawa we stayed at the Yuzawa Grand Hotel, an independent "Grand" hotel, not part of a chain, which can accommodate five hundred guests in its ninety rooms and six-hundred guests at the height of the New Year's holiday traffic. How? The hotel sleeps one-hundred skiers in the banquet hall.

The popularity of Yuzawa lies in the fact that it is only one hour by Bullet Train from Omiya Station in Tokyo's northeasternmost suburb.

Young people leave Tokyo after work on Saturday, get in a couple of hours of night skiing and then get up at dawn, ski all day and return to Tokyo Sunday night. You have to be young to do that for fun.

If you visit Tokyo in the December-to-April winter period, the closest skiing is Yuzawa—just don't go on the weekends.

An hour's bus ride from Yuzawa, unreachable by train, is Naeba, a larger ski center, host of the World Ski Cup in the late seventies.

At Naeba about thirty ski lifts serve the higher slopes and offer the longer runs. Two hotels, the Naeba Prince and its sister Prince hotel, the World Cup Hotel, can accommodate about eight-hundred people.

Yuzawa advertises itself as "White World" in the winter and "Green World" in the summer.

A cable car took us to the top of the mountain in five minutes to the edge of the largest park of alpine flowers in Japan from where we could also look over the entire valley.

A sports center in the valley includes eighteen tennis courts and an indoor arena.

Golf courses are available at both Yuzawa and Naeba—$50 on

weekdays and $70 on weekends.

The Grand Hotel's "Club Sunshine" was offering a topless review during our stay with five girls imported from Las Vegas. Walking down to the train station to return to Tokyo, we were picked up by two of the attractive, well-endowed show girls who were dying to speak English. One of them was six feet tall.

"I'm so tired of people staring at me," she said.

So I stopped.

By three o'clock we were back in Tokyo in the luxurious confines of the Akasaka Prince Hotel with six uninterrupted nights of non-packing, non-moving in front of us.

Touring a new country should be an adventure. You go everywhere and try to meet everyone, eat all of the different foods and try all of the accommodations. That's what travelling is all about.

But let's be honest. The quaint inns, the tatami-matted rooms, the different experiences of different hotels is all good stuff. But an attentive, well-managed twentieth century hotel is most satisfactory. Most satisfactory.

Addendum. The Love Hotels

As written earlier, the only accommodation we didn't try personally was the youth hostel. Not quite true.

There was another type of accommodation we didn't assess: the "love hotel."

Love hotels are part of the new Japan—a phenomenon since our last trip—mushrooming throughout the country, offering exotic bedrooms for those who would enjoy each other's company by the hour. It is currently estimated that there are 3,500 love hotels in operation.

Externally the love hotels often come in unusual shapes such as ships, castles, Arabian palaces, as suggested by their names: Love Boat, Cinderella Castle, Fantasy Land, Meguro Emperor. Garish signs and neon lights mark the properties and signs detail prices by the hour and by the night—a 'rest' or a 'stay.'

The city love hotels are known as *abec hoteru*. In the country, *moteru* are for those in cars.

Prices vary between Y3,500 to Y7,000 per hour. The ultimate love hotel reportedly costs almost Y15,000 and hour.

Entering a love hotel is marked with privacy. Money is exchanged without any staff being seen, only heard electronically. Communications is via microphone. Boards are provided to cover license plates for 'moteru' customers. Japanese ladies cover their heads with coats.

The decoration of the guest rooms vary wildly. Mirrored walls and ceilings, sauna baths, color video tape machines, waterbeds, rotating beds, harem decorations are among the attractions.

Daytimes and early evenings are the most popular times for a tryst and all day Sunday.

Why this social phenomenon?

Despite the secrecy and the suggestion of naughtiness, the love hotels are discussed quite openly and used by married couples as well as others for different reasons.

Young married couples living with parents in tight quarters certainly provide a percentage of the trade. Others are excited by the opportunity of sexual variation. Illicit office romances are encouraged by the opportunity of using the hotels.

We were at a dinner party, mostly of Westerners, when the subject came up.

One couple said, "We went on our anniversary. We were driving to Kyoto and stopped at a famous moteru and had to wait an hour and a half. We drank all of our champagne just waiting."

"When we got inside," the lady giggled, "all I could do was to go to sleep."

Another couple drove us back to the Imperial Hotel and, on the way, passed a famous love hotel in the Gotanda district decorated with turrets and other French chateau appointments.

"Stop the car," said the Lady Navigator. "Let's go look."

"Not with me you don't."

"I don't with anybody else," she said. "We are just going to peek in the door."

That's all we did. Peak. An unseen man said the place was full. Come back in an hour.

It was added to the list of the many things we have to do when we return back to Japan. The new Japan.

Thank You...

Researching Japan was a pleasure, particularly when so many people smoothed the path.

Mike Sano of Air New Zealand in Tokyo was particularly helpful. A whole team of JNTO people made influential contacts, arranged schedules, read copy, read galleys, provided back-up research material—Isokazu in Honolulu, Katsuhiko Narisada in San Francisco who provided updating data for the second edition, and Hideo Hamano, Takashi Nagaoka, Yasutake Tsukamoto in Tokyo were outstanding coordinators.

The Merle Boyers' experiences in Japan were most helpful.

Handy hotel people not mentioned in the book include Stan Takahashi and Jack Nishioka of Sheraton, Kojiro Muroya of the Imperial, Yosh Maki of the Akasaka Prince, Kenji Nakamoto of the Shiba Park Hotel, Shigeyuki Aoki, president of the Hotel Sendai Plaza.

A special toast goes to my Australian pals, Dr. Paul Matthews and Gwen Holdworth.

Not mentioned in the pages on Hanamaki was Hiroshi Itoh, our kind volunteer guide.

Toshiharu Akiba of the Tokyo Disneyland publicity section was an excellent source of information, as was Shigeo Yamada (Idaho-born) of Duty Free Shoppers.

The Lady Navigator is indebted to every policeman in Tokyo who re-directed her to intended destinations—and many seasoned Tokyo shoppers in Japan and the U.S.A., among them: Carolyn Daniel, Jill Little, Fumi Lopez, Cynthia Eyre, Norma Doty.

The list could go on for pages.

We are grateful for so many gracious assistants.

INDEX

Accommodations (also see Hotels), 14, 122, 146, 157, 178
Ainu, 173, 176, 183, 185, 191
Aizu-Wakamatsu, 258
Akan National Park, 174 (map), 193-199
Akasaka (see Tokyo)
Akihabara (see Tokyo)
Akita, xi, 212-215
Alps, 160, 163, 167-172
Animism, 177, 224
Antiques, 43, 168, 218, 228, 235, 259
Aomori, 202, 209
Asahikawa, 190-193
Asakusa (see Tokyo)
Asakusa Kannon Temple, 7
Asakusabashi (see Tokyo)
Ashinoko Skyline Drive, 67
Aso National Park, 103
Atomic Bomb, 91, 95-98, 133, 136-139
Attractions (man-made), 19-22, 163, 167, 179, 183, 185, 226
Automobile Rental (see Rental Car)
Azabu Juban (see Tokyo)

Bakurocho (see Tokyo)
Banshakus, 170
Bashi, 34
Basho, 244
Batchelor, Dr. John, 183
Bear Ranch (Hokkaido), 188
Bento, 187
Beppu, 101-104, 107
Bicyling, 85, 148, 166
Blakiston, Thomas Wright, 204
Boat Tours (also see Cruises), 153
Boy's Day, 107-110, 157

Buddhism, ix, 69, 75, 85, 86, 149, 151, 157, 229, 232, 236, 244, 250, 251
Bullet Train, 69, 70, 72, 218, 231, 258, 260
Businessman's Hotel, 154, 258
Bus Travel, 186-187, 196

Cameras, 7, 50
Cape Hinomisaki, 151, 152-154
Car Rental (see Rental Car)
Castles, 72, 78, 81, 128, 142-143, 148, 154, 156, 162, 254, 259
Cho, 34
Chome, 34
Clark, Dr. Wm. S., 184
Climate:
  Seasons, 6, 73, 173, 186, 254
  Effect on travel, 142, 145, 206, 223
Climbing, 173, 194, 225
Communications, 41, 113, 145, 150, 182
Costs vii, xii, xiii, 52, 111, 118, 120, 125, 129, 131, 145-148, 152, 168-170, 185, 192, 193, 203, 261
Crafts, 42-45, 49, 50, 115, 146, 149, 160-161, 163, 167, 187, 191, 213, 226, 240, 244, 246, 249
Credit Cards, 154
Cruises (also see Boat Tours), 60 153, 211, 216, 234, 235, 247
Cuisine, xiv, 1, 8, 12-18, 75, 82, 83, 90, 115-118, 123, 126, 133, 144, 149, 153, 166, 169, 177, 185-186, 190, 192, 203, 214, 218, 221, 247, 251, 253, 259

Cultural Parks, 163, 167, 226
Customs (Culture), vi, viii, 8, 22, 39, 57, 83-85, 90, 94, 106, 110-118, 120, 124, 126, 135, 142, 151-154, 164-170, 176, 182, 189, 192-194, 224, 227, 230-239, 259, 260
Currency, vii
Cycling (see Bicycling)

Daimyo, 1
Daisetsuzan National Park, 175 (map), 193-197
Dashi, 199
Date, Masamune, 236, 237
Deer Park (Nara), 85
Department Stores, 7-9, 15, 36-42, 46, 48, 50, 66, 82, 92, 161
Departo, 7, 240
Discount Programs, x, xii, 120
Disneyland, 19-22
Donjon, 82, 254, 255
Dori, 34
Driver's Licenses, 194, 201
Driving, 194, 201, 244-257

Echigo-Yuzawa, 259
Edo, 1
Electricity, 14
Ema, 169
Entertainment, 8, 124-127, 129, 144, 157, 163, 165, 189, 214, 222, 261
Expo '85, 29-31

Festivals, xiii, 107, 109, 110, 135, 166, 167, 179, 188, 198, 211, 213, 217, 220, 253, 255, 257
Ferry, 99, 131, 202, 209
Fishing, 60, 153, 173, 202, 223-225, 246
Five Lakes District, 66
Flea Markets, 43, 55-56
Food Specialties (see Cuisine)
Fukuoka, 141-146
Fukushima, 258
Funakata, 247
Furo, 74, 164

Gaijin, 78, 86
Gardens (also see Parks), 76, 112, 123, 129, 130, 134, 138, 144, 160, 162, 183, 185, 206, 240, 249
Gembikei Gorge, 232
Geography, ix, 101, 209
Gift Giving, 39, 57-58
Ginkakuji (Silver Pavilion), 72
Ginza, (see Tokyo)
Girl's Day, 110
Glover, Thomas Blake, 133-135
Golf, 60, 65, 66, 108, 111, 123, 131, 260
Goryokaku Fort, 202
Gotanda (see Tokyo)

Hagi, 146-150, 169
Hakadote, 177, 201-207
Hakata (see Fukuoka)
Hakone, 59-68
Hakone-machi, 59
Hamada, 150
Hanae Mori, 47, 52
Hanamaki Spa, 228, 230
Haori, 74
Hasekura, Tsunenaga, 237
Health Resorts (see Spas)
Hearn, Lafcadio, 154-156
Hibachi, 166
Hibiya Park (see Tokyo)

Hideyoshi, Toyotomi, 79, 81, 82, 156, 236, 237
Higashiyama, 258
Hiking, 60, 173, 200, 259, 210
Hiragana, vii,
Hiroshima, xi, 89, 171
History, ix, 1, 23, 69, 78, 85-86, 91, 94-95, 111-112, 122, 133, 136-139, 143, 160, 173, 176, 184, 202, 236, 258
Hokkaido, xi, xiv, 3, 58, 101, 173-207
Holidays (also see Festivals), 107-110, 157, 199
Home Visit Program, vii, ix, 93, 178, 181-182
Honshu, xi-xiv, 1-101, 146-172, 243
Horse Cart Tour, 205
Hospitality, 16, 120, 142, 150, 165, 169, 174, 179, 180, 185, 186, 198, 199, 242
Hotels, 1, 2-4, 43, 73, 79, 83-84, 91, 99, 101, 104, 108-109, 113, 122-124, 129, 131-133, 142-146, 157, 161-163, 187, 195, 198, 203, 213, 218, 223, 225, 230, 238, 241, 260
(Also See)
Businessmen's, 154, 258
Love, 234, 261
Magariya, 225-228
Minshuku, xiv, 89, 163-167, 225, 227
Pension, 203
Ryokan, xiv, 73, 76, 99, 215-218, 230-233, 241, 258

Ibusuki, 122-127
Ichinoseki, 231-233, 239

Iizaka, 258
Ikebukuro (see Tokyo)
Industry, 25-31, 82, 123, 138, 139, 154, 177, 187, 192, 202, 224, 240, 246, 248, 257
Information Sources, xii, 6, 7, 10, 11, 35, 40-41, 75, 116, 133, 161, 171, 178, 218, 234
International Arcade, 41
Interpreters, 136, 225, 244
Islands, xi, 204, 207
Iwadeyama, 239-240
Izumoshi, 151-154

JR (Japanese Railway), xii, 114, 131, 209
JNTO (Japan National Tourist Organization), vii, xii, xiii, 3, 6, 10, 22, 62, 75, 98
JTB (Japan Travel Bureau), xiv, 19, 26, 120
Japan Old Folk Craft & Antique Center, 49
Japanese baths, (See Furo)
Japanese Inn (See Hotels)
Jimbocho (see Tokyo)
Jimmu, 111

Kagoshima, 119-122
Kakunodate, 215-218
Kamaishi, 224
Kamakura, 22-24
Kamikaze, 143
Kaminoyama, 253-258
Kappabashi (see Tokyo)
Kanazawa, 160-163
Kanji, ix
Kanto Plains, 1
Karaoke, 168
Katakana, ix

Index

Kawayu Spa, 197, 198
Kimono, xii, 74, 81, 163, 168
Kinkakuji (Golden Pavilion)
Kirishima-Yaku National Park, 103, 121
Kitami Plain (Peppermint Valley), 196
Kobe, 202
Kodemma-Cho (see Tokyo)
Koide, 259
Kokeshi Dolls, 240, 244, 247
Kowakidani Spa, 65
Koyo, 253
Ku, 34
Kumamoto, 128, 129
Kurashiki, xi
Kyoto, xi, 1, 69, 87, 136, 159
 Katsura Imperial Villa, 73
 Kyoto Imperial Palace, 73
Kyushu, 128, 260

Lakes, 60, 66, 186, 199, 210, 212, 215
Language, ix, 16, 33, 69, 74, 77, 80, 82, 108, 113, 121, 143, 162, 213, 220, 235
Legends of Tono, 224, 227
Lookouts (see Scenic Lookouts)
Love Hotel, 234, 261

Maeda, 160
Magariya (see Hotels), 225-228
Manga, 113
Maps, iv
Marunouchi, (see Tokyo)
Masuda, 150
Matsue, 154-157
Matsumae, Yoshihiro, 176
Matsushima, 234-237

Meiji, 1, 63, 135, 162, 177, 202
Mikoshi, 198
Mineral Waters (see Spas), 101, 105, 132, 187
Mingei, 33, 244
Minshuku (see Hotels), xiv, 89, 163-167, 225, 227
Miyajima, 89, 98, 99
Miyake, Issey, 47
Miyako, 223-224
Miyanoshita, 60-68
Miyazaki, 107-119
Miyazawa, Kenji, 228-230
Monkey Forest (Beppu), 101
Morioka, xi, 218-223
Motorways, 257
Mountains, 121, 123, 129, 187, 194, 196, 202, 250
Mountain Shrines, 250
Mt. Fuji, 67
Mud Baths, 102
Museums, 5, 65, 86, 95, 105, 129, 137-138, 148, 152, 154-156, 163, 174, 183, 191, 202, 204, 211, 226, 244, 249, 254-255, 259

Naeba, 260
Nagasaki, xi, 92, 124, 133-134, 136, 139, 140, 141, 144, 202
Nara, 85-87
Narugo, 241
National Parks, 103, 121, 131, 163, 173, 175, 193-199
National Traits, 10, 12, 80, 99, 118, 209, 212
Nenokuchi, 210
Newspapers (In English), 128
Nihombashi (see Tokyo)
Niigata, 202

Nijo Castle, 78
Nikko, xi, 24, 72
Noboribetsu Spa, 185-190
Nopporo Forest Park, 174

Odashi, 150
Ochugen, 39
Ofuro (see Furo)
Oirase Valley, 210, 260
O-ishi, 16
Okayama, 160
Omiyage, 57
Oriental Bazaar, 46-47
Osaka, 79-82, 128, 136
Oseibo, 39

Pachinko, 116
Parks & Gardens, 5, 85, 86, 91, 92, 111, 129-133, 142-144, 160, 163, 167, 173-179, 183, 191, 206, 223
Pension (also see Hotels), 203
Peppermint Valley, 196, 260
Perry, Adm. Matthew, 117, 184, 202, 204-205
Population, ix, 1, 128, 173, 177, 218
Public Baths (see Spas)
Publications, 7-11, 40-41, 258

Rafting, 159
Railpass, (see JNR), xii, xiv, 120, 131, 171, 193, 200, 209, 215
Ramen, 13, 177
Religion, 85, 86, 121, 122, 132, 137, 139, 140, 149, 151, 157, 173, 184, 224, 226-227, 236
Rental Car, 193-200
Resorts, 60, 65, 99, 101, 122, 146
Restaurants, 3, 15, 17, 18, 83,

Index 269

144, 163, 179, 192, 221, 242, 246-248, 253, 259
Rikuchu Coast Nat'l Park, 223
Rishiri Island, 207
Robots, 29-30
Roppongi (see Tokyo)
Ryokan (see Hotels), ix, 73, 76, 99, 215-218, 230, 233, 241, 258

Sake, 191
Sakuraya Camera Shop, 7, 50
Samurai, 80
Sandbaths, 124-126
Sakata, 248-249
Sansa Dance, 220
Sapporo, xi, 174-185, 201
Scenic Drives, 65-68, 193, 196, 241
Scenic Highlights, 98, 160, 196, 210, 234, 259
Scenic Lookouts, 99, 124, 183, 186, 188, 191, 194, 197, 203
Science City, 29-31
Seikan Tunnel, 206
Sendai, xi, 233-242
Shi, 34
Shiba Park (see Tokyo)
Shibuya (see Tokyo)
Shikoku, xi, 142
Shimabara, 131
Shimenawa, 69
Shinjuku (see Tokyo)
Shintoism, ix, 69, 149, 151-153, 238, 251
Shio-sembei, 168
Shrines, 68, 69, 85, 99, 109, 130, 135, 148, 151-153, 158, 166, 183, 198, 204, 211, 250, 256
Shogunate (see Tokugawa

Index

Shogunate) 130, 137, 258
Shopping, 7-9, 15, 18, 32-58, 67, 72, 79, 82, 92, 115, 121, 149, 158, 161, 163, 167, 168, 179, 191, 206, 213, 235, 246, 259
 Bargains, 33, 51-55
 Crafts, 42-45, 49, 50, 115, 146,149, 160-161, 163, 167, 187, 191, 206, 213, 226, 240, 244, 246, 249
 Department Stores, 7-9, 15, 36-42, 46, 48, 50, 66, 82, 92, 161
 Marketplaces, 55, 163, 168, 205
 Tokyo, 32-58
 Wholesale, 51-57
Ski resorts, 254, 260, 241
Soba, 218, 221-222
Sotelo, Luis, 237
Sounkyo Gorge, 193-196
Spas, 24, 60, 101, 122, 132, 163, 185, 188-189, 193-198, 241, 254, 258
Special Events (see Festivals)
Sports (see individual listings)
Student Guides (Kyoto), 73, 76, 77, 79
Subways & City Trains, 9, 11, 180
Swimming, 173

Tange, Kenzo, 4
Takahata, 256
Takamatsu, 142
Takamura, Kotaro, 212, 229
Takayama, 163-172
Tansu, 241
Tatami, 74
Taxi, 12, 34, 59, 60, 129, 131

Telephone, 11
Temples, 5, 22, 69, 77-78, 85-86, 133, 140, 244, 250-251, 220, 232, 234, 237
Tendo, 244
TIC (see Tourist Information Center).
Tipping, 3
Tohoku, 209-242
Toilets, 21, 33, 72, 89
Tokyo, xii, 1-57, 261
 Department stores, 7-9, 15, 36-42
 Daimaru, 36, 42
 Hankyu, 36, 40
 Isetan, 7, 46, 50
 Keio, 7, 46
 Komatsu, 36
 Matsuya, 36, 38
 Matsuzakaya, 36
 Mitsukoshi, 7, 36, 38-40, 46, 48, 50
 Odakyu, 7, 40, 46
 Parco, 46
 Seibu, 40, 46, 48
 Sogo, 36
 Takashimaya, 36, 38-39, 41
 Tokyu, 36, 46, 48
 Wako, 36, 39, 41, 48
Day Tours:
 Disneyland, 19-22
 Nikko, 24-25
 Kamakura, 22-24
 Industrial Tours, 25, 27-31
 Flea Markets, 55-56
 Shopping, 32-58
 Tokyo Districts:
  Akasaka, 3, 9, 13, 18, 43
  Akihabara, 51-53
  Asakusa, 9, 37, 43

Asakusabashi, 53-54
Azabu Juban, 44-45
Bakurocho, 52-53
Ginza, 2, 14-16, 37
Gotanda, 262
Hibiya Park, 2
Ikebukuro, 48
Jimbocho, 49
Kappabashi, 33, 53, 55
Kodemma-Cho, 53
Marunouchi, 2, 37
Nihombashi, 36-43
Roppongi, 17, 43-44
Shiba Park, 5, 18
Shibuya, 9, 45-48
Shinjuku, 7, 49-50
Ueno Park, 9, 37
Subways & City Trains, 9, 11, 12
Tokugawa, Ieyasu, 78, 81, 176, 236
Tokugawa Shogunate, 1, 5, 24, 68, 132, 134, 176, 177, 202
Tottori, 158
Tourism, 64, 193
Tourist Information Center, 3, 6, 61, 41, 49, 69, 77, 78
Tourist Offices (Prefectures), vii, 178, 193, 219, 234, 257
Train Travel, 69, 70, 87, 107, 119, 121, 128, 131, 141, 146, 150, 157, 180, 200, 201, 259, 223
Translations (see Language).
Travel Tips, 3, 14, 35, 73, 99, 121, 141, 147, 156, 180, 186, 209, 258
Tsukiji, 8
Tsukuba, 29-31
Tsurugajo, 259

Tsuruoka, 249

U-Drive (see Rental Car)
Ueno Park (see Tokyo)
Ueno Station, 9
Uguisubari, 162
Ukiyo-e, 23,
Unzen National Park, 131-133

Volcanoes, 187, 198, 211

Winter Olympics (1972), 173, 179

Yamadera, 243
Yamagata, 243-257
Yanagida, Kunio, 224
Yasumiya, 210, 212
Yodobashi Camera, 7, 46, 50
Yokohama, 202
Yonezawa, 257-261
Yukata, xii, 45, 74, 124
Yumoto, 60

Xavier, St. Francisco, 122, 139

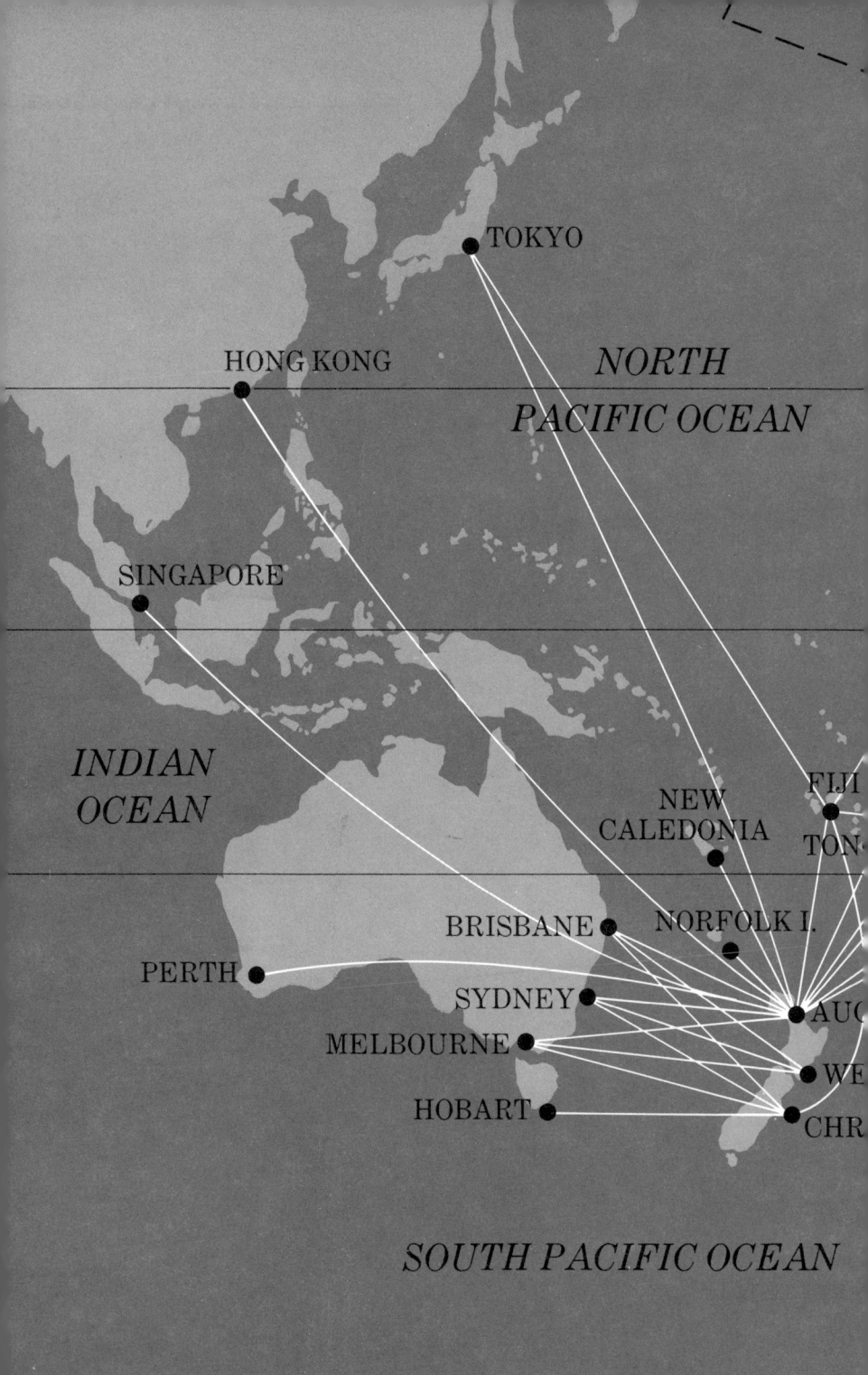

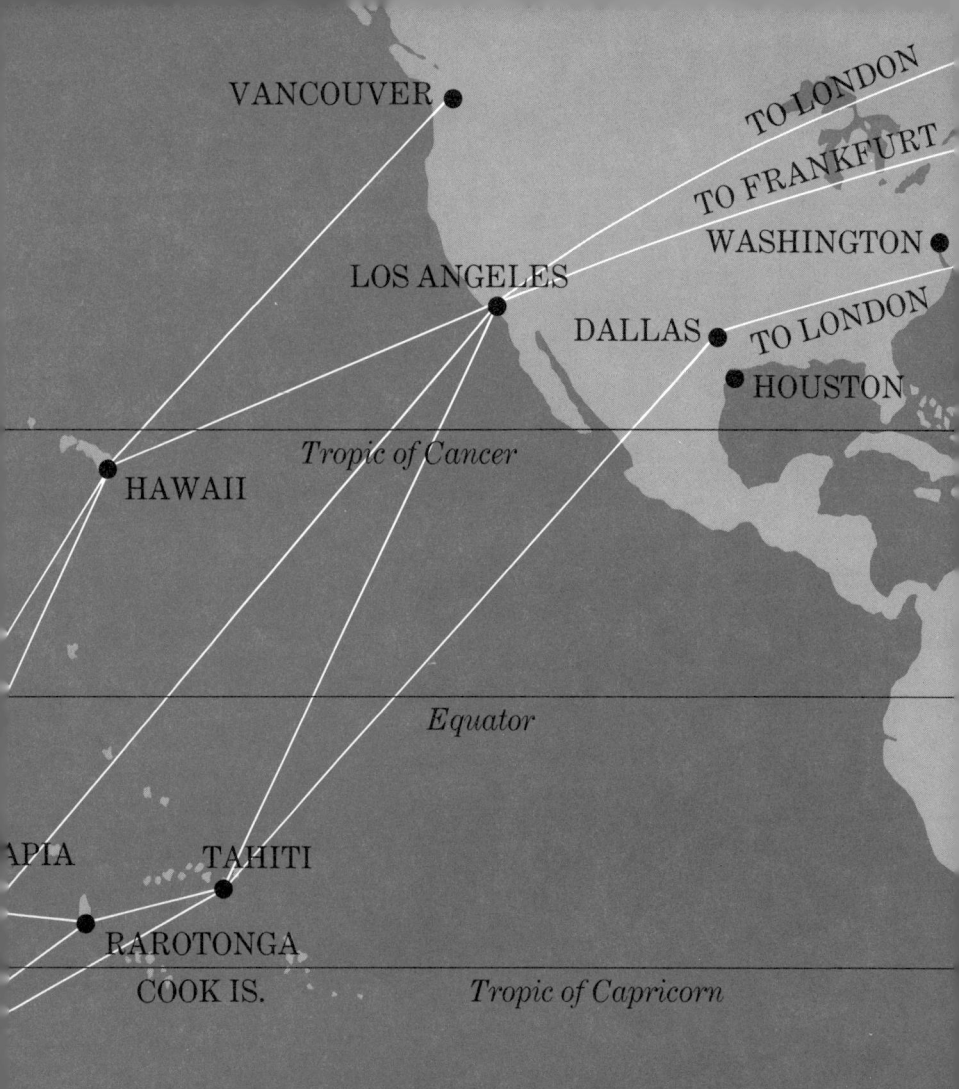

Air New Zealand International Route Network.